PENGUIN CLASSICS

THE DHAMMAPADA

VALERIE J. ROEBUCK was born in Hertfordshire in 1950. She studied at the University of Cambridge, where she was awarded a BA (Hons.) in Oriental Studies, specializing in Sanskrit and other Indian languages, and a PhD for a thesis on South Indian bronzes. A freelance scholar and lecturer, she is an Honorary Research Fellow of the University of Manchester and an Associate Member of the Centre for the History of Religion in Asia at Cardiff University. Dr Roebuck has a broad interest in Indian language, culture and religion. She is a Buddhist, practising and teaching meditation in the Samatha tradition, and is involved in interfaith work in Manchester. Her previous publications include *The Circle of Stars: An Introduction to Indian Astrology* (Element Books, 1992). She also translated the *Upaniṣads* for Penguin Classics.

The Dhammapada

Translated and edited with an introduction by
VALERIE J. ROEBUCK

PENGUIN BOOKS

PENGUIN CLASSICS

Published by the Penguin Group
Penguin Books Ltd, 80 Strand, London WC2R 0RL, England
Penguin Group (USA) Inc., 375 Hudson Street, New York, New York 10014, USA
Penguin Group (Canada), 90 Eglinton Avenue East, Suite 700, Toronto, Ontario, Canada M4P 2Y3 (a division of Pearson Penguin Canada Inc.)
Penguin Ireland, 25 St Stephen's Green, Dublin 2, Ireland (a division of Penguin Books Ltd)
Penguin Group (Australia), 250 Camberwell Road, Camberwell, Victoria 3124, Australia (a division of Pearson Australia Group Pty Ltd)
Penguin Books India Pvt Ltd, 11 Community Centre, Panchsheel Park, New Delhi – 110 017, India
Penguin Group (NZ), 67 Apollo Drive, Rosedale, North Shore 0632, New Zealand (a division of Pearson New Zealand Ltd)
Penguin Books (South Africa) (Pty) Ltd, 24 Sturdee Avenue, Rosebank, Johannesburg 2196, South Africa

Penguin Books Ltd, Registered Offices: 80 Strand, London WC2R 0RL, England

www.penguin.com

This translation first published in Penguin Classics 2010

020

Set in 10.25/12.25pt Postscript Adobe Sabon
Typeset by TexTech International
Printed in England by Clays Ltd, Elcograf S.p.A.

ISBN: 978-0-140-44941-9

www.greenpenguin.co.uk

FSC www.fsc.org MIX Paper from responsible sources FSC™ C018179

Penguin Books is committed to a sustainable future for our business, our readers and our planet. This book is made from Forest Stewardship Council™ certified paper.

Contents

Acknowledgements

I cannot even attempt to list the names of all the people who have helped me in the course of this work. First, there are those who inspired or encouraged me to take the task on, notably F. R. Allchin, Steve Farmer and J. R. Hinnells; and L. S. Cousins, without whose generous help I would hardly have dared to venture into the world of Pali and early Buddhism, after a previous existence specializing in Sanskrit. Les Callow should also be mentioned here, since he was the first person to suggest to me the idea of a Dhammapada translation, many years before. Then there are those who encouraged me when doubt set in – especially when I was finding it hard to discover a 'voice' in English for the Pali of the Dhammapada – among them Grevel Lindop and Tony Ellis, who read an early draft of the text and offered their criticisms of it as poetry in English.

It was very important for me to be able to discuss the work from the point of view of Buddhist teaching and practice, and I have been most grateful for discussions with friends who are meditators and sincere searchers within the Buddhist tradition, as well as, in some cases, scholars themselves – among them, Francis Beresford, Costel Harnasz, Usha McNab, Anne Schilizzi, Charles and Sarah Shaw, and many others who have taken part in study and practice groups to explore the Dhammapada.

Research into the Dhammapada and its related literature has taken me far beyond the realms of the Indian languages, into those of China and Tibet, which I regret I have never studied. I therefore owe my thanks to Max Deeg, Jungnok Park and Roland Steiner, scholars of these and other languages of Buddhism, who have been very generous in sharing their knowledge. The help of Kathy Lazenbatt of the Royal Asiatic Society has been indispensable in seeking out earlier translations of the Dhammapada into Western languages.

There are others, too, who have helped me via the various Indology lists on the internet, patiently answering my queries and helping me to find the books and articles I needed. Even a quick look at my email correspondence on Dhammapada topics reveals discussions with numerous scholars, including Jaymin Acharya, Stefan Baums, Peter Friedlander, Chris Haskett, Axel Michaels, Manish Modi, Walter Slaje, John D. Smith, Allen Thrasher, H. J. H. Tieken and Peter Wyzlic. For those whose names have been omitted, I want to assure them that their help is not forgotten. Needless to say, the use I have made of all this information, and the opinions expressed in the work, are entirely my own responsibility.

Much important research on the Dhammapada and its related literature is available only in German, another language that is regrettably unfamiliar to me. I therefore wish to express my heartfelt thanks to my German translator, Isabel Glasow, who has coped magnificently with densely written academic articles containing copious amounts of Sanskrit and Pali.

And thanks, as always, to my husband, Peter, for his unfailing love and support.

This work is dedicated to the memory of David Melling (1943–2004), philosopher, colleague and friend.

Valerie J. Roebuck
Manchester, January 2010

Pronunciation Guide

The following are the closest approximations in Received Standard English for the words from South Asian languages that are found in this book. The guide is designed primarily for Pali, but is also intended to provide some help with the Sanskrit (including Buddhist Hybrid Sanskrit) and Gāndhārī words that occur in the Introduction and Appendices.

VOWELS

a as in c<u>u</u>p, not as in c<u>a</u>p.
ā as in c<u>a</u>lm.
i as in p<u>i</u>ck.
ī as in p<u>ea</u>k.
u as in t<u>oo</u>k.
ū as in t<u>oo</u>l.
ṛ (Sanskrit only) is 'vocalic *r*' – *r* as a vowel. Originally it was probably pronounced as a trilled sound, like an *r* continued. Today, however, it is generally pronounced as a short *ri* sound, so *ṛddhi* sounds much like 'riddhi', and *ṛṣi*, 'sage', is often Anglicized as 'rishi'.
e as in b<u>a</u>ke.
ai (Sanskrit only) as in b<u>i</u>ke.
o as in b<u>oa</u>t.
au (Sanskrit only) as in b<u>ou</u>t.
a, *i*, *u*, *ṛ* are short vowels; *ā*, *ī*, *ū*, *e*, *ai*, *o*, *au* are long. In Pali only, *e* and *o* are shortened before double consonants, so that the *e* in *mettā* and the *o* in *gotta* are pronounced short, though the

resultant syllables are still long for stress purposes. (The length of syllables is important not only for knowing where to place the stress on words, but also for the metres used in poetry.)

CONSONANTS

k, *g*, *c*, *j*, *ṭ*, *ḍ*, *t*, *d*, *p*, *b* are unaspirated sounds: practically no breath escapes when they are pronounced, so they sound softer than their English equivalents. *kh*, *gh*, *ch*, *jh*, *ṭh*, *ḍh*, *th*, *dh*, *ph*, *bh* are aspirated: there is a noticeable escape of air, like an *h*, when they are pronounced. *kh*, *gh* etc. are written with single characters in the Indian scripts, and count as single sounds in pronunciation. Double consonants, such as *kka*, *kkha* etc., are fully pronounced, as in Italian.

kh as in blockhead, not as in loch.

gh as in egghead.

c as in chat, not as in cat (which would be spelled with a *k* in this system).

ch as in chat, but with a more marked escape of breath.

j as in lodge, not as in mirage.

jh as in bridgehead.

ph as in cuphook, not as in physics.

bh as in abhor.

There are two groups of *t* and *d* sounds. *t* and *d* are true dentals, pronounced with the tongue on the teeth, as in French. *ṭ* and *ḍ* are those distinctively Indian sounds, the retroflex consonants. In pronouncing them, the tongue starts from a position bent back against the roof of the mouth, and is brought slightly forward during speech, much as for *r*.

There is a similar relationship between dental *n* and retroflex *ṇ*, and between dental *s* (like English *s*) and retroflex *ṣ* (Sanskrit only – a soft *sh* sound). In Pali, there is also a retroflex consonant *ḷ*, as in *Pāḷi*.

th, *dh*, *ṭh*, *ḍh* are aspirated versions of the *t* and *d* sounds, as in pothook, bloodhound, not as in theme or this.

ś (Sanskrit and Gāndhārī) is a palatal *sh* sound, made with the tongue in the same place as for *j*, as in pushchair.

ñ comes before *c*, *ch*, *j* or *jh*, and sounds as in pi<u>n</u>ch, a<u>n</u>gel. In Pali, it can also occur on its own, doubled, or as an initial, when it is pronounced *ny*.

ṅ usually comes before *k*, *kh*, *g* or *gh*: it is the sound in pi<u>n</u>k, a<u>n</u>gle, ki<u>ng</u>.

ṃ nasalizes the preceding vowel, rather like the *n* in French *bon*.

v sounds somewhere between *v* and *w*, on its own sounding more like *v*, but after another consonant more like *w*.

h is pronounced with more resonance than is usual in English, while *ḥ* (Sanskrit only) is a slightly harsh breathy sound, most commonly at the end of a word (but cf. *duḥkha*, Pali *dukkha*).

STRESS ON WORDS

The stress on words in Pali and Sanskrit is determined by long and short syllables. For this purpose, a syllable containing a long vowel, or any vowel which is followed by more than one consonant, is long. A syllable containing a short vowel followed by a single consonant is short.

In a *two-syllable* word, the stress is always on the first syllable: <u>Ya</u>ma, <u>Bud</u>dha, *gati*.

In a *three-syllable* word, if the second syllable is long, it is stressed: *a<u>nic</u>ca, a<u>nat</u>tā*. If not, then the first syllable is stressed, regardless of length: *<u>nā</u>ginī, <u>A</u>rahat*.

In words of *four syllables* or more, if the second-last syllable is long, it is stressed: Moggall<u>ā</u>na. If not, then if the third-last syllable is long, that is stressed: Āj<u>ī</u>vika, Anāthapi<u>ṇ</u>ḍika. If that too is short, the fourth-last syllable is stressed, regardless of its length: <u>Dham</u>mapada, Dhammapada<u>ṭṭ</u>hakathā, <u>Ti</u>piṭaka. The stress on words in Pali and Sanskrit is not quite as heavy as that in English.

A NOTE ON GĀNDHĀRĪ

Gāndhārī, unlike Sanskrit and Pali, is known only from ancient manuscripts and has not survived in literary and liturgical use.

Moreover, while Sanskrit and Pali are traditionally written in scripts descended from Brāhmī, in which spelling corresponds more or less exactly to pronunciation, the surviving Gāndhārī texts are written in Kharoṣṭhī script, which does not always distinguish between short and long vowels, or single and double consonants. So while it seems probable that *abhiña* (Appendix I, v. 5) was in fact pronounced like its Pali equivalent *abhiññā*, and that *kama* (Appendix I, v. 20) was pronounced like Pali and Sanskrit *kāma*, we have no independent evidence for this.

Abbreviations

GDhp = Gāndhārī (Khotan) Dharmapada: see Brough 1962
PDhp = Patna Dharmapada: see Cone 1986 and 1989
SA = Saṃyutta Aṭṭhakathā (Saṃyutta Nikāya Commentary)
Uv = Udānavarga: see Bernhard 1965–90

Introduction

The Dhammapada is one of the best-known and best-loved works of Buddhist literature.[1] It forms part of the oldest surviving body of Buddhist writings, generally known as the Canon. This means that it is regarded as part of the authentic teaching of the Buddha himself, spoken by him in his lifetime, memorized, and compiled for oral transmission shortly after his death.[2]

The name 'Dhammapada' means a word or verse[3] of the Dhamma, the teaching of the Buddha. It has become the recognized title of the work, even in translation, though some have attempted to translate it.[4] The Dhammapada belongs to a type of composition that must be very ancient indeed: a collection of wise sayings in verse, attributed to a great teacher, and handed down among his followers.

There seem at one time to have been a number of versions of the Dhammapada, in different though closely related languages. The one translated here in full is in the Pali language, and belongs to the Pali Canon, the collection of scriptures recognized as authentic by followers of the Theravāda school of Buddhism.[5] But I have also included in the Appendices brief extracts from other early versions, to give some idea of the range of literature of this type that must once have existed.

The format of the Dhammapada is simple: it is a collection of verses, each consisting of four, or occasionally six, half-lines or *pādas*. Within the collection, the verses are arranged in chapters (*vagga*), each with a one-word title. Chapters may be named either from the format of the verses contained in them – for example Chapter 1, *Yamaka*, 'Twins' or 'Pairs', consisting mainly of contrasting pairs of verses – or from key words – for example Chapter 4, *Puppha*, 'Flowers', made up of verses which refer either to flowers in general or to particular kinds of flowers or perfumes. The titles help to give each chapter a loose theme, though the placing of verses in particular chapters sometimes seems a little arbitrary: for example, v. 325 appears to have nothing to do with the theme of Chapter 23, *Nāga*, 'The Elephant', other than the fact that it mentions another large animal, a 'great boar'. Many of the verses are capable of standing alone, while others form short sequences within the chapters; overall, the Dhammapada reads more like an anthology than a single long poem. Each verse or group of verses is now associated with explanatory material from a commentary, the Dhammapadaṭṭhakathā, which not only expounds its meaning but also describes the occasion on which the Buddha is said to have spoken the teaching.[6]

The verse forms used are not very elaborate. The metres of Pali verse, like those of classical Greek and Latin, are based on long and short syllables, not, like traditional English ones, on stress. Rhyme is not used, but alliteration is frequent. The majority of verses are in a metre known in Sanskrit as *śloka* or *anuṣṭubh*,[7] the basic medium for storytelling and instruction; but a variety of others are also used – often, it appears, for particular emotional effect.

As far as we can tell after an interval of more than two thousand years, the language used in the Dhammapada would not have struck its original hearers as difficult or obscure. Its diction seems generally clear and direct, though here and there we find examples of the puns and paradoxes so popular with ancient Indian authors.[8] Though there are some verses that now seem obscure, such difficulties generally seem to be the result of changes in language that caused the original meanings to be forgotten: the verse may then have been emended in the attempt to find meaning in it.[9] But, on the whole, the Dhammapada was and remains easy to understand and to memorize – qualities which have no doubt contributed to its popularity.

Like the language, the content has an accessible quality. The verses give ethical advice, or remind the hearer of the transience of life and the delusiveness of sense-desires. Some of the teaching is aimed primarily at monks and nuns (e.g. vv. 9–10, 73–5), and some at laypeople (e.g. vv. 303, 309–10); but most of it is clearly meant to be applicable to every would-be follower of the Buddha's path (e.g. vv. 127–8, 227–8). Indeed, much of the content of the Dhammapada would have been regarded as uncontroversial by members of any of ancient India's religious groups; and some of the verses are almost identical with ones found in Hindu or Jain texts.[10] But there are also verses and longer sequences that refer to specifically Buddhist themes, such as the qualities of the Buddha, or the Four Noble Truths (e.g. vv. 179–96). It is widely used in Theravāda countries as an accessible introduction to the Buddha's teaching.

THE LIFE OF THE BUDDHA

The life of the Buddha remains a subject of considerable debate among scholars. While very few would doubt that a genuine historical figure lies behind the teachings that bear that name, it is clear that in the millennia since his lifetime a considerable amount of legendary material has become attached to his story. The earliest and simplest narratives – those found in the Pali Canon – are principally interested in the quest leading up to his attainment of Buddhahood and his subsequent career as teacher. Many of the best-known stories of his life – for example the details of his birth and childhood – appear first in the commentaries. But modern attempts to find historical truth behind the legends have to reckon with the fact that even the canonical accounts include miraculous events such as prophecies and encounters with deities. The compilers of these ancient texts naturally saw and expressed the world in mythical and symbolic terms, not in modern rationalistic ones.

The following is a summary of the basic events of the Buddha's life, as generally accepted in the Buddhist world.[11] The Bodhisatta, or Buddha-to-be, was born in a royal family from the Sākiya[12] clan of north-east India, and was given the names

Siddhattha and Gotama.[13] He was known from the first to be no ordinary child. A sage who saw the newborn prince prophesied that he would be a great man, who would rediscover the Dhamma, found by all previous Buddhas, and teach it to the world. According to the commentarial versions, his father was aghast at the idea that his son might choose to become a wandering holy man, instead of the great ruler that he wished him to be, so he went to extreme lengths to ensure that his son would remain happily in the household life, providing him with every luxury, surrounding him solely with beautiful, healthy young people, and, when the time came, arranging a marriage for him with his cousin,[14] who eventually bore him a son, Rāhula.

Despite the efforts to shelter him from the suffering (*dukkha*) of life, the young prince came to see it all around him in the form of old age, sickness and death. Seeking to make an end of suffering, he left his wealth and status to become a wandering holy man. The commentarial accounts dramatize this in a series of encounters with an old man, a sick man, a corpse and a holy man,[15] and describe his night-time escape from a palace where he was effectively held prisoner. The canonical version simply says that he cut off his hair and beard, put on the ochre robe of a renunciant, and went forth into the homeless life, though his mother and father were reluctant and wept to see him go.[16]

In the Canon,[17] the Buddha describes his search for freedom from suffering. After leaving home, the young man sought out renowned meditation masters: first Āḷāra Kālāma, and then Uddaka Rāmaputta. He quickly learned everything that they could teach him. Āḷāra invited him to share the leadership of his group with him, and Uddaka even offered to hand over leadership of his group and follow him instead. But, although their meditation techniques could provide a temporary peace, they did not lead to complete freedom from suffering, so the Bodhisatta moved on.

He now undertook severe asceticism, deliberately subjecting his body to extremes of heat and cold, and starving himself nearly to death. This proved just as useless for his quest as the indulgence of his former princely life had been, so he gave it up and began once more to eat in moderation. A group of five ascetics who had been practising with him were disgusted at what they saw as a failure on his part, and abandoned him.

He travelled on to Gayā, in modern Bihar state. There, on the full-moon night of Vesākha (April–May), he sat beneath a pipal tree, making a determination to achieve liberation there, or die in the attempt. The Bodhisatta had remembered an occasion in his childhood when he had experienced a peaceful meditative state (*jhāna*) through observing his breath. He realized that this was the key to the practice that he needed: through the *jhānas* he could still his mind in order to penetrate to the cause of suffering.

By the end of that night he had understood the reality of suffering, and achieved the ultimate freedom, *bodhi*, often translated as 'enlightenment', but more accurately 'awakening'. Because of that, Gayā is now called Bodh (= Bodhi) Gaya, and[18] the tree under which he sat is called the Bodhi (or Bo) tree. He had now won the title of Buddha ('Awakened One'). He was thirty-five years old. From this point he is regarded as an enlightened being, free from suffering of the mind – though while he lived his body was still subject to old age, illness and eventual death.

The Buddha spent seven weeks at Gayā contemplating and organizing the insights he had reached, and then began to consider whether he should attempt to teach others. He knew that it would be a difficult task, since few would be able to understand the insights for which he had struggled so long. But a deity called Brahmā Sahampati approached him on behalf of all beings and requested him to teach the Dhamma. There were some beings, he said, who had little dust in their eyes, and would be able to understand it if the Buddha were to teach. Out of compassion, the Buddha agreed.

Looking around with the eye of wisdom, he searched for people capable of understanding his message. Āḷāra Kālāma and Uddaka Rāmaputta had both died, and as a result of their meditations were now in peaceful realms where, however, they could not become conscious of the Buddha's teaching. But the five companions who had practised asceticism with him were still alive and searching for liberation. Over the next few weeks the Buddha walked from Gayā to Sarnath (near Varanasi, in Uttar Pradesh) to see them. On the way he received alms from two merchants, Tapussa and Bhallika, who became the first lay Buddhists.

When the five ascetics saw him coming, they determined not to pay him the usual marks of respect, being still angry with his supposed lapse from asceticism; but, when he came closer, his presence was such that they could not help but show him reverence. To them he gave his famous first teaching, the Setting in Motion of the Wheel of Dhamma,[19] in the Deer Park at Isipatana, near Varanasi. He taught the Four Noble Truths, of suffering, the cause of suffering, the cessation of suffering, and the path leading to the cessation of suffering. First Koṇḍañña, then the rest of the five, attained liberation through the Buddha's teaching, and so became the first Arahats,[20] as well as the first monks, of his dispensation. Now all the Three Refuges of Buddhism were present in this world: the Buddha; the Dhamma, or Teaching, rediscovered by each Buddha; and the Saṅgha, or Community.

From then on the Buddha continued to travel around northern India on foot, teaching people of every possible class and background, and enabling many of them to reach high spiritual attainments. Among those who eventually achieved Arahatship through his teaching were many members of his family – though his jealous cousin Devadatta constantly plotted against him, seeking to wrest control of the Buddhist community for himself.

The Buddha had lived to the age of eighty when, feeling the effects of old age, he went to a grove of sal trees at Kusinārā (Sanskrit Kuśinagara, modern Kushinagar, Uttar Pradesh).[21] There he lay down on his right side under two trees, which shed blossoms on him, out of season. His last words to his followers were 'Conditioned things are by nature perishable. Attain your goal through awareness!'[22] After experiencing for the last time all the stages of *jhāna*, he passed away, entering *parinibbāna* – the end of rebirths and the complete cessation of suffering. The texts do not attempt to describe the condition of a being who has attained *parinibbāna*, since words no longer have any relevance in this case. His body was cremated, and his relics distributed among local rulers, who had them installed in *stūpas* (reliquary mounds) suitable for a great monarch.

Shortly after the Parinibbāna, a council was convened at which the monks recited together all that they had learned of the Buddha's teachings, so compiling what became the Pali Canon, to be memorized and handed on orally for the following centuries.

DATES

The Parinibbāna of the Buddha forms the basis of Buddhist chronology, but all the great schools of Buddhism seem to have had their own traditions concerning its date. Some Far Eastern schools placed it as early as 949 BCE,[23] while the Tibetans dated it to 881 BCE. The tradition handed down in the Theravāda world places the Parinibbāna in 543 BCE – a date that is increasingly accepted in the Buddhist world as a whole as a starting point for the Buddhist Era used in calendars. According to this tradition, the Buddha was born in 623 BCE, and attained awakening in 588 BCE. Many current scholars, however, would date the Parinibbāna as much as 150 years later – to around 400 BCE. This would date the Buddha's teaching career, and the presumed origins of the canonical literature, to the late fifth century BCE rather than the late seventh or early sixth century given by the Theravāda tradition.[24]

It is often said that the Pali Canon was not put into writing until the first century BCE, in Sri Lanka – a tradition that seems to be based on just two verses in the Dīpavaṃsa (*c.* fourth century CE), the traditional Pali chronicle of the island.[25] However, even if that is true for the Canon as a whole, it seems more than likely that Dhammapada verses, and similar poetic works, were committed to writing, separately or in groups, before that, as hearers would have had a strong motive to record them and share them with others.[26]

THE LANGUAGE OF THE DHAMMAPADA

Pali (*Pāḷi*) is one of the group of languages classified by scholars as 'Middle Indian' or 'Prakrit'.[27] These languages are descended from Sanskrit, or rather from the spoken Old Indian language of which Sanskrit was a refined version – just as the Italic languages, Italian, French, Spanish etc., are descended from the vernacular Latin spoken in the Roman Empire, rather than from the literary language of Virgil and Tacitus.

The Old and Middle Indian languages belong to the Indo-Iranian (or 'Indo-Aryan') branch of the Indo-European family, and so are distant relatives of English, Latin, Greek and indeed most of the languages of Europe. In consequence, certain words in Pali are likely to sound familiar to the English reader: for example, *mātā*, 'mother'; *pitā*, 'father'; *deva*, 'god' (cf. Latin *deus*); *dvi*, 'two'. The relationship between, say, English and Sanskrit or Pali is that of distant cousins. Claims that English is 'descended' from Sanskrit are pure fantasy. Both share a remote ancestor ('Proto-Indo-European') that ceased to exist in prehistoric times but has in part been reconstructed by philologists.

The Pali language originated in northern India in the centuries before the Common Era, but spread throughout the Theravāda Buddhist countries, first to southern India, and then to Sri Lanka and South East Asia, as a language of scholarship and religion. The early history of the language, and even its original name, is something of a mystery. The current use of the name 'Pali' is in fact the result of a misunderstanding. *Pāḷi* was originally the word for a text, as distinct from a commentary (*aṭṭhakathā*), so *pāḷi-bhāsā* meant 'the language of the sacred texts'. But by about the seventeenth century CE it had come to be understood as a name, 'the Pali language', and the usage has stuck. Its own speakers in ancient India seem to have called it *Māgadha-bhāsā*, meaning that it was the language of Māgadha in north-east India. But the name 'Māgadha' itself seems to have had a range of meanings. At times it referred to a small area around the city of Rājagaha (Sanskrit Rājagṛha, modern Rajgir, Bihar); at others to a large area under the suzerainty of the rulers of Pāṭaliputta (Sanskrit Pāṭaliputra, modern Patna, Bihar). Judging from surviving inscriptions, there was a wide degree of standardization in the language of the whole administrative area, with certain differences in local dialect which would not have prevented its being generally understood.[28] The language of the Pali Canon was therefore not simply one dialect among many, but a form of the lingua franca of a powerful empire, the first in fact that was used for official inscriptions in India. (Although Sanskrit is philologically older than Pali, its use in inscriptions is generally later.)

As long as the Pali Canon was the only early Buddhist Canon known to scholars, it was widely thought to be a literal record of the Buddha's own words; but, since the discovery of canonical material in other Middle Indian languages, scholars no longer consider this likely. However, even if the language of the surviving Pali texts is not exactly the same as that spoken by the Buddha in his lifetime, it is unlikely to be far removed from it. In fact the Buddha may well have taught in more than one dialect. According to tradition, he spent some forty-five years travelling over a wide area of northern India, speaking to people of all classes and backgrounds. Presumably he adapted the register and dialect of his speech according to his audience.[29]

As an educated man from an aristocratic family, the Buddha may well have known Sanskrit too; but if so he seems to have deliberately avoided using it as a teaching medium, presumably so that his teachings could reach the widest possible audience.

THE PALI CANON

In its original language, the Pali Canon is called the Tipiṭaka, 'Three Baskets',[30] because it consists of three large bodies of texts:

(i) the Vinaya Piṭaka, concerned with the disciplinary code, or Vinaya, for monks and nuns (but also including extensive narrative material about the life of the Buddha, giving the context in which these rules came to be made);

(ii) the Sutta Piṭaka, relating the Buddha's teachings in the form of connected dialogues and narratives;
(iii) the Abhidhamma Piṭaka, or advanced philosophical and psychological teachings, seeking to explain the true nature of our consciousness, and that which we regard as our 'self'.

The Sutta Piṭaka is the largest and best-known of the Baskets: many of the Buddha's most famous teachings come from this collection. It is itself divided up into five groups (*nikāya*), named according to the format of the texts within them:

(i) the Dīgha Nikāya, containing long (*dīgha*) discourses;
(ii) the Majjhima Nikāya, containing discourses of medium (*majjhima*) length;
(iii) the Saṃyutta Nikāya, containing connected (*saṃyutta*) discourses;
(iv) the Aṅguttara Nikāya, containing short discourses organized in numerical order (*aṅguttara*, 'longer by an item', 'graduated'), so that the first section is concerned with items that occur in 'ones', the second with 'twos', and so on up to 'elevens';
(v) the Khuddaka Nikāya, containing miscellaneous short (*khuddaka*) texts.

In comparison with the other Nikāyas, the Khuddaka contains a high proportion of works in verse, many of which have a popular character. It consists of fifteen books, of which the Dhammapada is one: others include the Sutta Nipāta, which contains many of the best-loved chants and blessings of Buddhism, and the Udāna, closely related in format and history to the Dhammapada.[31]

EARLY BUDDHIST SCHOOLS

The whole subject of the development of the early Buddhist schools is an intensely controversial matter, as well as a complex one, with ideas changing as new discoveries are made. There is no space here to cover the subject in the detail it deserves, but it is necessary to attempt a brief introduction in order to understand the world in which the Dhammapada literature took shape.

One obstacle to understanding lies in the terminology that has been used in much of the writing on the subject. Some earlier scholars used to use the word 'Hīnayāna' ('Lesser Vehicle') to refer to the early schools, even though this was a pejorative term invented by followers of the later Mahāyāna to distinguish these schools from their own 'Great Vehicle'. In recent decades it has come to be felt that this is unacceptable, and the term is now generally (though not universally) avoided; but this still leaves the question of what we *should* call them. The alternative terms 'Śrāvakayāna' ('The Vehicle of the Disciples') and 'non-Mahāyāna', though less offensive, are still inadequate, since all define the Theravāda and its sister schools through Mahāyānist eyes.

These terms also reflect a degree of confusion between, on the one hand, the geographical and cultural varieties of Buddhism and, on the other, the varieties of individual practice taught within them. In a tradition common, probably, to all Buddhist groups, there are said to be three spiritual paths, each leading to its own kind of liberation: (1) the way of the follower of a (Fully Awakened) Buddha, either in that Buddha's lifetime or through teaching handed down, leading to the liberation of the Arahat; (2) the way of individual practice, without such contact with a Buddha, leading to the liberation of the Paccekabuddha ('Individual Buddha' or 'Private Buddha'); and (3) the way of the Bodhisatta, leading to the liberation of the Sammāsambuddha or Fully Awakened Buddha, capable of being a world teacher, just like the 'Historical Buddha'. Though the Paccekabuddha and the Sammāsambuddha are said to have greater powers and attainments than the Arahat, all three are believed to have experienced a genuine awakening and release from suffering, from which the one who has attained it can never fall away. Each of the three kinds of enlightened beings may be described as a Buddha, or 'Awakened One', but when it is not further qualified the title generally refers to a Fully Awakened Buddha.

Properly speaking, the term 'Śrāvakayāna' refers to the first of these three paths to awakening; and the use of this term as a title for particular schools of Buddhism would seem to imply that those schools taught only the Arahat's path, and not those of the Private Buddha and the Fully Awakened Buddha. Yet the early schools taught all three of these paths, and all three are still known in the surviving representative of these schools, modern Theravāda Buddhism. Here, the path followed by the individual Buddhist is thought to depend on decisions made in the course of his or her spiritual life (which for Buddhists, of course, will be thought to include earlier lives). But it is generally felt that the way leading to Arahatship is suitable for the largest number of meditators, while relatively few will feel the call to make the greater, and more prolonged, commitment required to follow the paths leading to awakening as a Private or a Fully Awakened Buddha.

The innovation in the Mahāyāna school was not, then, the teaching of the Bodhisatta path, but the fact that this was recommended as a goal for all meditators, not just a minority who felt a particular vocation for it. Along with this went a downgrading of the attainment of the Arahat, which was no longer necessarily regarded as irreversible. Other common ideas about the distinctive character of early Mahāyāna – for example, that it was more open to laypeople, or to women, than the older schools – have been convincingly challenged by Paul Harrison.[32] For these reasons I prefer to follow him in calling the earliest pre- or non-Mahāyāna stages simply 'Mainstream Buddhism'.[33] This term is intended to reflect the situation just before and just after the start of the Common Era, and of course carries no implications about the mainstream character, or otherwise, of any later Buddhist schools, let alone of those in existence today.

The Mahāyāna branch separated from the Mainstream schools around the second century BCE, though the disputes that led to the split may have begun as much as two hundred years earlier. While all schools continued to accept the basic teachings of Buddhism, as expressed in their versions of the Canon, the Mahāyānists accepted in addition a number of later texts, such as the Prajñāpāramitā ('Perfection of Wisdom') Sūtras, which embodied distinctively Mahāyānist teachings. Though at first, judging by the evidence from inscriptions, and the reports of Chinese travellers, it was not very widespread,[34] Mahāyāna Buddhism eventually became the dominant tradition in much of Asia, developing into numerous different forms, such as the Zen and Pure Land schools of East Asia. From Mahāyāna, in turn, came other developments, such as the Vajrayāna, the Tantric form of Buddhism, particularly influential in Tibet and related cultural areas. It is worth remarking, however, that, though Mahāyāna Vinaya texts certainly existed, and survive in fragments, the monks and nuns of all current Buddhist communities use Vinaya texts inherited from the Mainstream schools.

Mainstream Buddhism now survives as a single but very widespread school: the Theravāda of Sri Lanka and South East Asia (Thailand, Burma, Cambodia, Laos). In ancient times, however, there are said to have been as many as eighteen or twenty Mainstream schools, of which the early Theravāda (sometimes called Vibhajjavāda (Vibhajyavāda), the Doctrine of Analysis) was just one. We have little information about most of them beyond their names, and brief mentions in the writings of other schools, so their teachings and history are often matters of debate. It appears that the differences between them could be based either on doctrine or on differing interpretations of the Vinaya, or on a combination of the two. Geographical factors also played their part, as different schools grew apart as they settled in different areas, or were influenced by the ideas and practices of their neighbours.

It is presumed that each of the Mainstream schools must once have had its own complete Canon; but the Pali Canon of the Theravādins is the only one to have survived complete, or practically so.[35] Of the other early Canons, some are now known only through archaeological relics, fragments on materials such as birch bark found for example in Central Asia, in the caves of the Silk Route, where discoveries continue to be made. (The climate of India itself is not very kind to ancient manuscripts.) Parts of others have survived through being incorporated into the literature of later, Mahāyāna, schools, either as complete texts or as substantial quotations. Thomas Oberlies has made an indispensable survey of the early Mainstream literature currently known, in which he seeks to assign each surviving text or fragment to one of the schools that is known from literature or inscriptions.[36]

Whereas the texts of the Mainstream schools were composed in Middle Indian languages, the Mahāyāna texts seem generally to have been composed in Sanskrit; and by about the fourth century CE the older texts included in the Mahāyāna collections were being translated into Sanskrit too. Buddhist Sanskrit takes a wide variety of forms, which range from a fairly standard form of Sanskrit – not much more 'unclassical' than, for example, the language of the great epics[37] – to a mixed language combining Sanskrit and Middle Indian elements. At its most extreme, the latter can resemble a language with Sanskrit word forms in a Prakrit grammar and syntax. Types of language towards this end of the spectrum are known to scholars as 'Buddhist Hybrid Sanskrit'.

From around the middle of the first millennium CE, as Mahāyāna Buddhism continued to spread outside India, the texts were further translated into non-Indian languages, including Tibetan, Chinese, Japanese and Mongolian. In many instances the Indian versions were subsequently lost, and the texts now survive only through the translations, particularly those in Tibetan or Chinese.

As far as can be ascertained, the structure of other Canons appears to have been similar to that of the Theravāda one, though it appears that there was a certain amount of variation, both in arrangement and in content.[38] Of the large body of literature that must once have existed, certain kinds of texts have survived in multiple versions. There are a number of versions of Vinaya texts – not surprisingly, as each school would have been concerned with regulating the behaviour of its monks and nuns. And of the Sutta/Sūtra texts, there are a striking number of versions of the Dhammapada or closely related works, suggesting that the popularity of this kind of literature began very early, and continued after the development of Buddhism into different schools.

DHAMMAPADAS, DHARMAPADAS AND UDĀNAS

A. Middle Indian Versions: Dhammapadas and Dharmapadas

We currently know of three distinct versions of the Dhammapada in Middle Indian languages:

(i) The Pali Dhammapada

Belonging to the Theravāda school, this forms the main subject of this book. It contains 423 verses, arranged in 26 chapters. No name is recorded for its compiler. The chapters do not seem to be in any obvious order, for example in terms of length, though the last chapter, on 'The Brahmin',[39] is much longer than any of the others. The oldest existing manuscripts date from around 1500 CE, but it is clear that the work was already being handed down in its present form, presumably in writing, at the time of the composition of the Dhammapadaṭṭhakathā, around 500 CE.

Other Middle Indian versions are usually called 'Dharmapada', from the form of the name in Sanskrit and some Prakrits:[40]

(ii) The Gāndhārī Dharmapada

We have the remains of two manuscripts of a Dharmapada in Gāndhārī, a Prakrit from Gandhāra (an area of what is now north-west India, Pakistan and a large part of Afghanistan). The first, and more substantial, version is the Khotan Dharmapada, usually known simply as *the* Gāndhārī Dharmapada. It survives as two portions of a single manuscript, found in Khotan, in Chinese Central Asia, in the 1890s and now divided between Paris and St Petersburg. Taken together, the portions appear to make up about five-eighths of the complete work: their condition suggests that the finder split up the original manuscript in order to sell it to two different collectors – with a big gap where he kept back a third part, hoping to find another buyer. When complete, the Khotan Dharmapada seems to have been in 26 chapters, arranged in order of length from the longest (on 'The Brahmin') to the shortest (title missing), and contained about 550 verses. The most up-to-date edition is still that of John Brough (Brough 1962), who also introduced it in his inimitable style. No translation appears to be available, but I have included a translation of an extract in Appendix I.

More recently, fragments were discovered of another version in Gāndhārī, now kept in the British Library and known as the London Dharmapada. It has been edited and translated by Timothy Lenz (Lenz 2003). It consists of a sequence of 13 verses, all of which are shared with the Khotan version, though with some slight changes in order. Most of them are on the theme of the snake that sloughs its skin (similar to the sequence from the Patna Dharmapada translated in Appendix II). It should be said, however, that the fragments are so tiny that in many cases one has to know what the verse ought to say before one can read it.

Both these manuscripts, written on birch bark in Kharoṣṭhī script, probably date from around the first century CE. The Khotan version is attributed, within the manuscript itself, to one Buddhavarman, but we do not know whether he was its editor or its compiler, or simply the copyist or even the owner of the copy.

The Gāndhārī Dharmapadas are believed to have belonged to the Dharmaguptaka sect, which was central to the spread of Buddhism to Central Asia and China. It gave great importance to the ideal of the Bodhisatta, and contributed largely to what was to become the Mahāyāna tradition of Buddhism. Chinese monks and nuns still follow the Dharmaguptaka Vinaya.[41]

Since Gāndhārī was the language of a distinct political area, well away from the original centre of Buddhism, perhaps we should view the Gāndhārī texts as translations into another Prakrit rather than simply alternative versions.

(iii) The Patna Dharmapada[42]

This was reportedly found in a monastery in Tibet in the 1930s, and we can only hope that it is still there.[43] All editors since then have worked from photographs taken at that time and kept in Patna, Bihar, in north-eastern India – hence the name. It is clearly not the most satisfactory arrangement. This is often described as a 'Sanskrit' or 'Buddhist Hybrid Sanskrit' Dharmapada; but Lenz describes it more accurately as 'a version written in a mixed dialect, showing Pāli, Prakrit and Sanskrit features'.[44] It seems quite likely that some of the more Sanskritic elements, such as the language of the chapter titles, are the result of editing by the copyists, since the manuscript itself is rather late – eleventh or twelfth century CE: after the Middle Indian languages had fallen out of vernacular use.[45] The Patna Dharmapada contains 414 verses, arranged in 22 chapters.

There is an excellent edition of this text by Margaret Cone, which originally formed part of her PhD thesis (Cone 1986) and was subsequently published as an edition of the *Journal of the Pali Text Society* (Cone 1989). A translation, included in the original thesis, sadly remains unpublished. I have included my own translation of one chapter of this text in Appendix II.

The Patna Dharmapada is plausibly attributed to the Sāmatiya sect,[46] which belonged to the Pudgalavāda tradition of Buddhism. The Pudgalavādins reinterpreted the 'no-self' (*anattā/anātman*) doctrine of Buddhism in ways that were felt by other Buddhists to be dangerously close to rejecting it. Whereas other schools maintained strictly that our sense of 'self' is purely illusory, the Pudgalavādins taught that there was a subtle entity (*pudgala*, Pali *puggala*, 'person') that continued from life to life. Although Pudgalavāda Buddhism was extremely widespread in India when Buddhism was still strong there, none of its schools survive today.

B. Sanskrit Versions: Udānavargas

With one small exception (see below), there are no surviving Sanskrit texts explicitly called 'Dharmapada': the equivalents surviving from the Sanskrit Canons are called 'Udānavarga'. The reasons for this are unclear. The word *udāna* (which is the same in Sanskrit and Pali) is generally used in canonical literature to refer to inspired utterances of the Buddha, often, but not necessarily, in verse.[47] So an Udānavarga (chapter of *udānas*) would be a collection of such utterances. In practice, the meanings of *udāna* and *dhammapada* would largely overlap: the utterances of the Buddha would certainly be words of *dhamma*, and vice versa.

The Pali Canon itself contains a text called the Udāna, part of the Khuddaka Nikāya. The Pali Udāna is of similar type to the Dhammapada, containing verses of the same kind, set in stories relating the circumstances in which they came to be spoken. (These resemble the ones in the Dhammapada Commentary, though without the background stories from previous lives.) However, it is a quite distinct text, sharing only a very few verses with the Dhammapada; and, although there is some overlap between the verses of the Sanskrit Udānavargas and the Pali Udāna, the Sanskrit Udānavargas resemble the Pali Dhammapada far more closely than they do the Pali Udāna.

The surviving Sanskrit Udānavarga texts seem to have belonged to the tradition of Buddhism called Sarvāstivāda, 'the doctrine (*vāda*) that everything (*sarva*) is (*asti*)', implying that past and future states exist in some subtle way within the present. The Sarvāstivādins had at least two versions of the Canon,[48] each of which has left us an Udānavarga. The Sarvāstivāda tradition was strong in Central Asia and Tibet, and, like that of the Dharmaguptakas, played an important part in the development of Mahāyāna Buddhism. Monks in the Tibetan tradition still follow the Sarvāstivādin Vinaya.

(i) Buddhist Hybrid Sanskrit Udānavarga

One version of the Udānavarga is represented by an incomplete and much damaged manuscript in Brāhmī script on poplar wood from Subaši, north-east of Kucā in present-day China, and now in the Bibliothèque Nationale, Paris. It dates from about the third–fourth century CE, and is in a distinctly non-classical form of Buddhist Hybrid Sanskrit. It appears to have consisted of some 33 chapters, which may originally have contained over 600 verses. It has been published, with an introduction and notes in French, by H. Nakatani (1987), but there appears to be no translation available in a European language.

(ii) Sanskrit Udānavarga

There is also a better-known Udānavarga composed in a more classical Sanskrit, represented now by various manuscripts and hundreds of fragments, as well as quotations in other works. The whole body of what survives has been edited by Franz Bernhard, with notes and introduction in German (Bernhard 1965–90). Again, there appears to be no translation available for this text. It is by far the longest of any of the surviving Dharmapada/Udānavarga texts, with some 971 verses in 33 chapters.

Verses in the Sanskrit Udānavarga often differ more markedly from their Pali equivalents than do those from the Buddhist Hybrid Sanskrit version. This generally appears to be because their compilers were more concerned with correct Sanskrit grammar and scansion, so that in translating them from whatever Middle Indian version they were using they had to adapt them to make them fit the metres of the verse.[49] Here and there, however, the differences may reflect alternative understandings of the verses.

The Sanskrit Udānavarga appears to have been compiled around the fourth century CE, by Dharmatrāta. It is known to have had a commentary, the Udānavargavivaraṇa ('Explanation of the Udānavarga'), by one Prajñāvarman, similar in format to the Dhammapadaṭṭhakathā. This commentary has disappeared in its original Sanskrit, but survives in Chinese and Tibetan translations.

(iii) Dharmapada Extracts

Yet another version, in what is very definitely a Buddhist Hybrid Sanskrit, is known from quotations in a Mahāyāna text called the Mahāvastu, a rare surviving text from the Lokottaravāda (or Lokuttaravāda) school.[50] The word *lokottara* means 'transcendent' (*loka-uttara*, 'beyond the world(s)'); and it is often confidently stated that the Lokottaravādins regarded the Buddha as an entirely transcendent being, and his actions in the human world as a show, created purely as a means of teaching. This position (comparable to the 'Docetism' of some early Christian sects) is indeed found in some later Mahāyānist schools, but it is probably anachronistic to read it into such an early phase of Buddhism. The issue referred to in the word *lokottara* seems in fact to have been the rather more subtle one of whether a Buddha's speech, as well as his mind, was 'transcendent' and not subject to conditions.[51] Since neither the Lokottaravādins themselves nor the larger Mahāsāṅghika tradition, to which they belonged, have left any contemporary descendants, the matter remains speculative.

The Mahāvastu ('Great Story'), which forms part of a lost Vinaya Piṭaka, is a long retelling of the life story of the Buddha. It contains several quotations explicitly said to be taken from a 'Dharmapada'. Generally these are single verses, all with equivalents in the Udānavarga, and one of which is found also in the Pali Dhammapada (v. 179).[52] But there is one much longer passage, in which the Buddha goes to visit a group of aged ascetics and spurs them to attain Arahatship by teaching them in a sequence of verses corresponding to the 'Thousands' (*Sahassa*) chapter (Chapter 8) of the Pali Dhammapada.[53] Interestingly, here the verses are also referred to as the 'Thousands', though the equivalent chapters of the Sanskrit and Buddhist Hybrid Sanskrit Udānas are called 'Repetition' (*Peyāla*), rather than 'Thousands' (*Sahasra*). I have included a translation of this passage, with its frame story, in Appendix III.

The Mahāvastu contains a further extended verse passage in which the Buddha gives a teaching to a boatman on the river Gaṅgā, who thereupon becomes a monk.[54] Many of the verses spoken there resemble ones in Dhammapada Chapter 25, 'The Monk' (*Bhikkhu*), including, appropriately, several variations on v. 369. Although this passage is not explicitly said to be from a Dharmapada, it seems more than likely that it is from the 'Monk' (*Bhikṣu*) chapter of such a text, as K. R. Norman suggests.[55]

The Mahāvastu in its present form is extremely difficult to date, with current estimates ranging from about the first to the fourth century CE. But in any case the sequences of verses quoted within it could well be considerably older.

C. Dharmapadas and Udānavargas in Chinese

There are four known Chinese translations or compilations of Dharmapada or Udāna material. Unlike the Indian versions, they are dated within the texts themselves. These dates are significant, because they show not only that the original text was in existence by then, but also that it was already sufficiently known and admired, even outside India, for people to want to translate it. A great deal of work remains to be done on these texts and their relationships, both between themselves and with their Indian originals, and few of them have been translated into any European language.

(i) The Fajü jing

This (Taisho 210) was translated and compiled in 224 CE by Weizhinan of the Wu dynasty. The title is the Chinese equivalent of *dhammapada*. It consists of verses only, the central core being more or less a translation of the Pali Dhammapada, or some closely related version. (It is not unheard of for Chinese translators to have worked from a Middle Indian language rather than Sanskrit: many of the early Chinese translations of Buddhist texts were from Gāndhārī.) This core is extended at beginning and end with further material (about a third of the total length of the work) added from elsewhere.

There is a readable modern translation of this text by Ven. K. L. Dhammajoti (1995), which however includes only the core 26 chapters (of 39) most closely corresponding to the Pali Dhammapada; a translation of the rest is planned.

(ii) The Faju piyu jing

This (Taisho 211) was compiled by Faju and Fali of the Jin dynasty, between 290 and 306 CE. It consists of selected stanzas from the Fajü jing together with a commentary, including frame stories, apparently drawing on Indian sources.

Translations of extracts from this text can be found in Beal's version (1878): there appears to be nothing more recent.

(iii) The Chuyao jing

Made by Zhu Fonian of the Qin dynasty in 383 CE, this (Taisho 212) is a translation of an old version of the Udānavarga together with a lost commentary by Dharmatrāta.

(iv) The Faju yaosong jing

This (Taisho 213) is a translation made by Tianxizai, between 980 and 999 CE, of the known Sanskrit Udānavarga, without a commentary.

D. Udānavarga in Tibetan

The Tibetan version is called *ched dubrjod pa'i tshoms*, the Tibetan equivalent of *udānavarga*. It appears to have been translated by Vidyāprabhākara, around the ninth century CE, from the Sanskrit Udānavarga, together with Prajñāvarman's commentary.

Somewhat confusingly, both translators of this version (Rockhill 1883 and Sparham 1983) entitle it 'Dhammapada', no doubt feeling that this would be more widely understood in the English-speaking world than 'Udānavarga'.

Although the various versions of the Dharmapada literature can be assigned with more or less certainty to specific schools of early Buddhism, there appears to be no evidence that the differences between them reflect doctrinal differences between those schools. But we should probably not expect such differences. Unlike, for example, the Abhidharma texts, the Dharmapada literature is concerned not with the more debatable areas of Buddhist philosophy, but with themes common to all the Buddhist traditions, particularly those of generosity, morality, diligence in practice, and the central importance of taking refuge in the Buddha, Dhamma and Saṅgha.

What is a Dharmapada?

From this brief overview, it will be seen that, despite their many similarities, the various Dharmapadas and Udānavargas are all distinct texts. The format remains constant, with the evocative chapter headings and the themed chapters, but the headings themselves can vary, and even when they are similar their order is different. (In any case, as Margaret Cone has pointed out,[56] some of the chapter headings are ones that we would expect to find in *any* compendium of Buddhist verse.) The different versions share a considerable body of verses, but the verses are not always assigned to the equivalent chapters within different versions. The lengths of the texts, when they were all complete, must have varied greatly, between the Sanskrit Udānavarga, with 971 verses in 33 chapters, and the Patna Dharmapada, with 414 verses in 22 chapters.

Clearly, some of the differences in length can be accounted for by repetition and expansion. For example, where the Pali Dhammapada has two verses (13–14):

As rain penetrates
An ill-roofed house,
Passion penetrates
An undeveloped mind.

As rain does not penetrate
A well-roofed house,
Passion does not penetrate
A well-developed mind,

the Patna Dharmapada has six (351–6) – three on the undeveloped and three on the well-developed mind, on the same pattern but with 'passion' replaced in subsequent verses by 'ill will' and 'delusion' – while the Udānavarga has twelve (31.11–22), with verses on 'pride', 'greed' and 'craving' added to the set. The format of the verses lends itself naturally to this kind of elaboration, and we can well imagine a monk adapting the verse to what he saw as the needs of a particular audience.

It is possible, indeed, that the order and number of verses assigned to different topics sometimes reflects local priorities; for example the prominence given to the chapter on 'The Brahmin' in the Gāndhārī Dharmapada may make us wonder whether there was a particular problem in that community with Brahmins who were trying to claim leadership on the strength of their birth, and needed to be reminded that, for Buddhists,

> You don't become a Brahmin
>   By matted locks, by lineage, or by caste:
> If you drive away evils on every side,
>   Small ones and great,
> Through driving away evils
>   You are called a Brahmin.
>
> (Appendix I.1)

But, whatever allowances we make for such forms of change and elaboration, it is not possible to trace these Dharmapadas back to one common original. The most that we can be confident of is that the Middle Indian versions represent an earlier stage of the creation of this literature, while the Sanskrit Udānavarga in its 33-chapter form represents a later stage, when the process of collection and expansion has been going on longer. But there is no certainty as to whether the Pali Dhammapada, or any of the others, is closer to an 'earliest' or 'most authentic' form of the text.

It does seem certain, however, that the *idea* of a Dharmapada was an ancient one – earlier than the division of the Buddhist tradition into different schools. Brough raises the possibility that, after the split, one school may have made a collection of Dharmapada type, and that others had then made their own compilations 'in order not to be outdone by their rivals'; but he at once dismisses this on the grounds that it would not produce the results that we actually find:

> On the evidence of the texts themselves it is much more likely that the schools, in some manner or other, had inherited from the period before the schisms which separated them, a definite tradition of a Dharmapada-text which ought to be included in the canon, however fluctuating the contents of this text might have been, and however imprecise the concept even of a 'canon' at such an early period.[57]

This seems a fair statement, on the basis of the material that is currently known to us. More doubtful is Brough's view that there are 'a few traces of deliberate sectarian rivalry' in the differences in arrangement between the Dharmapada texts:

> But when the last three titles in the Pali, Taṇhā, Bhikkhu, and Brāhmaṇa . . . appear in inverse order as the first three of the Prakrit, we can hardly help thinking that this was done quite deliberately, in order to be different from a rival sect . . . It is not impossible, therefore, that in a few instances a verse might have been placed in a given chapter simply because some other sect preferred to have it in another.[58]

Margaret Cone comments:

> Although it is feasible to suppose that the idea of a collection may have originated with one group, and that groups may have been influenced by what they heard others had done, there is no clear evidence of any closer relationship between any of the collections, not even of a deliberate difference in arrangement (although Brough . . . unconvincingly detects sectarian rivalry in the order of chapters in GDhp [the Gāndhārī Dharmapada]). With very few exceptions, each collection's choice of arrangement is easily explained and justifiable.[59]

Indeed, however strong the rivalries may have been, the main motivation in putting together and ordering any of the collections must have been to preserve as fully and accurately as possible the words of the Buddha, as that was understood by the compilers. Sectarian point-scoring would surely have had a lower priority.

To summarize, then: there must once have been a large body of oral literature in the form of verses, commonly known and recited. Some of these, expressing well-known bits of folk wisdom, were not specific to Buddhism, and were liable to turn up in Jain and Hindu literature too. Others had a specifically Buddhist message. Collections of such verses were already in existence before the various splits that gave rise to the different Mainstream schools. Those who compiled them seem to have known them either as Dhammapada/Dharmapada or Udānavarga, titles which for practical purposes were nearly synonymous.

Meanwhile, other verses carried on being handed down separately, or were found scattered through other Buddhist texts. For some centuries, such verses continued to be added to the collections as they were handed on. In the case of the Sanskrit Udānavarga and the Chinese translations, the process carried on longest; but the compilers were still often drawing on material that was genuinely ancient. However, at some point in each tradition it was decided that the collection was complete, a discrete item in a Canon of recognized teachings of the Buddha.

Study of the Dharmapada literature raises many questions about the nature and history of the oral tradition in Buddhism. What, for example, does all this variation tell us about its traditional attribution to the Buddha himself? Clearly, it does not rule it out, since the Buddha must have spoken a great many verses over the course of his forty-five years of teaching. (At that period, verse would have been thought at least as natural as prose as a way of conveying information that needed to be memorized.) It would not be surprising if sometimes he used or adapted verses that already existed in popular lore, or reused ones that he had previously composed, with variations to suit a new context; nor if some of those verses then returned to the folk tradition, and turned up again elsewhere.

But of course it is highly probable that verses spoken by others have ended up being attributed to the Buddha. Indeed, there are traditional precedents for such attributions; for example, in the commentary on Dhammapada v. 421, the Buddha hears a report of a teaching given by the Arahat nun Dhammadinnā, on which he comments, 'My daughter Dhammadinnā has explained it well: if I myself were to answer this question I would answer in just the same way.' As a result, Dhammadinnā's words are accounted 'Buddha's teaching' rather than 'Arahat's teaching'.[60] Such traditions would perhaps have made it acceptable up to a certain point to add new verses to the Dharmapada literature, so long as they were felt to have the authentic flavour of the Buddha's teaching.

COMMENTARIES

The name of the Commentary on the Pali Dhammapada, the Dhammapadaṭṭhakathā, is simply the Pali for 'Commentary on the Dhammapada'. Though not regarded as canonical, this Commentary is immensely popular. It includes some of the best-known stories[61] of the life of the Buddha and his early followers, such as the tales of Aṅgulimāla, the murderous bandit who became an Arahat, and of Kisā Gotamī and the mustard seed. Many of these stories have an inspirational quality, reminding the reader of the example of the Buddha's early followers, or warning against the errors of his opponents. Often, too, the Commentary seeks to describe the causes of these events, in terms of the actions of the characters in previous lives.[62]

The Dhammapadaṭṭhakathā was composed in what is now Sri Lanka, and was apparently largely based on material already existing in the vernacular language of the island, presumably a Sinhala Prakrit.[63] It is attributed in one manuscript to the great commentator Buddhaghosa (fourth or fifth century CE).[64] Though K. R. Norman seems on the whole to accept this attribution (albeit with reservations),[65] other scholars have doubted it, preferring to date the Commentary a little later than Buddhaghosa.[66] In any case, it was certainly written the better part of a millennium after the period in which the main stories are set. However, the actual custom of commentating on the Dhammapada verses must go back to their beginning, since some of them would be hard to understand without such a commentary, while a few would seem to be positively dangerous (e.g. vv. 97, 294–5). The Commentary draws on a wide range of material, including earlier canonical literature, and popular stories with a strong element of folklore (magic rings, self-filling rice pots, etc.). I have not translated the commentarial material, since to do so would have expanded this book to many times its present length;[67] however, I have included summaries of the principal stories, since they are vital to our understanding of how the Dhammapada has been thought about and used in the Buddhist tradition – and how it continues to be used.

To get a flavour of the Commentary, it is worth seeing what the commentator has done with the two famous verses with which the Dhammapada begins:

manopubbaṅgamā dhammā manoseṭṭhā manomayā
manasā ce paduṭṭhena bhāsati vā karoti vā
tato naṃ dukkham anveti cakkaṃ va vahato padaṃ.

manopubbaṅgamā dhammā manoseṭṭhā manomayā
manasā ce pasannena bhāsati vā karoti vā
tato naṃ sukham anveti chāyā va anapāyinī.

Fore-run by mind are mental states,
    Ruled by mind, made of mind.
If you speak or act
    With corrupt mind,
Suffering follows you,
    As the wheel the foot of the ox.

Fore-run by mind are mental states,
    Ruled by mind, made of mind.
If you speak or act
    With clear mind,
Happiness follows you,
    Like a shadow that does not depart.

This is a clear statement of the law of *kamma*, as it is understood in the Buddhist tradition: that it is the *intention* with which an act is performed that causes its consequences. The stories in the Dhammapadaṭṭhakathā are chosen to reinforce this message. That accompanying the first verse concerns a blind monk who is an Arahat. One day as he walks he is seen to be crushing many small insects under his feet; but because of his blindness he does not realize it. His fellow monks complain to the Buddha that he has committed the severe offence of taking life – enough to warrant expulsion from the Order. But the Buddha explains that, as there was no intention to kill, the monk has committed no fault.

The story on the second verse concerns a sick youth who is the son of a miser. The father refuses to spend money on a doctor until it is too late, and the boy dies; but, because he has mentally taken refuge in the Buddha, he is reborn in a heavenly state. Appearing to his former father in his divine new form, he causes him to mend his ways.

These are the bare bones of the stories, and their message seems clear; but, in the Commentary as we have it, the first story in particular is much elaborated. In it, we hear of two brothers, Mahāpāla and Cullapāla.[68] Mahāpāla becomes a monk in middle age, and makes a determination to spend the *vassa* (the three-month retreat of the rainy season) without lying down, sitting up even to sleep – a form of ascetic practice. But he contracts an eye disease. A physician prescribes an ointment, but instructs him to lie down while he uses it: if he does not do so, says the doctor, he will certainly go blind. Even after three separate warnings, Mahāpāla refuses this advice and keeps to his vow. He loses his sight, but gains Arahatship at the same moment.

The other monks wish to know the reason for this, and the Buddha explains that in a previous existence Mahāpāla was a physician. A poor woman came to him for a cure for an eye disease; she promised that, if he were to cure her, she and her children would become his slaves. But when she recovered she did not want to keep her word, so she pretended that the medicine had not worked after all. Then the physician in revenge gave her another ointment, which made her go blind. As a result of this, he became blind in a number of later existences – yet another illustration of *kamma* in action.

What one feels about the likelihood of all this will depend, of course, on one's own views about *kamma* and rebirth. But, as a story, it seems so grim that it threatens to overbalance the message of the verses. Moreover, persisting in a vow at the cost of losing one's eyesight does not seem entirely in keeping with the Middle Way, which shuns the extreme of asceticism as well as that of self-indulgence. But I do not think the commentator is prescribing such a course of action for the reader (or hearer): rather, he is setting up an extreme example of one of the Buddhist virtues, the perfection of commitment or *adhiṭṭhāna*, just as the Jātaka tales tell of extreme acts of generosity or self-sacrifice in the previous lives of the Buddha. And the idea that a person may give up physical sight to gain a higher kind of vision seems to have an archetypal resonance: we may think, for example, of the Norse god Odin, who sacrificed one of his eyes to drink from the spring of wisdom. There is also the consolatory aspect, found in many of these stories, that, despite his wicked action in a previous life, with all its heavy consequences, Mahāpāla in his last life was able to overcome all his defilements and attain the perfect peace and freedom of Arahatship.

A similar pair of verses is found in the other extant Dharmapadas, though not generally at the beginning. We find them in the Sanskrit Udānavarga (31.23–4) and the (Khotan) Gāndhārī Dharmapada (201–2), in both cases with variant readings: in place of 'made of mind' (Pali *manomayā*) we have 'swift as mind' (Sanskrit *manojavāḥ*, Gāndhārī *maṇojava*), and in place of 'Like a shadow that does not depart' (Pali *chāyā va anapāyinī*) we have 'Like a pursuing shadow' (Sanskrit *chāyā vā hy anugāminī*, Gāndhārī *chaya va aṇukamiṇi*).[69]

According to the Chinese commentary translated by Beal (1878), and based presumably on that of Prajñāvarman, the verses refer to two young merchants who hear the Buddha's teaching, but respond to it in different ways. One rejects it, gets drunk, and goes to sleep by the roadside, with the result that in the morning he is killed by the wheels of the other merchants' wagons. The other is more moderate in his drinking, and is protected as he sleeps by the Four Kings, the guardian deities of the four directions. He is taken up by a wealthy merchant, who has noticed that the shadow of a tree continues to fall on him even when the sun has moved round the sky – a story told elsewhere of the Buddha-to-be as he meditates under a rose-apple tree while still a boy. So the second merchant goes on to make his fortune.

In this case, the stories seem to have been made up on the basis of the verses (perhaps even slightly mistranslated or misunderstood),[70] rather than the other way round. But elsewhere the Chinese commentaries (which, as we have seen, date from roughly the same period as the existing Pali one) seem to have preserved understandings that have been lost in the Pali version.[71]

Though perhaps we should not make too much of this until more research has been done on the Chinese commentarial literature, the stories presumably also reflect the circumstances in which they were told. While a monk teaching in Sri Lanka would draw on stories of the monastic life there, and the agricultural community that surrounded him, one who was teaching in towns on the Silk Route might well draw on tales of merchants and travellers – people like many of those in his audience.[72] But both would also have had memories well stocked with accounts, from the early Canons and elsewhere, of the life of the Buddha and the first men and women who followed him.

The story of Mahāpāla illustrates an important theme in the Dhammapadaṭṭhakathā: the moment of realization of one of the higher states, as the mind becomes successively free from the 'fetters' (*saṃyojana*): the state of the Stream-Enterer (whose mind is for the first time turned unalterably towards liberation), Once-Returner, Non-Returner, or Arahat – the last being a fully liberated being, freed from all fetters and no longer liable to fall into states such as fear, anger or desire. This liberation does not make him or her a colourless character, and the Arahats in these stories all have their own qualities and special talents. For example, although Arahats are by definition free from fear, in the story accompanying v. 177 the former bandit Aṅgulimāla is shown to have a special power over wild elephants, perhaps because he has made a particular effort to develop loving kindness. Certain of the Arahats and other leading followers of the Buddha appear repeatedly in the Commentary: among them are the two chief monks Sāriputta, noted for his wisdom, and Moggallāna, noted for his psychic powers; Ānanda, the Buddha's faithful attendant; and the generous lay followers Anāthapiṇḍika and Visākhā. These and many others clearly had a firm place in popular consciousness, and were instantly recognized when they appeared as characters in these stories.[73]

THE DHAMMAPADA AS LITERATURE

Among all the doubts about the relationships between the different versions of the Dhammapada and Udānavarga, one thing remains clear: this literature was immensely popular. It was loved, memorized and commented on in widely diverse countries and languages, and in many different schools of Buddhism; and it continues to be so.[74] Today, the Pali Dhammapada is still one of the most read and quoted Buddhist texts, within the Theravādin community and outside it. So it is worth considering the nature of its appeal.

John Brough, the editor of the Gāndhārī Dharmapada, was less than enthusiastic about the qualities of the Dharmapada texts as literature:

> In cultural conditions where the cliché, and particularly the religious cliché, was not so much tolerated as venerated, and where many existing verses could with the greatest of ease be broken into usable quarters, it is understandable that a considerable treasure-house of versified tags was ready to hand for any monk zealous to compose. Now and then a monk might be a poet, and here and there among the Dharmapada verses we have the good fortune to inherit some fragments of excellent poetry. But we should not expect to find very much. Poetry is not an easy art, and good poets are always rare. To build from other men's bricks and sanctified clichés is tolerably simple; and many a monk entirely devoid of poetic ability was readily persuaded that his verses were no worse than those of his neighbour.
>
> The resulting vast accumulations of insipid mediocrity which piety preserves are by no means peculiar to Buddhism . . . Buddhism has its own share of great art; but we do no service to Buddhism or to its genuine art if we magnify the literary worth

> of a text beyond its deserts . . . Distinguished scholars (not themselves Buddhists) have indeed written with liberal hyperbole of the 'profound moral value' of the Pali *Dhammapada*, and have rated it among the masterpieces of Indian literature. Here I politely dissent. Those who write in this way can hardly have made any serious comparison with great literature; nor could anyone with a sense of literary values describe the whole collection in terms scarcely merited by its best parts, if he had himself lived day and night close enough to these verses for long enough to arrive at an assessment of his own disencumbered of hearsay.[75]

But since I too have now spent a certain amount of time with these verses, I feel emboldened to disagree with my first Professor of Sanskrit. Clearly, taste is at issue here, and no doubt John Brough was temperamentally attracted to polished, classical works of literature, of the kind that he himself translated in his wonderful *Poems from the Sanskrit* (1968). But the Dhammapada, in all its forms, retains a strong kinship with oral literature.

Few, I think, would deny that oral literature can have its own masterpieces: we need only think of folk ballads such as 'Sir Patrick Spens' or lyrics such as 'The Lyke-Wake Dirge'. No one thinks it is a blemish in such works if they contain repetitions or set phrases. For that matter, I doubt whether anyone thinks the worse of Homer because of his use of such set expressions as 'the wine-dark sea' or 'wily Odysseus', designed to fit as neatly into the Greek hexameter line as 'that one I call a Brahmin' (*tam ahaṃ brūmi brāhmaṇaṃ*) does into the *śloka*.[76] On the contrary, they are rightly regarded as part of his charm.

The Dhammapada originated in an age when verse was the main means of retaining and handing on knowledge, and its primary purpose was to convey its message in clear, memorable terms. In this it succeeds admirably. Indeed, if one has lived with it for a while, it becomes quite difficult not to keep quoting it. There is its realistic attitude to unfair criticism (vv. 227–8):

This is an ancient truth, Atula,
    Not just for today:
Folk blame the one who sits silent;
    They blame the one who says a lot;
They blame the one who says little, too –
    No one in this world is not blamed.

There never was, there never will be,
    Nor is there found today
A person who is altogether blamed
    Or altogether praised.

On the ways in which quarrels, between people or nations, are perpetuated, and the only way to end them (vv. 3–5):

'He insulted me, he struck me,
    He defeated me, he robbed me':
For those who get caught up in this,
    Hatred does not cease.

'He insulted me, he struck me,
    He defeated me, he robbed me':
For those who do not get caught up in this,
    Hatred ceases completely.

For never here
    Do hatreds cease by hatred.
By freedom from hatred they cease:
    This is a perennial truth.

On the devastating way in which death intervenes in human plans (v. 47):

While a man gathers flowers,
    His mind attached to this and that,
Death carries him away
    As great a flood takes a sleeping village.

Its earthy, proverbial-sounding verses on the perils of adultery (vv. 309–10) seem to me very far from Brough's 'other men's bricks and sanctified clichés':

Four things happen to the reckless man
Who goes with the wife of another:
Ill fortune earned; disturbed sleep;
Third, blame; and fourth, a hell world –

Ill fortune earned, and an evil destination:
Small pleasure for frightened man with
frightened woman –
And the king imposes a heavy punishment.
So a man shouldn't go with the wife of another.

In the original, the whole rhythm of the verses (the longer *triṣṭubh-jagatī*[77] rather than the *śloka*) suggests agitation, and in line 2 of the second verse the masculine and feminine forms of *bhīta*, 'frightened', seem to huddle together as though listening for an angry husband coming home:

cattāri ṭhānāni naro pamatto
āpajjati paradārūpasevī:
apuññalābhaṃ na nikāmaseyyaṃ
nindaṃ tatīyaṃ nirayaṃ catutthaṃ,

apuññalābho ca gatī ca pāpikā
bhītassa bhītāya ratī ca thokikā
rājā ca daṇḍaṃ garukaṃ paṇeti,
tasmā naro paradāraṃ na seve.

(The inflected nature of Pali enables the poet to vary the word-order without obscuring the meaning of the sentence.)

The imagery of the Dhammapada tends to be simple and immediate. Many of its similes are taken from nature: from the sun, moon and weather; from rocks, mountains and lakes. Various trees and plants are mentioned, each with associations familiar to the original hearer, just as a reader of English poetry would recognize the distinct characters and associations of the oak, yew, lily or rose. We hear of the bamboo, which flowers rarely and then dies; of the sweet-scented jasmine; and of course of the lotus, which grows pure and fragrant out of muddy water. Among animals, we hear of migrating geese, of herons fishing in ponds, of monkeys, hares, spiders and bees – the last being pointed out as the model for the way in which a monk should live, supported by his lay followers, but not exploiting them (v. 49):

> In the village, a sage should go about
> Like a bee, which, not harming
> Flower, colour or scent,
> Flies off with the nectar.

There are numerous references to domesticated creatures such as cattle, horses and mules.[78] The elephant, a much-loved animal, has a chapter of its own (Chapter 23).

There are many references to the world of work. Farming (particularly cattle-keeping) naturally predominates, but we find references also to craft skills such as carpentry (vv. 80, 145), arrow-making (vv. 80, 145), silversmithing (v. 239) and garland-making (vv. 44–5, 53).[79] From the less respectable parts of society, we hear of the cheating gambler (v. 252) and the professional criminal (v. 97).

The arts of war provide a useful source of similes for the resolution and skills necessary for the meditator who seeks to conquer the defilements. We hear, for example, of the need to guard one's own actions as one would guard a border town (v. 315). In battle, the bow is the principal weapon (indeed the only one mentioned in the Dhammapada). A warrior might ride into battle on horseback, on an elephant, or (like the heroes of the Mahābhārata) in a chariot – in which case the charioteer also plays a vital part, controlling the horses so that the warrior can use his weapons (vv. 94, 222).

Secular power is embodied in the king and his officers, while the religious establishment is represented by the Brahmins, the priestly class who are responsible for carrying on the ritual practices based on the traditions of the Vedas. But outside the settled life of the household there is another class of religious practitioner, who has (at least in theory) given up all worldly ties. Such wanderers, often called *samaṇa* (Sanskrit *śramaṇa*),[80] are of many kinds, some of them following extreme ascetic practices, wandering naked, or eating next to nothing. The Buddhist monks (*bhikkhu*)[81] are marked out by their shaven heads and their yellow or orange robes. They are enjoined not to follow such extreme practices, but to live in a modest, disciplined way, striving ceaselessly towards liberation. The Dhammapada has strong warnings for those monks who wear the robe and accept the alms of lay supporters but do not practise as they should (v. 308). Though the monastic life is regarded as particularly conducive to spiritual attainment (v. 99), we are reminded that those living the household life may also reach such attainments (v. 142).

The existence of gods and other non-human beings is taken for granted. Normally they are mentioned in a general way, as a group (vv. 94, 420), but a few are mentioned by name, notably Maghavan (known elsewhere as Sakka), the king of the gods (v. 30), and Brahmā, a deity of the higher realms (vv. 105, 230).[82] The forces that bind beings to *saṃsāra* – the realm of rebirth – are embodied in the figure of Māra, the tempter (vv. 7–8, 34, 37, 40, 46, 57, 105, 175, 274, 276, 337, 350). Death, the inevitable consequence of living in that realm, is also personified (vv. 46–8, 170, 287), and often identified with the god Yama, in myth the ruler and judge of the dead (vv. 44–5, 235, 237).

Although the gods are thought to have far longer and happier lives than human beings, their condition is not fundamentally different from our own: indeed, human beings can win divine status in a future life through morality and generosity (vv. 30, 224). All conditioned states, including existences in heaven or hell worlds, are impermanent, and the state of a liberated human being is greater than that of any deity (cf. vv. 94, 105, 230).

The dangers and seductions of *saṃsāra* are portrayed as fever (v. 90), poison (vv. 123–4), captivity (v. 346), or the threat of attack from bandits (v. 123). Its suffering is compared to that of a fish on land (v. 34) or of birds caught in a net (v. 174). The quest for liberation is often pictured, naturally, as a path to be followed (Chapter 20, *passim*), or as a river to be crossed (vv. 85–6). More unexpectedly, perhaps, the understanding that comes (or not) as one tries to live the spiritual life can be expressed in terms of something as simple and homely as eating soup (vv. 64–5):

Even if lifelong
  A fool attends upon a wise man,
He no more knows *dhammas*
  Than a spoon knows the flavours of soup.

Even if for a moment
  An intelligent man attends upon a wise man,
He quickly knows *dhammas*
  As the tongue knows the flavours of soup.

The basic simplicity of the Dhammapada style does not exclude certain kinds of artfulness, including word games and puns of an extremely elaborate kind (see the section on 'Translating the Dhammapada', below). But most characteristic is a straightforwardness of word and thought that yet suggests great possibilities for reflection, as we see in the famous summary of the teaching of the Buddhas – not just one, but all Awakened Ones (v. 183):

Not to do any evil;
  To undertake what is good;
To purify your own mind:
  This is the teaching of the Buddhas.

sabbapāpassa akaraṇaṃ kusalassa upasampadā
sacittapariyodapanaṃ etaṃ buddhāna sāsanaṃ.

At such moments, the Pali Dhammapada has a lean, spare beauty that is all its own.

TRANSLATING THE DHAMMAPADA

There have been countless translations of the Pali Dhammapada. It is generally stated that the first version in a European language was a Latin version, published in 1855, by the pioneering Danish scholar Michael Viggo Fausbøll, which in turn profoundly influenced the first English translation, by the great Max Müller, published in the series 'The Sacred Books of the East' in 1881.

This is probably true if we consider only translations of the complete text. However, both Fausbøll and Müller acknowledge a debt to an earlier English version, by the Revd Daniel John Gogerly, a London-born Methodist missionary to Sri Lanka, who was also a serious scholar of Pali and Buddhism. Gogerly's version, of the first eighteen of the twenty-six chapters, was originally published in 1840 in a Methodist journal called *The Friend*.[83] Despite some misunderstandings of Buddhist philosophy, Gogerly shows a sympathy, remarkable for his time, for the ethical teachings of the Dhammapada, and his work deserves not to be forgotten.

Since the age of these pioneers, the Dhammapada has been translated into a remarkable number of languages. An exhibition of manuscripts and published editions of Buddhist texts held at the Staatsbibliothek, Munich, in 2005 included a translation into Polish, dated 1925, one into Yiddish, dated 1958, and one into Turkish, dated 1982.[84] There have also been numerous versions in English, many of them still in print – which naturally leads to the question of why it seemed necessary to undertake a new one.

The existing versions tend to fall into two main categories. On the one hand are those designed primarily for devotional purposes, aimed at committed Buddhists – the sort of book that a Buddhist might keep on his or her bedside table for inspiration. In this type of translation, explanations of doubtful points tend to be traditionally based.[85] Other versions have a more scholarly flavour, but are still firmly rooted within the Pali commentarial tradition. A particularly fine example of this kind of translation is that of J. R. Carter and M. Palihawadana (1987). On the other hand there are the academic translations, of which the great current example is that of K. R. Norman (*The Word of the Doctrine*, 1997), which draws on the latest scholarship on the Dhammapada and the related texts. It is an awe-inspiring work of scholarship, but its renderings are highly literal, and its style is not aimed at the general reader.

Both Carter and Palihawadana's and Norman's translations – and numerous others, listed in the Bibliography – have been indispensable to me in working on the text. But it still seemed to me that there was room for a new translation, drawing on up-to-date scholarship but combining it with readability. I also wanted to provide some sense of the body of literature to which the Pali Dhammapada belonged, giving the general reader some access to such works as the Gāndhārī and the Patna Dharmapadas, of which there are either no translations at all or ones available only in specialist academic works. So in a series of appendices following the main body of the book I have included translations of extracts from three other extant versions.

In producing the present translation, my first aim was of course to express as accurately as possible the meaning of the original text, as far as we can currently ascertain it. But, along with this, I was also concerned to convey, if I could, something of the feeling of the original, the way in which it would have struck its early hearers in the Pali – something that is perhaps even harder to ascertain, but that still seemed worthwhile to attempt.

In the first place, this meant that I was committed to a verse translation, whereas most previous versions of the Dhammapada have been in prose. A rhymed version, or any other formal type of English verse, would have been impossible while retaining the nuances of meaning, but I have tried to represent the form and feeling of the verses in stanzas of free verse of a similar shape to the originals. So where the original verse has four *pādas*, I have used four lines; where it has six *pādas*, six lines. But the content is not necessarily divided up between the lines in the same way as it divides between the *pādas* in Pali: the syntax of the two languages is so different that to attempt to do this would create a forced or unnatural effect.

The Dhammapada presents a number of special challenges to the translator. Pali, like other ancient Indian languages, reflects a culture with different assumptions from the modern English-speaking world (even including modern India). Often, to make sense of a verse for the contemporary reader, I have had to add a word or two implied, but not stated, in the original. Where I have done this, I have mentioned the fact in the notes.

I wanted to keep the plain-spoken, sometimes even colloquial, feeling of the original, and to avoid writing 'Buddhist Hybrid English'[86] – that language in which things are never 'lucky' or 'good', always 'auspicious' or 'meritorious'. I also wanted to avoid scattering the text with untranslated Pali terminology; but in some cases there is simply no single English equivalent for a Pali term. A particularly difficult case is *dhamma*, which has a number of technical meanings, ranging from 'mental state' (or even 'thing') to *the* Dhamma – the teaching of the Buddhas. Even when the word is used in the former senses, however, there is still a sense that the 'small-d' *dhamma* is an instance or expression of the 'capital-d' Dhamma. In the translation, where there *is* a usable English equivalent I have translated the 'small-d' *dhamma* with the meaning that it bears in its context, while leaving the 'capital-d' Dhamma as it is. It should be remarked, however, that Pali in its original scripts has no equivalent of upper- and lower-case letters, so this too may sometimes be a matter of interpretation. So again I have mentioned such decisions in the notes.

Although I have tried to keep close to the structures of the original, there are many usages in Pali that, though possible, would be awkward in English, giving the impression that the original was awkward too, rather than clear and lucid as it generally is. One particularly pressing question was how to translate impersonal constructions, which are far more common in Pali than in English. The 'one' construction tends to sound over-formal, or even clumsy, in verse, and current spoken English prefers 'you'. So, after considerable reflection, I decided that I would normally translate such constructions with 'you': 'you should make an effort' rather than 'one should make an effort.' There seemed little danger of causing misunderstanding, since in the Dhammapada there generally *is* an element of advice or warning to the hearer in such expressions; but, for those who are happier knowing such things, where the 'you' *is* a genuine second-person form – with the Buddha addressing some person or group of people – I have mentioned the fact in the notes.

The Dhammapada also makes frequent use of a structure in which a verb is expressed once, but is meant to be understood two or three times; for example, in its very first verse, we have

> Suffering follows you,
>   As the wheel the foot of the ox.

Here I felt that the reader would readily understand the last line to mean 'as the wheel [follows] the foot of the ox [that draws the cart]', so I have kept the usage – especially as the language of the poem itself here feels a little unusual and arresting. But elsewhere I have adapted it to what I have felt would be the current English usage, by adding the verb that is to be understood. For example, for v. 252 I have written

> Others' faults are easy to see,
>   While your own are hard to see.
> The faults of others
>   You winnow like chaff;
> You hide your own
>   As a cunning gambler hides a bad throw

rather than

>   . . . . . .
>   As a cunning gambler a bad throw.

Pali also makes great use of constructions involving the 'absolutive' or 'indeclinable participle': 'having done this, one is freed.' Where I have felt that English would more naturally say 'if you do this, you'll be freed,' this is how I have translated it. Similarly, I have often translated passive verbs ('this is done by me') into the active ('I do this').

A particular problem in translating the Dhammapada is its fondness for puns, which in ancient India could be used as a means of conveying serious truths: see for example the complex plays on words for 'wood' and 'desire' in vv. 283–4, 344. A Tudor poet might just have managed to make something of this (perhaps speaking of the 'woodness', i.e. madness, of desire); in modern English, however, puns are primarily viewed as a way of making jokes, and I have scarcely attempted to reproduce them, except in a very limited way (see vv. 256–7). Generally I have had to settle on one of the meanings for the translation, and explain the rest in the notes. The culminating horror for the translator is v. 97, with a sequence of epithets which apply, on the surface, to a master criminal, but on deeper reflection to an enlightened saint. In this case the only solution I could find was to provide two complete translations, with explanations in the notes.

But, despite the above, the most pervasive challenge of all in translating the Dhammapada is its sheer straightforwardness. There are some verses of great simplicity which are immensely touching in the original, but quite impossible to translate without losing most of their power – for example vv. 42–3:

Whatever an enemy can do to an enemy,
Or a rival to a rival,
A wrongly directed mind
Will do worse to you than that.

What mother or father cannot do,
Or any other kin,
A rightly directed mind
Will do better for you than that.

diso disaṃ yan taṃ kayirā
verī vā pana verinaṃ
micchāpaṇihitaṃ cittaṃ
pāpiyo naṃ tato kare.

na taṃ mātā pitā kayirā
aññe vāpi ca ñātakā
sammāpaṇihitaṃ cittaṃ
seyyaso naṃ tato kare.

With no similes or ornaments and the plainest of vocabulary, these verses leave the translator absolutely nowhere to hide. In the original, they are capable of bringing a tear to the eye; but it would be too much to expect a translation to do the same.

I hope, however, that, in order to experience this work to best effect, the reader will pause from time to time and speak some of the verses aloud. This was, after all, how the original was meant to be experienced; and in my translation I have tried to be true to that fact.

NOTES

1. Since these works were transmitted orally, perhaps for some centuries, before being put into writing, the word 'literature' in this context is not meant to be restricted to things which were written down.
2. On the life of the Buddha, see below.
3. Some have also sensed a pun on *dhammapatha*, 'way or path of the *dhamma*', but this seems less likely (Mizuno 1979: 255–6).
4. For example K. R. Norman's translation (Norman 1997) bears the title *The Word of the Doctrine*. However, this follows the general practice of the Pali Text Society, in which editions of original texts are called by their Pali titles, and translations have their titles translated into English.
5. Theravāda (Sanskrit Sthaviravāda), 'The Doctrine of the Elders', also known as the Southern school, has long been the predominant form of Buddhism in Sri Lanka, Burma, Cambodia and Thailand, with communities also in Laos, Malaysia and Bangladesh, and now a following in the West. For more on the Theravāda traditions, see below.
6. Or one of his followers spoke it with the Buddha's endorsement. For more on the Dhammapadaṭṭhakathā, see below, 'Commentaries'.
7. Pali *vatta* or *anuṭṭhubha*; but the Sanskrit terms are more widely understood. This verse form could be said to be the equivalent in Sanskrit and Pali of the iambic pentameter in English.
8. And such a trial to the translator: see e.g. v. 97 and notes, and vv. 283–4 and notes. (Puns may also have been intended in places where they are no longer readily detected: for a likely example, see vv. 44–5 and notes.)

9. See for example the notes on v. 175.
10. I have noted a few such examples (e.g. vv. 70, 109, 131, 200, notes), but have not attempted to be comprehensive.
11. For the version found in the Dhammapada Commentary, see the notes on vv. 11–12.
12. In Sanskrit, Śākya – hence the title, often used of the Buddha in Mahāyāna texts, of Śākyamuni, 'Sage of the Śākyas'.
13. In Sanskrit, Siddhārtha Gautama. Siddhattha means '[He] who has accomplished his aim'; Gotama is the name of his family's *gotta* or lineage. It remains unclear why the Sākiyas, a proudly Khattiya clan, claimed membership of a Brahmin *gotta* (see the notes to v. 393). Their marriages were certainly not arranged according to Brahmanical *gotta* rules.
14. The later commentaries call her Yasodharā (Sanskrit Yaśodharā), 'Fame-bearer', but canonical texts use other names, most often simply 'the Mother of Rāhula'.
15. However, the Dīgha Nikāya (2.23–30, from Sutta 14, the Mahāpadāna Sutta) describes such a series of encounters in the early life of a previous Buddha, Vipassin.
16. Since we are told elsewhere (e.g. Dīgha Nikāya 2.14; Sutta 14: Mahāpadāna Sutta) that his mother, Māyādevī, had died shortly after his birth, the 'mother' referred to here must be his step-mother, Mahāpajāpati (Sanskrit Mahāprajāpatī/Mahāprajāvatī), who brought him up as her own.
17. Majjhima Nikāya 1.161–75, esp. 1.163–73 (Sutta 26: Ariyapariyesanā Sutta); ibid. 1.238–51, esp. 1.241–51 (Sutta 36: Mahāsaccaka Sutta).
18. The accounts of his struggles in terms of the attack by Māra are found first in the commentaries: see the story segment of the notes on vv. 11–12.
19. Dhammacakkapavattana Sutta, found in both the Vinaya Piṭaka (Vinaya 1.10–12) and the Sutta Piṭaka (Saṃyutta Nikāya 56.11).
20. For specialist terms see the Glossary.
21. Dīgha Nikāya 2.72–168 (Sutta 16: Mahāparinibbāna Sutta).
22. *vaya-dhammā saṅkhārā. appamādena sampādetha.* A powerful saying that does not lend itself easily to translation. '*Saṅkhāras* are *vaya-dhamma* [i.e having the nature (*dhamma*) of passing away (*vaya*)]. Bring about success by means of awareness [*appamāda* – see the notes for Chapter 2].'
23. Dates are given in the form BCE (Before Common Era) and CE (Common Era), rather than BC and AD.

24. For recent thinking on the dates of the Buddha see Bechert 1991–7, Cousins 1996 and Prebish 2008.
25. Dīpavaṃsa 20.20–21: see K. R. Norman 1983: 10–11, Roth 2000: 64. The idea that a council was held for this purpose is debatable.
26. I am grateful to L. S. Cousins for this observation.
27. The word 'Prakrit' (Sanskrit *prākṛta*) denotes a vernacular language, as distinct from Sanskrit (*saṃskṛta*, 'perfected'), the language of culture. Though Pali certainly belongs in that category, it is often treated as distinct from other Middle Indian languages, in expressions such as 'Prakrit and Pali'.
28. However, the language of the Pali texts differs in a number of ways from the language of surviving inscriptions from that area, generally known as 'Māgadhī'. Māgadhī has some distinctive features, such as the use of 'l' in certain positions where other Middle Indian languages, including Pali, would normally have 'r'. Some 'Māgadhisms' are preserved in the Pali Canon, along with forms from other early dialects (K. R. Norman, 1983: 4–5).
29. See further K. R. Norman 1980, and, for another view, Ven. Thanissaro Bhikkhu, <http://www.accesstoinsight.org/tipitaka/kn/dhp/dhp.intro.than.html>, section on 'Historical Notes'.
30. Sanskrit Tripiṭaka. As is usual in discussing Theravāda Buddhism and its texts, where the Pali and Sanskrit forms of a word differ, I use the Pali form: hence *dhamma* rather than *dharma*, *nibbāna* rather than *nirvāṇa*. (Some words, such as *buddha*, literally, 'awakened one', and *vinaya*, 'discipline', are the same in both languages.) The Sanskrit alternatives are given in the Glossary, for those who are more accustomed to seeing them.
31. Though this is now the most widely accepted arrangement, historically there have been others, including one in which both the Vinaya and the Abhidhamma texts were included in the Khuddaka Nikāya (Norman 1983, 8).
32. Harrison 1987.
33. Harrison 2005: 168, 169.
34. Harrison 1987: 80.
35. There is a little room for doubt, because two later Pali works, the Nettippakaraṇa and the Peṭakopadesa, thought to have been written around the start of the Common Era, illustrate their arguments by quoting extracts from the Pali Canon. Among these are a number of passages that are no longer present in the Pali Canon as we have it – many of them verses of Dhammapada

type. Some, however, consider that these texts were drawing on another version of the Canon.

36. Oberlies 2003–4.
37. The great Sanskrit epics, the Mahābhārata and the Rāmāyaṇa, contain a large number of non-standard grammatical forms, suggesting their own strong links with the oral tradition.
38. The Sanskrit equivalents of the various parts of the Tipiṭaka/Tripiṭaka are: (1) Vinaya Piṭaka; (2) Sūtra Piṭaka; (3) Abhidharma Piṭaka. In the Mahāyāna schools, the constituent parts of the Sūtra Piṭaka were generally called *āgama* ('tradition') rather than *nikāya*: the Dīrghāgama, Madhyamāgama, Saṃyuktāgama, Ekottarāgama/Ekottarikāgama (*ekottara*/*ekottarikā*, 'more by one') and Kṣudraka. (The term *nikāya* is still found within the Mahāyāna texts, and *āgama* within the Theravāda, but as less common alternatives.) Not all Canons had Kṣudraka as a separate Āgama: some placed their Kṣudraka-type material elsewhere.
39. I have used the older Anglicized form 'Brahmin' in preference to the more correct 'Brāhmaṇa' in the present work because it seemed to fit more happily into the verse of the translation itself, where it is many times repeated. Once I had made that decision, it seemed better to use it in the Introduction too, to avoid the confusion of having two different translations for the same word.
40. The variant spelling 'Dharmmapada' is also frequently found in manuscripts.
41. Indeed, the Dharmaguptaka lineage has achieved a certain prominence in recent years, since it is the only one that appears to have retained an unbroken tradition of Bhikṣuṇī ordination – *bhikṣuṇī* (Pali *bhikkhunī*) meaning a fully ordained nun. According to most traditions, a *bhikṣuṇī* could be ordained only by a Buddha (see the story for v. 391) or by a quorum of existing *bhikṣuṇīs* in association with the monks, not by monks alone. So in modern times some women from other Buddhist traditions have gone to the Chinese nuns for ordination, while continuing to follow their own doctrinal traditions.
42. Skilling (1997) prefers to call it the Patna Dhammapada, because *dhamma* is the form used in the body of the text.
43. There is some doubt about its present whereabouts: see Roth 2000: 5–6, 91–2. Facsimiles of the manuscript are included at the end of the same book (plates 2–14).
44. Timothy Lenz, with contributions by Andrew Glass and Bhikshu Dharmamitra, *A New Version of the Gāndhārī Dharmapada and a Collection of Previous-Birth Stories: British Library*

Kharoṣṭhī Fragments 16 + 25 (Seattle and London: University of Washington Press, 2003), p. 12.

45. The Prakrits seem to have been falling out of use – or, rather, developing into later languages called Apabhraṃśas – by around the fourth–sixth century CE.
46. By Peter Skilling (1997). The name of this school is found in a number of variants, including 'Sāṃmatīya' (Skilling's preferred spelling).
47. It is perhaps related to *udāna*, 'up-breath', one of the five 'breaths' of ancient Indian physiology (Roebuck 2000: xviii; 2003: xxx–xxxi and references given there). In this case, it would resemble the Western idea of 'inspiration', but seen as coming up from within the speaker rather than down from above.
48. Some have taken references in texts to 'Mūlasarvāstivāda' ('Root-Sarvāstivāda') to refer to a separate school; but Fumio Enomoto (2000) has convincingly demonstrated that this is simply an honorific name for the Sarvāstivāda school itself. (See also Fuktta 2003: xxi.)
49. Cone 1986: lviii.
50. *Lokottara* is the Sanskrit, *lokuttara* the Middle Indian form. The Lokottaravāda was an offshoot of the Mahāsāṅghika ('of the Great Order'), the earliest proto-Mahāyānist movement to have broken away from the early Mainstream schools in the disputes that led to the development of the Mahāyāna schools.
51. The point at issue in these controversies is the nature of a Fully Awakened Buddha after his attainment of liberation but before his *parinibbāna*. How far is he part of the transcendent (*lokuttara*) realm, and how far is he still part of the worldly (*lokiya*) realm of *saṃsāra*, where existence is shaped by conditions and is subject to suffering (*dukkha*)? The various schools tried to answer this question, according to their own interpretations of Abhidhamma philosophy, in relation to the triad of body, speech and mind. According to Mainstream Buddhist ideas, the body of the Buddha is still in some sense part of the conditioned realm, since it is subject to old age, illness and death, but his mind is completely free of it. For example when the Buddha was wounded by Devadatta's rock (v. 90, story), he felt physical pain, conditioned by the injury, but he did not experience mental anguish conditioned by that, as hatred, aversion etc. could no longer arise in his mind. The question of speech was a particularly knotty one, since the acts of speaking and hearing are in part physical, but the thought that inspires them may be transcendent.

Unlike the Theravādins, the Lokuttaravādins seem to have held that the Buddha's speech was entirely *lokuttara*, regardless of whether he was teaching the Dhamma or speaking of everyday matters. For these and related controversies, see Cousins 1991.

52. See v. 179 and note.
53. Mahāvastu 3.434–7.
54. Ibid. 3.421–3.
55. K. R. Norman 1983: 60 and notes.
56. Cone 1986: lix.
57. Brough 1962: 27.
58. Ibid.: 28–9.
59. Cone 1986: lix.
60. They are included in the Majjhima Nikāya (1.299–304; Sutta 44: Cūḷavedalla Sutta).
61. I use the words 'story' and 'tale' as literary terms for this kind of narrative, with no implications as to whether or not they are 'true' in a historical sense. (In fact I think it likely that many of these narratives had a factual basis; but, since on the whole they concern the kind of people who do not leave archaeological records, we are unlikely ever to know how much.)
62. There is therefore some overlap with the Jātaka, the collection of stories of previous births of the Buddha found in the Khuddaka Nikāya. However, these two sources do not always agree on which 'stories of the present' link with which stories of previous lives. (On Jātaka stories, see Shaw 2006b.)
63. Carter and Palihawadana 1987: 3–6.
64. Perhaps best known as the author of the *Visuddhimagga*, 'The Path of Purification', a manual for meditators (Ñāṇamoli 1975).
65. K. R. Norman 1983: 121.
66. Buddhaghosa's own date is slightly doubtful. Since there is a late-fifth century Chinese translation of the commentary on the Vinaya, definitely attributed to him, he cannot be later than that date, but he could be earlier. The safest suggestion would seem to be that he was active around the late fourth century CE.
67. The English translation of the Dhammapadaṭṭhakathā, Burlingame's *Buddhist Legends*, comes to three substantial volumes (Burlingame 1921): it is concerned with the stories, and omits the material explaining the meaning of each verse. Carter and Palihawadana (1987) translate the commentarial explanations of the meaning of the verses, but omit the stories.
68. 'Big Protector' and 'Little Protector'. The adjectives *mahā* and

culla (also spelled *cūḷa* or *cūla*), 'great' and 'small', are often prefixed to the names of older and younger brothers and sisters (cf. notes on vv. 18, 25), though *mahā* is also used to distinguish great persons such as Arahats from others with the same name (e.g. Mahā Moggallāna, Mahā Kassapa).

69. The equivalent is also found in Pali in the Peṭakopadesa version: see note 35, above.

70. Though the Fajü jing, as translated by Dhammajoti (1995: 104), seems to remain close to the Pali version:

> Mind is the origin of events
> They have] mind as the chief, and are mind-impelled.
> If one harbours an evil thought in the mind
> And then speaks or acts;
> Suffering pursues one necessarily,
> As a cart [necessarily] rolls over the track.
>
> Mind is the origin of events
> They have] mind as the chief, and are mind-impelled.
> If one harbours a good thought in the mind
> And then speaks or acts;
> Happiness pursues one necessarily,
> As a shadow [necessarily] follows its substance.

71. See for example the notes on v. 97.

72. Carter and Palihawadana (1987: 6–7) comment on the effect of the background on the Commentary, but with reference to the explanations of the meanings of the verses rather than the stories: 'Another area for further inquiry is the extent to which the commentary "reduces" the sense of the *Dhammapada* verses and offers a narrow monastic meaning, addressed primarily to bhikkhus (buddhist monks), or a sectarian meaning attuned exclusively to the teachings of the Theravada school.'

73. I have included some of the frequently occurring names in the Glossary, but for comprehensive information on all the proper names in the Pali Canon and commentaries, see Malalasekhara 1937–8. The online version is particularly useful to the non-specialist reader, since it is organized in the order of the Roman alphabet, while the print version uses Pali word-order.

74. For some of the translations of the Dhammapada into different Western languages, see Grönbold and Dachs 2005: 140ff.

75. Brough 1962: xxi. He does go on to concede that 'a reasonable

critic will readily admit that there are many attractive things here' and that it is not nearly so bad as what he calls 'the unrelieved doggerel of the *Dharma-samuccaya*' (ibid.), a later text with related content.

76. See the notes on vv. 385–6.
77. Pali *tiṭṭhubha-jagatī* – but the Sanskrit terms are generally used.
78. If we include the rest of the Dharmapada literature, the range of animals mentioned becomes wider. In the Udānavarga, for example, we find mentions of the lion, deer and tortoise, among others. The snake – surprisingly absent from the Pali Dhammapada – seems to put in an appearance in most of the other extant Dharmapadas, and has its own chapter in the Patna Dharmapada (see Appendix II). Interestingly, there seems to be no mention of the smaller domestic animals, the dog, cat or mongoose, or even of the talking birds often kept as pets in classical India. (In the Dhammapada Commentary, all sorts of animals appear, including dogs and cats – the former generally as working animals kept by huntsmen.)
79. We also find the potter's wares, which would have been ubiquitous in ancient India (vv. 40, 121–2), but no reference to their making. However the Udānavarga (1.12) has the potter, too:

    Just like a clay vessel
        Made by a potter,
    Each life of a mortal
        Ends in breaking.

80. Literally, 'striver', and possibly the origin of the (adopted) English word 'shaman'. (The word appears to have spread in its Prakrit form, *śamaṇa*, under Buddhist influence, into the languages of Central Asia, from which it entered Chinese (as *shamen*) and Japanese (as *shamon*). It is thought to have entered English via Tungus and Russian; but the matter remains controversial. (See Carmen Blacker, *The Catalpa Bow: A Study of Shamanistic Practices in Japan* (London: George Allen & Unwin, 1975), pp. 23, 317–18.)
81. There is no specific mention in the text of nuns (*bhikkhunī*), though they play a prominent part in the Commentary.
82. Or perhaps one of a class of deities described as living in their own high heavens, the 'Formless Realms'.
83. D. J. Gogerly, 'The *Dhammapada* or "Footsteps of Religion"', first published in 1840 in the journal *The Friend* in Colombo, and

reprinted in A. S. Bishop (ed.), *Ceylon Buddhism: Being the Collected Writings of Daniel John Gogerly*, 2 vols. (Colombo: The Wesleyan Methodist Bookroom; London: Kegan, Paul, Trench, Trübner & Co., 1908), II, 249–92. This version is also available at<http://www.bodhgayanews.net/pdf/gogerly_dhammapada.pdf>. For other translations by Gogerly see <http://www.sacred-texts.com/journals/ja/tbg.htm>.

84. Grönbold and Dachs 2005: 140ff.

85. One that I have found particularly helpful is that of Narada Thera (1993).

86. Paul Griffiths (1981) has an excellent analysis of the problem, though I do not agree with his solution, which is to edit and study, rather than translate, the more intractable texts. In my experience, there are few better ways of studying a text than trying to translate it.

Bibliography

Basak, Rādhāgovinda (ed.), 1963–8. *Mahāvastu avadānam* (Sanskrit and Bengali; pref. and introd. in English), 3 vols., Calcutta Sanskrit College Research Series nos. 21, 30, 63. Calcutta (= Kolkata): Calcutta Sanskrit College (Śaka years 1884–90, = 1963–8 CE)

Beal, Samuel (tr.), 1878. *Texts from the Buddhist Canon: Commonly known as Dhammapada, with Accompanying Narratives*, tr. from the Chinese, Trübner's Oriental Series II. London: Trübner & Co.

Bechert, H. (ed.), 1980. *The Language of the Earliest Buddhist Tradition* (= *Die Sprache der ältesten buddhistischen Überlieferung*). Göttingen: Vandenhoeck & Ruprecht

—— (ed.), 1991–7. *The Dating of the Historical Buddha* (= *Die Datierung des historischen Buddha*), 3 vols. Göttingen: Vandenhoeck & Ruprecht

Bernhard, F. (ed.), 1965–90. *Udāna-varga*, 3 vols., Abhandlungen der Akademie der Wissenschaften in Göttingen, Philologisch-Historische Klasse, Folge 3, nos. 54, 187. Göttingen: Vandenhoeck & Ruprecht

Brough, John (ed.), 1962. *The Gāndhārī Dharmapada*, London Oriental Series, vol. 7. London: School of Oriental and African Studies (repr. New Delhi: Motilal Banarsidass, 2001)

—— (ed. and tr.), 1968. *Poems from the Sanskrit*. Harmondsworth: Penguin

Burlingame, E. W. (tr.), 1921. *Buddhist Legends Translated from the Original Pali Text of the Dhammapada Commentary*, 3 vols., Harvard Oriental Series, nos. 28–30. Cambridge,

Mass.: Harvard University Press (repr. Oxford: Pali Text Society, 1993–5)

Carter, John Ross, and Palihawadana, Mahinda, 1987. *The Dhammapada*. New York and Oxford: Oxford University Press

—— 2000. *The Dhammapada*, New York and Oxford: Oxford University Press (a paperback version of the translation of the verses from the preceding item, but without the extensive commentary)

Cone, M., 1986. *The Patna Dharmapada*, unpublished PhD dissertation, University of Cambridge

—— 1989. 'Patna Dharmapada', *Journal of the Pali Text Society*, 13: 101–217

Cousins, L. S., 1991. 'The "Five Points" and the Origins of the Buddhist Schools', in Tadeusz Skorupski (ed.), *The Buddhist Forum*, vol. 2, pp. 27–60. London: School of Oriental and African Studies

—— 1995. 'Person and Self', in *Buddhism into the Year 2000*, pp. 15–31. Bangkok: Dhammakāya Foundation

—— 1996. 'The Dating of the Historical Buddha: A Review Article', *Journal of the Royal Asiatic Society*, 3rd series, 6, 1: 57–63; online at <http://indology.info/papers/cousins/>

Cousins, L. S., Kunst, A., and Norman, K. R. (eds.), 1974. *Buddhist Studies in Honour of I. B. Horner*. Dordrecht: D. Reidel

Daw Mya Tin, 1990. *The Dhammapada: Verses and Stories*. New Delhi: Sri Satguru Publications

Dhammajoti, K. L., 1995. *The Chinese Version of Dhammapada*. Kelaniya: The Postgraduate Institute of Pali and Buddhist Studies

Duerlinger, James, 2003. *Indian Buddhist Theories of Persons: Vasubandhu's 'Refutation of the Theory of a Self'*. London and New York: Routledge

Enomoto, Fumio, 2000. '"Mūlasarvāstivādin" and "Sarvāstivādin"', in Christine Chojnacki et al. (eds.), *Vividharatnakaraṇḍaka: Festgabe für Adelheid Mette*, pp. 239–50. Swisttal-Odendorf: Indica et Tibetica Verlag

Fausbøll [sometimes spelled Fausböll], Michael Viggo (ed. and tr.), 1855. *Dhammapadam* (Latin tr.). Copenhagen ('Haunia'): Reitzel

Fick, Richard, 1920. *The Social Organisation in North-East India in Buddha's Time*, tr. Shishirkumar Maitra. Calcutta (= Kolkata): University of Calcutta

Fišer, Ivo, 1954. 'The Problem of the Seṭṭhi in Buddhist Jātakas', *Archiv Orientální*, 22: 238–66

—— 1979. 'Pāli averaṁ, Dhammapada 5', in A. K. Narain (ed.), *Studies in Pali and Buddhism: A Memorial Volume in Honor of Bhikkhu Jagdish Kashyap*, pp. 93–7. New Delhi: B. R. Publishing Corporation

Friedlander, Peter G., 2007. 'Dhammapada: Translations and Recreations', in R. Palapathwala and A. Karickam (eds.), *One Word, Many Versions*, pp. 54–76. Tiruvalla-1, Kerala: Dr Alexander Marthoma Centre for Dialogue

—— 2009. 'Dhammapada Traditions and Translations', *Journal of Religious History*, 33, 2: 218–37

Fukita, Takamichi, 2003. *The Mahāvadānasūtra: A New Edition Based on Manuscripts Discovered in Northern Turkestan*. Göttingen: Vandenhoeck & Ruprecht

Griffiths, Paul, 1981. 'Buddhist Hybrid English: Some Notes on Philology and Hermeneutics for Buddhologists', *Journal of the International Association of Buddhist Studies*, 4, 2: 17–32

Grönbold, G., and Dachs, K., 2005. *Die Worte des Buddha in den Sprachen der Welt/The Words of the Buddha in the Languages of the World: Tipiṭaka, Tripiṭaka, Dazangjing, Kanjur*, catalogue of an exhibition held at Bayerische Staatsbibliothek, Munich, 27 January–20 March 2005. Munich: Bayerische Staatsbibliothek

Hara, M., 1992. 'A Note on Dhammapada 97', *Indo-Iranian Journal*, 35, 2/3: 179–91

Harris, E., 2006. *Theravada Buddhism and the British Encounter: Religious, Missionary and Colonial Experience in Nineteenth Century Sri Lanka*. London: Routledge

Harrison, Paul, 1987. 'Who Gets to Ride in the Great Vehicle? Self-image and Identity among the Followers of the Early Mahāyāna', *Journal of the International Association of Buddhist Studies*, 10, 1: 67–90

—— 2005, 'Searching for the Origins of the Mahāyāna: What Are We Looking For', in Paul Williams (ed.), *Buddhism: Critical Concepts in Religious Studies*, vol. 3, pp. 164–80. London: Routledge (first published in *Eastern Buddhist*, new series, 28, 1 (1995): 48–69)

Hinüber, Otto von, and Norman, K. R., 1995. *Dhammapada*. Oxford: Pali Text Society

Jones, J. J. (tr.), *c.* 1949–56. *The Mahāvastu: Translated from the Buddhist Sanskrit*, 3 vols., Sacred Books of the Buddhists nos. 16, 18, 19. London: Pali Text Society; Boston: Routledge & Kegan Paul

Lenz, Timothy (with Andrew Glass and Bhikshu Dharmamitra), 2003. *A New Version of the Gāndhārī Dharmapada and a Collection of Previous-Birth Stories: British Library Kharoṣṭhī Fragments* 16 + 25. Seattle and London: University of Washington Press

Malalasekhara, G. P., 1937–8. *Dictionary of Pāli Proper Names*, 2 vols. Oxford: Pali Text Society; repr. in 3 vols. 1997; online at <http://www.palikanon.com/english/pali_names/dic_idx.html>

Mizuno, Kōgen, 1979. 'Dharmapadas of Various Buddhist Schools', in A. K. Narain (ed.), *Studies in Pali and Buddhism: A Memorial Volume in Honor of Bhikkhu Jagdish Kashyap*, pp. 255–67, New Delhi: B. R. Publishing Corporation

Müller, F. Max (tr.), 1881. *The Dhammapada: A Collection of Verses: Being One of the Canonical Books of the Buddhists*, Sacred Books of the East, vol. 10, pt 1. Oxford: Clarendon Press

Nakatani, H. (ed.), 1987. *Udānavarga de Subaši, Edition critique du manuscrit sanskrit sur bois provenant de Subaši, Bibliothèque nationale de Paris, Fonds Pelliot*, Publications de l'Institut de civilisation indienne, nos. 53–4 (the first volume contains the transliterated text, the second photographs of the original manuscript). Paris: Collège de France

Ñāṇamoli, Bhikkhu (tr.), 1975. *The Path of Purification (Visuddhimagga) by Bhadantācariya Buddhaghosa*. Kandy: Buddhist Publication Society

Narada Thera, 1993. *The Dhammapada: Pāli Text and Translation with Stories in Brief and Notes*. Taipei: Buddha

Educational Foundation (first published as *The Dhammapada. Translated with Notes by Narada Thera. With a Foreword by Bhikkhu Kassapa and Introduction by E. J. Thomas.* London: John Murray, 1954)

Norman, H. C. (ed.), 1906 (repr. 1992). *Dhammapadatthakathā. The Commentary on the Dhammapada*, 4 vols. Oxford: Pali Text Society

Norman, K. R., 1979. 'Dhammapada 97: A Misunderstood Paradox', *Indologica Taurinensia* 7: 41–8 (= K. R. Norman 1991: 187–93)

—— 1980, 'The Dialects in Which the Buddha Preached', in H. Bechert (ed.) 1980: 61–77 (= K. R. Norman 1991: 128–47)

—— 1983. *Pāli Literature: Including the Canonical Literature in Prakrit and Sanskrit of All the Hīnayāna Schools of Buddhism*, History of Indian Literature, vol. 7, fasc. 2. Wiesbaden: O. Harrassowitz

—— 1991. *Collected Papers*, vol. 2. Oxford: Pali Text Society

—— (tr.), 1997. *The Word of the Doctrine (Dhammapada).* Oxford: Pali Text Society

Oberlies, Thomas, 2003–4. 'Ein bibliographischer Überblick über die kanonischen Texte der Śrāvakayāna-Schulen des Buddhismus (ausgenommen der des Mahāvihāra-Theravāda)', *Wiener Zeitschrift für die Kunde Südasiens*, 47: 37–84

Prebish, Charles S., 2008. 'Cooking the Buddhist Books: The Implications of the New Dating of the Buddha for the History of Early Indian Buddhism', *Journal of Buddhist Ethics*, 15; online at <http://www.buddhistethics.org/15/prebish-article.pdf>

Priestley, Leonard C. D. C., 1999. *Pudgalavāda Buddhism: The Reality of the Indeterminate Self.* Toronto: University of Toronto, Centre for South Asian Studies

Radhakrishnan, S., 1950 (repr. 1999). *The Dhammapada.* New Delhi: Oxford University Press (a Hindu philosopher's understanding of the Dhammapada)

Rau, W., 1959. 'Bemerkungen und nicht-buddhistische Sanskrit-Parallelen zum Pāli-Dhammapada', in Claus Vogel (ed.), *Jñānamuktāvalī. Commemoration Volume in Honour of Johannes Nobel on the Occasion of his 70th Birthday*

Offered by Pupils and Colleagues, Sarasvati-Vihara Series no. 38, pp. 159–75. New Delhi: International Academy of Indian Culture

Rhys Davids, T. W., and Stede, William (eds.), 1972. *The Pali Text Society's Pali–English Dictionary*. London and Boston: Routledge & Kegan Paul, for the Pali Text Society, London (a reprint of the original 1921–5 edition)

Rockhill, W. Woodville (tr.), 1883. *Udânavarga: A Collection of Verses from the Buddhist Canon, Compiled by Dharmatrâta. Being the Northern Buddhist Version of Dhammapada. Translated from the Tibetan of the Bkah-hgyur. With Notes and Extracts from the Commentary of Pradjnâvarman*, Trübner's Oriental Series. London: Trübner & Co.

Roebuck, V. J. (ed. and tr.), 2000. *The Upaniṣads, Translated and Edited with an Introduction*. New Delhi: Penguin Books India

—— 2003. *The Upaniṣads*. London: Penguin Books (a revised edition of the previous item)

Roth, G., 1976. 'Dhammapada Verses in Uttarajhāyā 9', *Sambodhi* (Ahmedabad: L. D. Institute of Indology), 5, 2–3 (special issue in memory of Dr A. N. Upadhye): 166–9

—— 2000. *Discussions about Patna Dharmapada*. Patna: Patna Museum

—— (ed.), 1980. 'The Patna Dharmapada', in H. Bechert (ed.) 1980: 93–135

Saddhātissa, H. (tr.), 1994 (repr. 1998). *The Sutta-Nipāta*. Richmond, Surrey: Curzon Press

Salomon, R., 1998. *Indian Epigraphy: A Guide to the Study of Inscriptions in Sanskrit, Prakrit, and the Other Indo-Aryan Languages*. Oxford: Oxford University Press; New Delhi: Munshiram Manoharlal Publishers

Samtani, N. H. (ed.), 1989. *Amalā Prajñā: Aspects of Buddhist Studies: Professor P. V. Bapat Felicitation Volume*, Bibliotheca Indo-Buddhica no. 63. New Delhi: Sri Satguru Publications

Sanderson, Alexis, 1995. 'The Sarvāstivāda and its Critics: Anātmavāda and the Theory of Karma', in *Buddhism into the Year 2000*, pp. 33–65. Bangkok: Dhammakāya Foundation

Senart, Emile, 1882–97. *Le Mahâvastu. Texte sanscrit publié pour la première fois et accompagné d'introductions et d'un commentaire*, 3 vols. Paris: Société asiatique; online at <http://www.sub.uni-goettingen.de/ebene_1/fiindolo/gretil/1_sanskr/4_rellit/buddh/mhvastuu.htm>.

Shaw, Sarah, 2006a. *Buddhist Meditation: An Anthology of Texts from the Pāli Canon.* London and New York: Routledge

—— 2006b. *The Jātakas: Birth Stories of the Bodhisatta.* New Delhi: Penguin Books India

Singh, R. S., 1978, 'Botanical Identity and a Critical Appreciation of *Māluvā Latā* as Evinced in the Buddhistic Pali Literature', online at <http://www.new.dli.ernet.in/rawdataupload/upload/insa/INSA_1/20005af5_139.pdf>

Skilling, Peter, 1997. 'On the School-affiliation of the "Patna Dhammapada"', *Journal of the Pali Text Society*, 23: 83–122

—— 2006. 'Daśabalaśrīmitra on the Buddhology of the Sāṃmitīyas', *Nagoya Studies in Indian Culture and Buddhism* (Nagoya University Association of Indian and Buddhist Studies), 25: 99–123

Sparham, Gareth (tr.), 1983. *The Tibetan Dhammapada. In the Language of India: Udanavarga; in the Language of Tibet: Ched.du.brjod.pai.ts'oms; in English: Compilations of Indicative Verse. Compiled by Dharmatrata.* New Delhi: Mahayana Publications

Taisho = J. Takakusu, K. Watanabe (eds.), *Taisho-shinshu-daizokyo.* Tokyo: Taisho Issaikyo Kankokai, 1961–78 (Japanese standard print version of the Chinese Tripiṭaka)

Thanissaro Bhikkhu, 'Dhammapada: Historical Notes'; online at <http://www.accesstoinsight.org/canon/sutta/khuddaka/dhp/history.html>. (This website is highly recommended for all matters connected with Buddhism in the Theravāda tradition.)

Thomas, Edward J., 1927 (rev. edn 1931), *The Life of Buddha as Legend and History.* London: Kegan Paul, Trench, Trübner & Co.; New York: Alfred A. Knopf

Vogel, J. P., 1962. *The Goose in Indian Literature and Art*, Memoirs of the Kern Institute no. 2. Leiden: E. J. Brill

Walshe, Maurice (tr.), 1987. *Thus Have I Heard: The Long Discourses of the Buddha. A New Translation of the Dīgha Nikāya*. London: Wisdom Publications

Watanabe, K., 1994. 'Avoiding all Acts by Both Buddha and Mahāvīra', *Bulletin d'Etudes Indiennes*, 11–12 (1993–4): 229–32

DHAMMAPADA CHANTING

A number of recordings are available of the Dhammapada being chanted in Pali. Mp3 files of each chapter, chanted in Sinhalese style by Ven. Weragoda Sarada Maha Thero with spoken translation, can be downloaded from <http://www.buddhanet.net/e-learning/buddhism/dhammapada.htm>.

Note on the Text

The text I have worked from is that of the Pali Text Society (Hinüber and Norman 1995).

There are two different systems of numbering in use for the verses of the Dhammapada: a continuous numbering, 1–423, that runs throughout the work, and a separate numbering within each chapter. So the same verse could be referred to either as 326 or as 23.7. Since references in other texts are usually to the continuous numbering, I have used that as my main system, but noted the numbers in the alternative system at the beginning of each chapter.

To avoid scattering the pages of the translation with superscript numbers, and allow the reader to experience the verses undistracted if he or she wishes, I have keyed the endnotes to the numbers of the verses themselves. Comments there are headed by a brief quotation of the words being commented on.

THE DHAMMAPADA

CHAPTER 1
TWINS
(1.1–20)

1. Fore-run by mind are mental states,
   Ruled by mind, made of mind.
If you speak or act
   With corrupt mind,
Suffering follows you,
   As the wheel the foot of the ox.

2. Fore-run by mind are mental states,
   Ruled by mind, made of mind.
If you speak or act
   With clear mind,
Happiness follows you,
   Like a shadow that does not depart.

3. 'He insulted me, he struck me,
   He defeated me, he robbed me':
For those who get caught up in this,
   Hatred does not cease.

4. 'He insulted me, he struck me,
   He defeated me, he robbed me':
For those who do not get caught up in this,
   Hatred ceases completely.

5. For never here
   Do hatreds cease by hatred.
By freedom from hatred they cease:
   This is a perennial truth.

6. Others do not understand
 That we must control ourselves here:
But for those who do understand this –
 Through it, their quarrels cease.

7. If you live contemplating the fair,
 Unrestrained in senses,
Not knowing moderation in food,
 Dull, of weak effort,
Māra overthrows you
 As the wind an ill-rooted tree.

8. If you live contemplating the foul,
 Well restrained in senses,
Knowing moderation in food,
 Confident, raising effort,
Māra does not overthrow you,
 As the wind a rocky mountain.

9. If someone who is not freed from stain
 Puts on the yellow robe,
Devoid of self-control and truthfulness,
 He's not worthy of the yellow robe.

10. But if someone has got rid of the stains,
 Well established in the precepts,
Endowed with self-control and truthfulness,
 He indeed is worthy of the yellow robe.

11. Those who imagine value where there's none,
 And don't see value where there's value,
Do not understand value –
 Dwellers in the realm of wrong thought.

12. Those who perceive value where there's value,
 And no value where there's none,
Understand value –
 Dwellers in the realm of right thought.

13. As rain penetrates
An ill-roofed house,
Passion penetrates
An undeveloped mind.

14. As rain does not penetrate
A well-roofed house,
Passion does not penetrate
A well-developed mind.

15. He is sorry here; after death he is sorry;
In both places the evil-doer is sorry.
He is sorry, he is tormented,
Seeing his own action was defiled.

16. He is happy here; after death he is happy;
In both places the doer of good is happy.
He is happy, he is joyful,
Seeing his own action was pure.

17. He suffers here; after death he suffers;
In both places the evil-doer suffers.
He suffers, thinking, 'I have done wrong';
And going to a bad place he suffers
even more.

18. He rejoices here; after death he rejoices;
In both places the doer of good rejoices.
He rejoices, thinking, 'I have done right';
And going to a good place he rejoices
even more.

19. Though you recite much scripture,
If you are unaware and do not act according
You are like a cowherd counting others' cattle,
Not a sharer in the wanderer's life.

20. Though you recite little scripture,
If you go from *dhamma* to *dhamma*,
Abandoning passion, hatred and delusion,
Rightly knowing, with well-freed mind,
Not clinging either here or in the other world,
You are a sharer in the wanderer's life.

CHAPTER 2
AWARENESS

(2.1–12)

21. Awareness is the place of the deathless;
    Unawareness is the place of death.
The aware do not die;
    The unaware are as though dead already.

22. Knowing this especially
    About awareness, the wise
Delight in awareness,
    Taking pleasure in the realm of the Noble Ones.

23. Those who constantly practise meditation,
    Ever firm in their endeavour,
Those wise ones touch *nibbāna*,
    The unsurpassed peace of *yoga*.

24. If you're effortful and mindful,
    Pure in deed, acting with consideration,
Controlled, living by the Dhamma,
    And aware, your fame will increase.

25. By effort, awareness,
    Restraint and self-control,
The wise one should make an island
    Which the flood will not overwhelm.

26. Foolish, unwise folk
    Indulge in unawareness.
The wise one guards awareness
    As the finest treasure.

27. Do not indulge in unawareness,
    Or closeness with sense-pleasures.
For aware, meditating,
    You'll gain great happiness.

28. When a learned one
    By awareness wards off unawareness,
He ascends the palace of wisdom,
    And, sorrowless, observes the sorrowful folk,
Wise watching fools, as one on a mountain
    Sees those on the ground.

29. Aware among the unaware,
    Fully awake among the sleeping,
The wise one goes, leaving them behind
    As a swift horse leaves a weak horse behind.

30. By awareness Maghavan
    Became the chief of the gods.
Folk praise awareness.
    Unawareness is always blamed.

31. The monk who delights in awareness,
    Seeing the danger in unawareness,
Moves like a fire,
    Burning up fetters small and great.

32. The monk who delights in awareness,
    Seeing the danger in unawareness,
Not liable to fall back,
    Is close to *nibbāna*.

CHAPTER 3
THE MIND

(3.1–11)

33. The wise one makes straight
    The trembling, fickle mind –
So hard to guard, so hard to control –
    As the fletcher makes straight the arrow.

34. Like a fish thrown on land,
    Drawn out of its watery home,
This mind thrashes around
    To escape the rule of Māra.

35. The mind is hard to restrain, light,
    Flying where it will.
Control of it is good.
    Mind controlled brings happiness.

36. Mind is most hard to see, most subtle,
    Flying where it will.
The wise one should guard it.
    Mind guarded brings happiness.

37. Mind is far-travelling, a solitary mover,
    Bodiless, a cave-dweller.
Those who restrain it
    Will get free of Māra's bonds.

38. If your mind is unsteady,
If you do not know the true Dhamma,
If your composure is disturbed,
Your wisdom will not become complete.

39. If your mind is not troubled,
If your thought is not perturbed,
If you've left behind good and evil,
Wakeful, you'll have no fear.

40. Knowing that this body is like a pot,
Fortifying the mind like a city
You should fight Māra with the weapon of wisdom.
You should guard your territory without resting.

41. Soon, alas, this body
Will lie on the earth,
Abandoned, consciousness departed,
Like a useless log of wood.

42. Whatever an enemy can do to an enemy,
Or a rival to a rival,
A wrongly directed mind
Will do worse to you than that.

43. What mother or father cannot do,
Or any other kin,
A rightly directed mind
Will do better for you than that.

CHAPTER 4
FLOWERS

(4.1–16)

44. Who will conquer this earth,
    And this world of Yama with its gods?
Who will pluck the well-taught word of Dhamma
    As a skilled one plucks a flower?

45. The Learner will conquer this earth,
    And this world of Yama with its gods.
The Learner will pluck the well-taught word
        of Dhamma
    As a skilled one plucks a flower.

46. Knowing that this body is like foam,
    Understanding it has the nature
        of a mirage,
You should cut off the flower-spikes of Māra,
    And go where the King of Death can't
        see you.

47. While a man gathers flowers,
    His mind attached to this and that,
Death carries him away
    As a great flood takes a sleeping village.

48. While a man gathers flowers,
    His mind attached to this and that,
Unsatisfied in his desires,
    The Ender overpowers him.

49. In the village, a sage should go about
Like a bee, which, not harming
Flower, colour or scent,
Flies off with the nectar.

50. You should not look at
Others' faults,
Things done or not done by others,
But at things done or not done by yourself.

51. Like a beautiful flower,
Colourful but scentless,
The well-taught word is fruitless
For one who does not practise.

52. Like a beautiful flower,
Colourful and fragrant,
The well-taught word is fruitful
For one who practises.

53. Just as you can make
Many kinds of garlands from a heap of flowers,
There is much good that can be done
By one born mortal.

54. The scent of flowers is not blown against the wind –
Not sandalwood or *tagara* or jasmine.
But the scent of the good is blown against the wind:
A good man perfumes all directions.

55. Sandalwood, *tagara*,
Lotus and jasmine:
Among all kinds of scents,
The scent of virtue is unsurpassed.

56. Of little range is the scent
That is *tagara* or sandalwood.
But the scent of the virtuous
Is wafted among the gods, supreme.

57. Māra doesn't find the path
Of those who practise virtue,
Living in awareness,
Freed by right understanding.

58. Just as a lotus,
Sweet-scented, ravishing,
Grows on a heap of refuse
Flung on the high road,

59. A disciple of the Fully Awakened
Shines out through wisdom
Among the blind multitude,
The refuse of beings.

CHAPTER 5
FOOLS

(5.1–16)

60. Long is night for the wakeful;
    Long is a league for the weary.
Long is *saṃsāra* for fools
    Who do not know the true Dhamma.

61. If, as you travel, you meet
    None better than yourself, or equal,
You should steadfastly travel alone.
    There's no companionship with fools.

62. A fool is troubled, thinking,
    'I have sons, I have wealth';
But even himself doesn't belong to himself –
    Let alone sons, let alone wealth.

63. The fool who knows his folly
    Becomes wise by that fact.
But the fool who thinks he's wise –
    He's called 'a fool' indeed!

64. Even if lifelong
    A fool attends upon a wise man,
He no more knows *dhammas*
    Than a spoon knows the flavours of soup.

65. Even if for a moment
An intelligent man attends upon a wise man,
He quickly knows *dhammas*
As the tongue knows the flavours of soup.

66. Fools, lacking intelligence,
Go on with a self that's like an enemy,
Doing evil action
Which bears bitter fruit.

67. That action that's done is not good
That you repent when you've done it –
If, weeping, with tear-stained face
You experience its working-out.

68. That action that's done is good
That you don't repent when you've done it –
If happy and cheerful
You experience its working-out.

69. Until the evil ripens
The fool thinks it's honey-sweet;
But when the evil ripens
The fool's plunged into suffering.

70. Though month after month he eats
Food with the tip of a *kusa*-grass blade,
A fool's not worth a sixteenth part
Of those who've mastered *dhammas*.

71. For an evil deed that is done does not ripen
The same day, as milk curdles:
It follows the fool, burning,
Like a fire covered with ashes.

72. A fool gets a reputation for knowledge
Only to his disadvantage:
It destroys the fool's bright part
And causes his head to split.

73. He may wish for respect among bad people,
Precedence among the monks,
Lordship in the dwelling places,
Honour among the families of others.

74. '*I* did this – so let
Both laymen and renouncers think;
Let me be in charge
Of everything, things to be done or not done.'
Such is the fool's intention.
His desire and pride increase.

75. One is the way that leads to gain,
Another the way to *nibbāna*.
Understanding this,
The monk who is a disciple of the Buddha
Should not delight in honour,
But devote himself to solitude.

CHAPTER 6

THE WISE MAN

(6.1–14)

76. If you see a wise man who
Sees your faults, tells what is blameworthy,
You should keep company with such a one
As a pointer-out of treasures:
If you keep company with such a one
It becomes better, not worse, for you.

77. He should teach, instruct,
Deter from unmannerly behaviour.
For then he becomes dear to the good,
Not dear to those not good.

78. You shouldn't keep company with evil friends;
You shouldn't keep company with the
worst of men.
Keep company with good friends;
Keep company with the best of men.

79. The Dhamma-drinker sleeps happily
With clear mind.
The wise man always delights
In the Dhamma taught by the Noble Ones.

80. Irrigators lead the water;
Fletchers shape the arrow;
Carpenters shape the wood;
The wise control themselves.

81. As a solid rock
Is not moved by the wind,
The wise are not shaken
Amid blame or praise.

82. Just like a deep lake,
Clear and undisturbed,
The wise grow peaceful
On hearing Dhamma teachings.

83. Good people go everywhere;
The good don't boast, from desire for sensual things;
Touched by happiness or sorrow,
The wise do not display excitement or depression.

84. One who would not, for his own sake or another's,
Seek a son, wealth, a kingdom,
Nor seek his own success through injustice,
Is virtuous, wise and just.

85. Few among humans are those folk
Who cross to the other shore:
These other people
Just run along the bank.

86. But those folk who follow the Dhamma
When the Dhamma has been rightly taught
Will go to the other shore.
The realm of death is very hard to cross.

87. Leaving dark states,
The wise one should develop the bright,
Coming from home to homelessness,
Into solitude, where it's hard to find enjoyment.

88. There, leaving sense-pleasures, owning nothing,
He should seek enjoyment;
The wise one should purify himself
From afflictions of the mind.

89. Those whose minds are rightly developed
In the enlightenment factors,
Who, not clinging, rejoice
In the cessation of clinging,
Who are radiant, with defilements extinguished:
These have attained *nibbāna* in the world.

CHAPTER 7
THE ARAHAT

(7.1–10)

90. No fever is found
    In one who has travelled the road,
Who, sorrowless, freed in every way,
    Has destroyed all bonds.

91. The mindful make effort:
    They do not delight in a dwelling.
As geese leave a pool,
    They give up any kind of home.

92. Those who do no hoarding,
    Who fully understand food,
Whose range is liberation,
    Empty and signless –
Their path is as hard to follow
    As that of birds in the sky.

93. One whose defilements are exhausted,
    Who is unattached to food,
Whose range is liberation,
    Empty and signless –
His track is as hard to follow
    As that of birds in the sky.

94. One whose senses have attained calm
    Like horses well trained by a charioteer,
Whose pride has gone, who is free from defilements –
    Such a one even the gods envy.

95. Like the earth, such a one has no ill will:
True to his vows, he's like a royal pillar,
A mudless pool.
Such a one has no more wanderings in *saṃsāra*.

96. Calm is the mind
And calm the speech and actions
Of such a one, perfectly calm,
Who is freed through right knowledge.

97. That man who's faithless,
Ungrateful, a burglar,
Who's blown his chances, an eater of forbidden food,
He's a brave fellow indeed.

[alternatively]

That man who's desireless,
Who knows the unmade, a breaker of links,
Who's gone beyond chances, who's got rid of desire,
He's a fine person indeed.

98. Wherever Arahats live,
In village or forest,
In valley or hill –
What a lovely place it is!

99. Lovely are the forests
Where folk find no delight.
Those free from passion *will* find delight there:
They don't seek for sensual things.

CHAPTER 8
THOUSANDS

(8.1–16)

100. Better than a thousand sayings
  Made up of useless words
Is one word of meaning
  Which calms you to hear it.

101. Better than a thousand verses
  Made up of useless words
Is one word of verse
  Which calms you to hear it.

102. Better than speaking a hundred verses
  Made up of useless words
Is one word of Dhamma
  Which calms you to hear it.

103. Though you might conquer in battle
  A thousand times a thousand men,
You're the greatest battle-winner
  If you conquer just one – yourself.

104. Better to conquer yourself
  Than these other creatures.
If a person is self-controlled,
  Behaving always with restraint,

105. Neither god nor spirit,
Not Māra and Brahmā together,
Can turn to defeat
The victory of such a one.

106. You could sacrifice with a thousand offerings
Month by month for a hundred years;
But if you were to pay homage to a
developed person
Once, just for a moment,
That homage would be better
Than that hundred-year sacrifice
would be.

107. A person could tend the fire in the forest
For a hundred years;
But if he were to pay homage to a developed
person
Once, just for a moment,
That homage would be better
Than that hundred-year sacrifice
would be.

108. Whatever sacrifice or offering in the world
One might offer for a year, seeking merit,
All that is not worth a quarter as much
As reverence to those who are upright.

109. For one whose behaviour is respectful,
Who constantly honours his elders,
Four things increase:
Life-span, beauty, happiness and strength.

110. Better than living a hundred years
Ill behaved, unconcentrated,
Is living for one day
Well behaved, a meditator.

111. Better than living a hundred years
Unwise, unconcentrated,
Is living for one day
Wise, a meditator.

112. Better than living a hundred years
Lazy, without effort,
Is living for one day
Steadfastly making effort.

113. Better than living a hundred years
Not seeing arising and passing away
Is living for one day
Seeing arising and passing away.

114. Better than living a hundred years
Not seeing the deathless state
Is living for one day
Seeing the deathless state.

115. Better than living a hundred years
Not seeing the supreme Dhamma
Is living for one day
Seeing the supreme Dhamma.

CHAPTER 9
EVIL

(9.1–13)

116. Make haste in what is right;
    Defend the mind from evil.
If you are slow in doing good,
    Your mind will take delight in evil.

117. If a person does evil,
    He should not do it repeatedly;
He should not set his will upon it:
    It's painful to accumulate evil.

118. If a person does good,
    He should do it repeatedly;
He should set his will upon it:
    It's pleasant to accumulate good.

119. An evil person sees good
    So long as the evil does not ripen;
But once the evil action ripens
    The evil person sees evil.

120. A good person sees evil
    So long as the good does not ripen;
But once the good action ripens
    The good person sees good.

121. You should not think lightly of evil
('It will not come to me').
By the falling of drops of water
A water-pot is filled;
The fool is filled with evil
Though he practise it little by little.

122. You should not think lightly of good
('It will not come to me').
By the falling of drops of water
A water-pot is filled;
The wise one is filled with good
Though he practise it little by little.

123. As a merchant with a small caravan but great wealth
Would avoid a dangerous road,
As one wishing to live would avoid poison,
You should avoid evil actions.

124. If there is no wound in your hand
You can carry poison in your hand.
Poison does not attack one who is unwounded.
There is no evil for one who does not do evil.

125. The one who does harm to a harmless person
Who is pure and faultless,
Evil comes back to that one, the fool!
Like fine dust thrown into the wind.

126. Some find a womb;
Evil-doers go to hell;
Those who go well go to heaven;
Those free from defilements attain *parinibbāna*.

127. Not in the sky, nor in the middle of the ocean;
Not inside a mountain cave –
There is no place on earth where you can stand
And escape from evil action.

128. Not in the sky, nor in the middle of the ocean;
Not inside a mountain cave –
There is no place on earth where you can stand
Where death will not overcome you.

CHAPTER 10
THE ROD

(10.1–17)

129. All beings tremble at the rod;
All are afraid of death.
Seeing their likeness to yourself,
You should neither kill nor cause to kill.

130. All beings tremble at the rod;
Life is dear to all.
Seeing their likeness to yourself,
You should neither kill nor cause to kill.

131. The one who, desiring happiness for himself,
Harms with the rod
Beings who desire happiness
Will have no happiness hereafter.

132. The one who, desiring happiness for himself,
Does not harm with the rod
Beings who desire happiness
Will have happiness hereafter.

133. Do not speak harshly to anyone:
Those spoken to will answer back.
For angry speech is painful:
Retribution may reach you.

134. If, like a cracked gong,
You don't let yourself make a noise,
You have attained *nibbāna*:
There is no arrogance in you.

135. Just as a cowherd with his rod
Drives his cattle to pasture,
Old age and death
End the lives of living things.

136. Now when a fool does evil,
He does not understand.
By his own actions the ignorant one
Is burnt as if by fire.

137. Whoever with the rod does harm
To rodless ones who do no harm
Will soon come to one or other
Of these ten states:

138. He'll experience sharp pain, loss,
Bodily injury,
Serious disease,
Or disturbance of mind,

139. Trouble from the king,
Grave slander,
Loss of relatives,
Or destruction of goods;

140. Or else blazing fire
Will burn down his house.
On the breaking-up of the body,
That unwise one goes to hell.

141. Neither going naked, nor matted locks,
nor mud,
Nor fasting, nor lying on the bare
ground,
Nor dust, nor dirt, nor striving in squatting
posture
Can purify the mortal who has not
gone beyond doubt.

142. Even though you wear fine clothes, if you
live peacefully,
Calmed, controlled, disciplined, living
the holy life,
Laying aside the rod in dealing with all beings,
You are a Brahmin, a wanderer, a monk.

143. Is there any person in the world
Restrained by honour
Who avoids blame
As a thoroughbred horse avoids the whip?

144. Just like a thoroughbred horse touched
by the whip,
Be energetic and swift.
By faith, morality and effort,
Concentration and investigation
of *dhammas*,
Endowed with knowledge and conduct,
mindful,
You will abandon this suffering,
great though it is.

145. Irrigators lead the water;
Fletchers shape the arrow;
Carpenters shape the wood;
The true control themselves.

CHAPTER 11

OLD AGE

(11.1–11)

146. What's the laughter, why the joy,
     When the world is ever burning?
Plunged into darkness,
     Won't you look for a lamp?

147. See this painted shape –
     A compound mass of sores,
Diseased, with many imaginings –
     In which there's no permanent abiding.

148. This form is worn out,
     A nest of diseases, very frail.
This mass of decay will break down,
     For life ends in death.

149. What delight is there, once you've seen
     These dove-coloured bones
Cast away
     Like gourds in autumn?

150. A city made of bones
     Plastered with flesh and blood,
In which lurk old age and death,
     Pride and hypocrisy!

151. Even finely painted royal chariots wear out:
Just so the body grows old.
The Dhamma of the good does not grow old.
Indeed, the good make it known to the good.

152. A person of little knowledge
Grows old as a plough-ox grows old.
His flesh increases:
His wisdom does not increase.

153. I wandered without respite
A journey of many births,
Seeking the house-builder.
Painful is birth again and again.

154. House-builder, I have seen you:
You shall not build a house again.
All your rafters are broken:
Your ridge-pole is destroyed.
The mind, freed from conditioned things,
Has reached the end of cravings.

155. Those who have not practised the holy life,
Who have not gained wealth in youth,
Waste away like old herons
At a pond that has lost its fish.

156. Those who have not practised the holy life,
Who have not gained wealth in youth,
Lie like wasted arrows,
Lamenting for things past.

CHAPTER 12
SELF

(12.1–10)

157. If you hold yourself dear
        You should keep yourself well guarded.
A wise one should keep awake
        During one or other of the three watches.

158. First he should establish himself
        In what is proper,
And then teach another:
        That way a wise one will not be defiled.

159. You should do yourself
        As you teach another;
Well tamed, tame others –
        For self, they say, is hard to tame.

160. Self is protector of self:
        What other protector could there be?
With your self well tamed
        You find a protector who's hard to find.

161. By self evil is done:
        It is born of self, arisen from self.
It crushes the ignorant
        As a thunderbolt crushes a gemstone.

162. The one whose extreme bad conduct spreads
over him
Like a *māluvā* creeper over a sal tree
Does to himself
What an enemy would like to do.

163. Things that are wrong and bad for you
Are easy to do;
What is both good for you and right
Is most difficult to do.

164. The unwise one who,
Because of wrong view,
Reviles the teaching of the Arahats,
The Noble Ones who live by Dhamma,
Ripens only to his own destruction
Like the fruit of the bamboo.

165. By self alone evil is done;
By self one is defiled.
By self evil is not done;
By self one is purified.
Purity and impurity are individual matters:
No one can purify another.

166. You should not neglect your own benefit
For another's benefit, great though it be.
Understanding your own benefit,
You should pursue your own benefit.

CHAPTER 13
THE WORLD

(13.1–12)

167. You shouldn't follow a lesser Dhamma
Or live in unawareness.
You shouldn't follow wrong views
Or be attached to the world.

168. You should stand up, be aware,
Practise the Dhamma well.
One who practises the Dhamma sleeps happily
In this world and the next.

169. You should practise the Dhamma well,
Not practise it badly.
One who practises the Dhamma sleeps happily
In this world and the next.

170. You should see the world
As a bubble, a mirage.
If you look on it like this
The King of Death can't see you.

171. Come, see this world
Like a painted royal chariot.
Where the foolish sink down,
The wise have no attachment.

172. But whoever was unaware before
And afterwards becomes aware
Illuminates this world
Like the moon freed from a cloud.

173. Whoever has done an evil deed
But covers it with a virtuous one
Illuminates this world
Like the moon freed from a cloud.

174. This world has gone blind:
Few here see.
The rare one makes for heaven,
Like a bird freed from a net.

175. Geese go by the sun's path;
Mages go through the sky.
Conquering Māra with his army,
The wise go forth from the world.

176. If a person speaks falsely,
Though he transgresses just one *dhamma*,
There is no evil he won't do,
Rejecting the other world.

177. Misers don't go to the world of the gods –
Indeed, fools don't praise giving.
But the wise one, sharing the joy of giving,
Through that becomes happy in the other world.

178. Better than sole rulership of the earth,
Or going to heaven,
Or lordship over all the worlds
Is the fruit of Stream-Entry.

CHAPTER 14
THE BUDDHA

(14.1–18)

179. The one whose victory cannot be undone,
Whose victory does not go anywhere
in the world –
By what path will you lead him,
The trackless Buddha of infinite range?

180. The one for whom there is no attachment,
with its net,
No craving to lead him anywhere –
By what path will you lead him,
The trackless Buddha of infinite range?

181. Even the gods envy
The mindful Fully Awakened Ones,
Who are wise, intent on meditation,
Delighting in the calm of non-attachment.

182. Hard to reach is the human state,
Hard the life of mortals.
It's hard to hear the true Dhamma,
Hard for Buddhas to arise.

183. Not to do any evil;
To undertake what is good;
To purify your own mind:
This is the teaching of the Buddhas.

184. Patience, endurance, is the highest asceticism;
Nibbāna, say the Buddhas, is supreme.
One who harms others is no renouncer;
Injuring others, one is no true wanderer.

185. Not blaming, not harming,
Restraint in the monastic rule,
Knowing moderation in eating,
Secluded lodging,
Exertion in higher thought:
This is the teaching of the Buddhas.

186. 'Not by a rain of gold pieces
Is satisfaction found in sense-pleasures.
Sense-pleasures are painful and have little
sweetness':
Knowing this, the wise one

187. Takes no delight in sense-pleasures,
Even heavenly ones:
The disciple of the Fully Awakened
Delights in the destruction of craving.

188. People struck by fear
Seek many kinds of refuge:
Mountains and woods,
Groves, trees and shrines.

189. This is not the safe refuge;
This is not the supreme refuge.
Not by going to this refuge
Are you freed from all suffering.

190. But the one who has gone for refuge
To the Buddha, Dhamma and Saṅgha
Sees with right wisdom
The Four Noble Truths:

191. Suffering, the arising of suffering,
    The overcoming of suffering,
And the Noble Eightfold Path
    Which leads to the ceasing of suffering.

192. This is the safe refuge;
    This is the supreme refuge.
By going to this refuge
    You are freed from all suffering.

193. A thoroughbred man is hard to find:
    He's not born just anywhere.
The family in which that steadfast one is born
    Prospers happily.

194. Happy is the arising of Buddhas,
    Happy the teaching of the true Dhamma,
Happy the unity of the Saṅgha,
    Happy the asceticism of the united ones.

195. If you honour those worthy of honour –
    Whether Buddhas or their disciples –
Who have gone right beyond proliferation
    And crossed over grief and lamentation;

196. If you honour ones like that,
    Who have attained *nibbāna* and are
        afraid of nothing,
It is not possible for your merit
    To be measured by anyone – so great it is.

CHAPTER 15
HAPPINESS

(15.1–12)

197. Ah, how happily we live,
Without hatred among those who hate!
Without hatred we dwell
Among people who hate.

198. Ah, how happily we live,
Healthy among the sick!
Healthy we dwell
Among people who are sick.

199. Ah, how happily we live,
Carefree among the careworn!
Carefree we dwell
Among people who are careworn.

200. Ah, how happily we live,
We who own nothing!
We shall feast upon joy
Like the Radiant Gods.

201. The victor breeds hatred;
The defeated sleeps in pain.
The calmed one sleeps happily,
Leaving behind victory and defeat.

202. There is no fire like passion,
No fault like quarrelling,
No pain like the aggregates,
No happiness greater than peace.

203. Hunger is the worst disease,
Conditioned things the greatest grief:
When you know this truly,
Nibbāna is the greatest happiness.

204. Health is the best possession,
Contentment the greatest wealth;
Trust is what makes the truest kin;
Nibbāna is the greatest happiness.

205. Savouring the taste of solitude
And the taste of calm
You become free of fear and free of evil,
Savouring the taste of joy in the Dhamma.

206. It's good to see the Noble Ones,
Ever pleasant to live with them:
If you never see a fool
You'll always be happy.

207. The one who keeps company with fools
Will be sorry for a long time.
It's painful to live with fools,
Like being always with an enemy.
But a wise man is pleasant to live with,
Like meeting your kin.

So:

208. If someone is steadfast, intelligent and learned,
Patient under his burden, true to his word, noble,
Keep company with such a good, wise man
As the moon keeps to the zodiac path.

CHAPTER 16
THE DEAR

(16.1–12)

209. If you apply yourself to distraction
And not to concentration,
If you abandon the goal – clinging to what's dear –
You'll envy the one who applies himself
to the goal.

210. Never associate with those who are dear
Or with those who are not dear.
Not seeing dear ones is painful,
And so is seeing those not dear.

211. So don't hold anything dear,
For losing what's dear is an evil:
There are no ties for those
To whom nothing is dear or not dear.

212. From the dear comes grief;
From the dear comes fear.
If you're freed from the dear
You'll have no grief, let alone fear.

213. From affection comes grief;
From affection comes fear.
If you're freed from affection
You'll have no grief, let alone fear.

214. From pleasure comes grief;
From pleasure comes fear.
If you're freed from pleasure
You'll have no grief, let alone fear.

215. From desire comes grief;
From desire comes fear.
If you're freed from desire
You'll have no grief, let alone fear.

216. From craving comes grief;
From craving comes fear.
If you're freed from craving
You'll have no grief, let alone fear.

217. The one who's endowed with good character
and insight,
Who's firm in the Dhamma, a truth-speaker,
Who does his own work –
Folk will hold him dear.

218. The one who has aroused a wish for the Undeclared
Should be filled with that consciousness,
His mind not bound to sense-pleasures.
Then he's said to be 'heading upstream'.

219. When a man who has been long abroad
Comes safe from far away,
His friends, relations and well-wishers
Welcome him on his arrival.

220. Just so, when someone who has done good actions
Goes from this world to the next,
His good actions receive him as relatives receive
A dear one on his arrival.

CHAPTER 17
ANGER

(17.1–14)

221. You should give up anger, abandon pride,
Go beyond all fetters.
If you do not cling to name and form,
Possessing nothing, sorrows cannot attack you.

222. The one who controls anger that's arisen
Like a chariot going off-course
I call a charioteer.
Other folk are merely rein-holders.

223. By freedom from anger you should conquer anger,
By good conquer what is not good,
By giving conquer miserliness,
By truth the teller of lies.

224. You should tell the truth, not get angry,
Give when asked, even if there's not much:
By these three practices
You will go among the gods.

225. Those sages who abstain from harm,
Ever restrained in body,
Go to the imperishable state,
Where those who go don't grieve.

226. In those who are ever wakeful,
Learning by day and night,
Committed to *nibbāna*,
The defilements go to rest.

227. This is an ancient truth, Atula,
Not just for today:
Folk blame the one who sits silent;
They blame the one who says a lot;
They blame the one who says little, too –
No one in this world is not blamed.

228. There never was, there never will be,
Nor is there found today
A person who is altogether blamed
Or altogether praised.

229. But the one whom the wise praise
When they've observed him day after day,
One of flawless conduct, wise,
Endowed with wisdom and morality –

230. Who would dare to blame him,
An ornament of new gold?
Him the gods, too, praise:
He is praised even by Brahmā.

231. You should guard against anger in the body;
You should be restrained in body.
Giving up misconduct of the body,
You should practise good conduct with the body.

232. You should guard against anger in speech;
You should be restrained in speech.
Giving up misconduct of speech,
You should practise good conduct with speech.

233. You should guard against anger in the mind;
You should be restrained in mind.
Giving up misconduct in the mind,
You should practise good conduct with the mind.

234. The wise are restrained in body,
Restrained in speech as well.
The wise are restrained in mind.
Indeed, they are thoroughly restrained.

CHAPTER 18
RUST

(18.1–21)

235. Now you are like a withered leaf.
     Yama's servants wait on you.
You stand at the start of an undertaking,
     And you've no provision for your journey.

236. So make an island for yourself.
     Strive quickly: become wise.
With rust blown away, stainless,
     You will go to the Noble Ones' celestial land.

237. Now you have reached old age.
     You are on your way to meet Yama.
There's no lodging for you on the way,
     And you've no provision for your journey.

238. So make an island for yourself.
     Strive quickly: become wise.
With rust blown away, stainless,
     You will not go to birth and old age again.

239. Gradually, little by little,
     Moment by moment, the wise one
Should blow away his own impurity
     As a smith does that of silver.

240. As rust that's arisen from iron,
Once arisen from it, eats it away,
His own actions lead to an evil destination
The one who misuses the requisites.

241. For texts, not practising is the rust;
For houses, lack of exertion.
Laziness is the rust of beauty;
Unawareness the rust of a guard.

242. The rust of a woman is misconduct;
Miserliness is the rust of a giver.
All evil ways are rusts,
In this world and the next.

243. A worse rust than this rust
Is ignorance, the worst rust.
Get rid of this rust
And be rustless, monks.

244. It's easy to live like a shameless person,
A crow-hero,
Offensive, presumptuous,
Proud and corrupt.

245. But it's hard to live like a modest person,
Always seeking what's pure,
Sincere, not proud,
Of pure life, insightful.

246. Whoever in this world
Takes life, speaks falsehood,
Takes what is not given,
Resorts to another's wife,

247. And whatever man
Gives himself up to strong drink,
By doing that he digs up his own root,
Right here, in this world.

248. Know this, my friend:
Evil states are unrestrained.
May greed and wrongdoing
Not deliver you to long suffering.

249. Indeed, people give according to
Their faith, to their clarity of mind.
Whoever is discontented about this,
About the food and drink of others,
Does not, day or night,
Achieve concentration.

250. But the one in whom this is cut off,
Pulled up, root and all,
Day or night
Achieves concentration.

251. There is no fire like passion,
No grip like hate,
No net like delusion,
No river like craving.

252. Others' faults are easy to see,
While your own are hard to see.
The faults of others
You winnow like chaff;
You hide your own
As a cunning gambler hides a bad throw.

253. If you contemplate the faults of others,
Always seeking cause for offence,
Your defilements increase:
You're far from the destruction of the defilements.

254. In the sky there is no track;
Outside the Order there is no true wanderer.
Folk delight in proliferation;
Tathāgatas are free from proliferation.

255. In the sky there is no track;
Outside the Order there is no true wanderer.
Conditioned things are not eternal;
In the Buddhas there is no disturbance.

CHAPTER 19
THE JUST

(19.1–17)

256. Someone is not a justice
Because he tries a case in haste:
The learned one, who looks into
What's the case and not the case,

257. Who not hastily but justly,
Fairly, leads others –
Protected by the Dhamma, the wise one
Is called a justice.

258. Someone is not learned
Because he talks a lot:
One who's patient, free from hatred and fear,
Is called learned.

259. Someone is not a Dhamma-bearer
Because he talks a lot:
If someone hears just a little
But experiences the Dhamma with his body,
He indeed is a Dhamma-bearer –
One who isn't careless of the Dhamma.

260. Someone is not an Elder
Because his hair is grey.
He's just had a long life.
He's called 'grown old in vain'.

261. If truth and Dhamma are in someone,
Non-violence, self-restraint and control,
Then, steadfast and free of defilements,
He indeed is called an Elder.

262. A man does not become fine
Merely through speaking fine words
Or through his attractive appearance
If he's a jealous, grasping rogue.

263. But the one in whom this is cut off,
Pulled up, root and all –
That wise one, free from fault,
Is called fine indeed.

264. Someone doesn't become a wanderer by shaving his head
If he's undisciplined and tells lies.
How can he be a wanderer
If he's full of desire and greed?

265. But if he lays evils to rest,
Small ones and great, completely,
Because he's laid evils to rest
He's called a wanderer.

266. Someone does not become a monk
Just because he begs alms from others;
If he takes on the household way of life,
He's not a monk, for all that.

267. The one who, living the holy life,
Wards off both good and evil,
And moves in the world with consideration,
Is called a monk indeed.

268. Not by silence does someone become a sage
If he's foolish and ignorant.
A wise one who, as though holding scales,
Takes up the better choice

269. And avoids evil – he's a sage:
He's a sage because of that.
If he understands both in the world,
He's called a sage because of that.

270. Someone does not become noble
By harming living things.
Through not harming any living things
He is called noble.

271. Not through precepts and observances alone,
Nor yet by much learning,
Or attainment of concentration,
Or dwelling in seclusion,

272. Do I reach the happiness of freedom from desire
Not experienced by worldly folk;
Nor has a monk attained confidence
If he has not achieved the destruction of
the defilements.

CHAPTER 20
THE PATH

(20.1–17)

273. The Eightfold Path is the best of paths,
    The Four Sayings the best of truths,
Freedom from passion the best of states,
    The Seer the best of two-footed beings.

274. This is the path – there is no other –
    For the purification of seeing.
Enter upon this one:
    This is the thwarting of Māra.

275. If you enter upon this path,
    You'll make an end of suffering –
The path I taught you
    Once I'd understood the easing of darts.

276. *You* have to make the effort:
    The Tathāgatas are the teachers.
Meditators who enter upon the path
    Are freed from Māra's bonds.

277. 'All conditioned things are impermanent.'
    When by wisdom you see this,
You grow weary of suffering.
    This is the path to purity.

278. 'All conditioned things are suffering.'
When by wisdom you see this,
You grow weary of suffering.
This is the path to purity.

279. 'All *dhammas* are without self.'
When by wisdom you see this,
You grow weary of suffering.
This is the path to purity.

280. If at the time for striving he does not strive,
Gives in to lethargy though young and strong,
That idle, lazy man, with lowered thoughts
and mind,
Does not by wisdom discover the path.

281. Guarding your speech, restrained in mind
And body too, you should do no unskilful act.
Purifying these three ways of action,
You'll reach the path taught by the sages.

282. From practice arises wisdom;
From not practising, decrease of wisdom.
Knowing this twofold path
Leading to gain and loss,
You should establish yourself in such a way
That your wisdom increases.

283. Cut down the wood, not the tree.
From the wood arises danger.
Cut down wood and brushwood
And be free from the wood, monks.

284. As long as any tiny bit of brushwood
Of a man towards women is not cut down,
He has a mind in bondage,
Like a sucking calf towards its mother.

285. Cut off affection towards yourself
As you'd pluck an autumn lily with
your hand.
Develop the path to peace,
The *nibbāna* taught by the Well-Gone.

286. 'I'll live here in the rainy season,
Here in the winter and summer,'
The fool thinks:
He does not see his danger.

287. If a man's intoxicated by sons and cattle,
His mind attached to this and that,
Death carries him away
As a great flood takes a sleeping village.

288. Sons cannot protect you,
Nor father, nor any relatives.
When you are assailed by the Ender
There's no protection in your kin.

289. Knowing this for a fact,
The wise one, restrained by good conduct,
Should quickly clear
The path that leads to *nibbāna*.

CHAPTER 21

MISCELLANEOUS

(21.1–16)

290. If, by giving up happiness from material things,
He might see a great happiness,
A wise man, looking to the great happiness,
Would give up happiness from material things.

291. If you seek your own happiness
By causing pain to others,
Then, caught up in attachment to hatred,
You won't be freed from hatred.

292. For what should be done is cast aside,
But what should not be done is done.
In those who are arrogant and unaware
The defilements increase.

293. But for those in whom mindfulness of body
Is ever rightly undertaken,
Who do not practise what should not be done,
Who persevere in what should be done,
Who are mindful and wise,
The defilements go to rest.

294. After killing mother and father
And two royal kings
And destroying a kingdom with its tax-gatherers,
The Brahmin walks unharmed.

295. After killing mother and father
And two Brahmin kings
And destroying a tiger-man as fifth,
The Brahmin walks unharmed.

296. Gotama's disciples
Are always wide awake:
Both day and night they are ever
Mindful of the Buddha.

297. Gotama's disciples
Are always wide awake:
Both day and night they are ever
Mindful of the Dhamma.

298. Gotama's disciples
Are always wide awake:
Both day and night they are ever
Mindful of the Saṅgha.

299. Gotama's disciples
Are always wide awake:
Both day and night they are ever
Mindful of the body.

300. Gotama's disciples
Are always wide awake:
Both day and night their minds
Delight in non-violence.

301. Gotama's disciples
Are always wide awake:
Both day and night their minds
Delight in meditation.

302. It's hard to go forth, hard to find pleasure;
Houses are hard to live in and painful;
It's painful to live with people who are different;
The wayfarer is beset with suffering.
So you shouldn't be a wayfarer,
And you won't be beset with suffering.

303. One who is faithful, endowed with good conduct,
Who has attained fame and wealth,
Whatever country he goes to
He is honoured there.

304. Though far away, the good shine out
Like Mount Himavat.
The bad are not seen even here,
Like arrows shot by night.

305. One who sits alone, sleeps alone,
Walks alone unwearying,
Alone controls himself,
Will find pleasure in the forest.

CHAPTER 22
HELLS

(22.1–14)

306. The one who says what is not goes to a
hell world;
So does the one who does something
and says he doesn't.
Both these, when they die, become equal
Men of low conduct, in the other world.

307. Many with the yellow robe on their backs
Are of evil character and uncontrolled.
Through their evil actions, the evil
Are reborn in a hell world.

308. Better to eat a ball of iron
Hot as flames of fire
Than to eat the alms of the kingdom
While immoral and uncontrolled.

309. Four things happen to the reckless man
Who goes with the wife of another:
Ill fortune earned; disturbed sleep;
Third, blame; and fourth, a hell world –

310. Ill fortune earned, and an evil destination:
Small pleasure for frightened man with
frightened woman –
And the king imposes a heavy punishment.
So a man shouldn't go with the wife
of another.

311. Just as *kusa* grass, when wrongly grasped,
Cuts your hand,
The wanderer's life, wrongly undertaken,
Drags you to a hell world.

312. Any action that's slack,
Any vow that's defiled,
Any spiritual practice that's doubtful
Doesn't bear much fruit.

313. If it needs doing, do it;
Undertake it steadfastly –
For a slack ascetic
Just scatters more dust on himself.

314. A bad deed is better not done –
You repent a bad deed afterwards.
A good deed is better done –
One you won't repent when you've done it.

315. Guard yourselves
Like a border city,
Guarded inside and out.
Don't let the moment escape you.
Those who miss the moment regret it
When they're consigned to a hell world.

316. They are ashamed of what is not shameful
And not ashamed of what is shameful:
From taking up wrong views
Beings go to to a bad destination.

317. Seeing danger where there is no danger
And not seeing danger where danger exists,
From taking up wrong views
Beings go to a bad destination.

318. Imagining fault where there is no fault
And not seeing fault where fault exists,
From taking up wrong views
Beings go to a bad destination.

319. But perceiving fault where fault exists
And no fault where there is no fault,
From taking up right views
Beings go to a good destination.

CHAPTER 23
THE ELEPHANT

(23.1–14)

320. Just as an elephant in battle
  Endures arrows shot from the bow
I will endure abusive speech –
  For people in general are ill behaved.

321. Folk take the tamed one into battle;
  The king mounts the tamed one.
The tamed one, who endures abusive speech,
  Is the best among human beings.

322. Fine are tamed mules
  And thoroughbreds from Sindh
And great tusker elephants;
  But the self-tamed is finer than these.

323. Not by these mounts
  Can you go to the place where none has gone
As you'll go by a well-tamed self,
  Tamed by means of tamed.

324. The tusker called Dhanapālaka
  Hard to control, exuding pungent *must*,
Eats not a morsel in captivity.
  The tusker remembers the elephant-forest.

325. While he is lazy, gluttonous,
A sleeper, rolling about as he lies,
Like a great boar fed on grain,
The fool comes to a womb again and again.

326. Once this mind roamed about
As it wished, as it wanted, as it liked.
Today I will control it properly
As a mahout controls an elephant in *must*.

327. Take delight in awareness:
Guard your own minds.
Lift yourselves out of the bad road
Like the tusker sunk in the mud.

328. If you find a skilful companion
Who walks with you, well behaved and wise,
You should walk with him, joyful and mindful,
Overcoming all dangers.

329. If you don't find a skilful companion
Who walks with you, well behaved and wise,
Then, like a king leaving conquered territory,
You should walk alone, like an elephant
in an elephant-forest.

330. It's better to walk alone:
There's no companionship with fools.
You should walk alone and do no evil,
With few wants, like an elephant in
an elephant-forest.

331. When need arises, companions are pleasant;
Pleasant is contentment with this and that;
At life's end, merit is pleasant;
Pleasant is the abandoning of all suffering.

332. Pleasant in the world is caring for your mother;
Pleasant, too, caring for your father;
Pleasant in the world is caring for wanderers;
Pleasant, too, caring for Brahmins.

333. Pleasant is good conduct continued to old age;
Pleasant is firm faith;
Pleasant is the winning of wisdom;
Pleasant is not doing evil.

CHAPTER 24
CRAVING

(24.1–26)

334. If a person walks unaware
His craving grows like a *māluvā* creeper.
He jumps hither and thither
Like a monkey seeking fruit in a wood.

335. If someone is overpowered
By this fierce craving, the clinging to the world,
His sorrows increase
Like *bīraṇa* grass after rain.

336. But if someone overpowers
This fierce craving, hard to overcome in the world,
His sorrows fall away from him
Like a water-drop from a lotus.

337. So I say to you, venerable sirs,
As many as are met together here:
Dig up the root of craving
As one seeking the *usira* root digs up *bīraṇa* grass.
Don't let Māra break you,
As a flood breaks a reed, again and again.

338. Just as a tree, if its root is undamaged and firm,
Even when cut down, grows again,
So, when the tendency to craving is not rooted out,
Suffering springs up again and again.

339. If the thirty-six streams that flow towards enchanting things
Are strong in someone,
Floods, imaginings of passion,
Carry off that person of wrong views.

340. The streams ever flow,
The creeper sprouts and stands tall.
When you see that the creeper has grown up,
Cut out its root with wisdom.

341. For a person, there are wide-flowing
And lovely delights.
Those folk who depend on pleasure, seekers of happiness,
Undergo birth and old age.

342. Those who are subject to craving
Crawl around like a trapped hare.
Bound by fetters and bonds, for a long time
They undergo suffering again and again.

343. Those who are subject to craving
Crawl around like a trapped hare.
So a monk should put away craving
If he desires his own freedom from passion.

344. Come, see the man
Who, without brushwood, and committed to the wood,
Freed from the wood, runs back to the wood!
Though freed, he runs back to his bonds.

345. That's not a strong bond, say the wise,
One made of iron, wood or rope.
The longing for jewelled earrings,
Affection for children and wives –

346. This is a strong bond, say the wise,
Heavy, hard to escape for the slack.
But, cutting even this, folk go forth,
without longing,
Leaving sensual pleasure behind.

347. Those who are attached to passion follow a stream
They have made for themselves, as a spider
follows its web.
But, cutting even this, the wise go on, without
longing,
Leaving all suffering behind.

348. Let go what's before, let go what's after,
Let go what's in the middle: cross to the
other shore!
With your mind freed on all fronts,
You won't come to birth and old age again.

349. If a person is churned up by thoughts
Of strong passion, dwelling on the fair,
His craving grows yet more:
He makes the bond strong.

350. But the one who delights in calming his thoughts –
Who, ever mindful, contemplates the foul –
He will finish it.
He will cut Māra's bond.

351. The one who has reached the goal, fearless,
Without craving, flawless,
Has cut out the darts of existence.
This accumulation is his last.

352. The one without craving, without clinging,
Skilled in etymology and words,
Who knows the order of letters
And what comes before and after:

He, with his last body,
Is very wise, a great person –
So he is called.

353. All-conquering, all-knowing am I,
Undefiled among all *dhammas*,
All-renouncing, released through the destruction of craving.
I myself have understood, so to whom should I point as teacher?

354. The gift of Dhamma conquers all gifts;
The flavour of Dhamma conquers all flavours;
The pleasure of Dhamma conquers all pleasures;
The destruction of craving conquers all suffering.

355. Riches destroy the fool,
But not the one who seeks the other shore.
Through craving for riches, the fool
Destroys himself as he does others.

356. Fields are spoiled by weeds;
These folk are spoiled by passion –
So a gift to those without passion
Bears great fruit.

357. Fields are spoiled by weeds;
These folk are spoiled by hatred –
So a gift to those without hatred
Bears great fruit.

358. Fields are spoiled by weeds;
These folk are spoiled by delusion –
So a gift to those without delusion
Bears great fruit.

359. Fields are spoiled by weeds;
    These folk are spoiled by desire –
So a gift to those without desire
    Bears great fruit.

CHAPTER 25
THE MONK

(25.1–23)

360. Restraint of the eye is good;
 Good is restraint of the ear;
Restraint of the nose is good;
 Good is restraint of the tongue;

361. Restraint of the body is good;
 Good is restraint of speech;
Restraint of mind is good;
 Good is restraint all round.
Restrained all round, a monk
 Is freed from all suffering.

362. Restrained of hand, restrained of foot,
 Restrained of speech, best of restrained ones,
Delighting inwardly, concentrated,
 Alone, contented – that one they call a monk.

363. The monk who is restrained of mouth,
 A gentle speaker, not puffed up,
Who illuminates the meaning and the Dhamma –
 His speech is sweet.

364. Dwelling in Dhamma, delighting in Dhamma,
 Contemplating Dhamma,
Mindful of Dhamma, a monk
 Does not abandon the true Dhamma.

365. You should not despise your own gains,
Nor live envying those of others.
Envying others' gains, a monk
Does not attain concentration.

366. If a monk, even with small gains,
Does not despise his own gains,
Him the gods praise
As one of pure livelihood, unwearied.

367. One who has no possessiveness at all
In regard to name or form,
And does not grieve for what is not,
He is called a monk.

368. The monk who dwells in loving kindness,
Confident in the Buddha's teaching,
Attains the peaceful state,
The blissful stilling of conditioned things.

369. Monk, bail out this boat!
Once bailed, it will go lightly for you.
Cutting off both passion and hatred,
You will go to *nibbāna*.

370. Cut off five, give up five,
Develop five to the highest.
The monk who has gone beyond the five bonds
Is called 'crosser of the flood'.

371. Monk, meditate! Don't be unaware.
Don't let your mind wander in the strand of sense-pleasure.
Don't recklessly swallow an iron ball.
Don't, as you burn, cry, 'This is suffering!'

372. There's no meditation in one without wisdom,
Or wisdom in one who doesn't meditate.
The one in whom are both meditation and wisdom
Is close to *nibbāna*.

373. The monk who with calm mind
Has entered an empty house,
Who has right insight into *dhammas*,
Has joy beyond the human.

374. Whenever he contemplates
The arising and passing away of the aggregates
He gains joy and happiness.
That is the 'deathless' for those who know.

375. So this is how the wise monk
Can make a beginning here:
Guarding of the senses, contentment,
Restraint in the monastic rule.
Find friends who are good for you,
Of pure livelihood, unwearied.

376. You should have generous habits,
Be skilled in good conduct.
Then, rich in happiness,
You'll make an end of suffering.

377. As the jasmine sheds
Its withered blossoms,
You should let go
Of passion and hatred, monks.

378. Peaceful in body, peaceful in speech,
Peaceful in mind, concentrated,
A monk who has rejected the world's meat
Is called 'at peace'.

379. By self urge on yourself;
    By self examine yourself.
Then, self-guarded and mindful,
    You'll live happily, monk.

380. For self is the lord of self;
    Self is the refuge of self.
So control yourself
    As a merchant controls a fine horse.

381. The monk who's rich in happiness,
    Confident in the Buddha's teaching,
Attains the peaceful state,
    The blissful stilling of conditioned things.

382. The monk who, while still young,
    Applies himself to the Buddha's teaching
Illuminates this world
    Like the moon freed from a cloud.

CHAPTER 26

THE BRAHMIN

(26.1–41)

383. Strive, and cut across the stream;
Drive away sense-pleasures, Brahmin.
Knowing the destruction of conditioned things,
You'll know the unmade, Brahmin.

384. When, among twofold states,
A Brahmin goes to the other shore,
Then, once he knows,
All fetters go to rest.

385. The one for whom there is neither
The far shore, nor the near shore, nor
both the far and near shores,
Free of fear, unfettered,
Him I call a Brahmin.

386. The one who sits meditative, free from stain,
Whose task is done, who's free from
defilement,
Who has reached the supreme goal,
Him I call a Brahmin.

387. By day, the sun shines;
By night, the moon gleams;
In his armour, the warrior shines;
Meditating, the Brahmin shines;
But ever, night and day,
The Buddha shines with his radiance.

388. One's called 'Brahmin' for getting rid of evil;
One's called 'wanderer' for equable conduct;
For getting rid of one's own stain
One's called 'renouncer'.

389. A Brahmin should not strike a Brahmin,
Nor unleash his anger against him.
Shame on him who strikes a Brahmin!
More shame on him who unleashes his anger!

390. This is of no small benefit to a Brahmin,
To have restraint of mind about things that are dear.
The more the will to harm ceases,
The more is sorrow calmed.

391. The one who does no wrong
Through body, speech or mind,
Restrained in the three ways,
Him I call a Brahmin.

392. The one from whom you can learn the Dhamma
Taught by the Fully Awakened One
You should honour with reverence
As a Brahmin honours the sacrificial fire.

393. You don't become a Brahmin
By matted locks, by lineage, or by caste:
The one in whom are truth and Dhamma,
He's pure, and he's a Brahmin.

394. Fool, what use are your matted locks,
Your antelope-skin garment?
There's a mess inside you:
You clean the outside.

395. The person who wears clothes from a dust-heap,
Lean, a tracery of veins,
Meditating alone in the wood,
Him I call a Brahmin.

396. But I don't call someone a Brahmin
Because he's born of a Brahmin womb
or mother:
If he owns anything
He's just a man who says 'good sir'.
One who owns nothing, without clinging,
Him I call a Brahmin.

397. One who has cut all fetters,
Who is unafraid,
Who has gone beyond bonds, unfettered,
Him I call a Brahmin.

398. One who's cut the strap and the girth,
The thong with its attachments,
Who's pushed up the door-bar, awakened,
Him I call a Brahmin.

399. One who, though innocent, endures
Abuse, beating and imprisonment,
Whose strength is patience, whose army is
his strength,
Him I call a Brahmin.

400. One who's not angry, keeping his vows,
Keeping morality, free from lust,
Tamed, bearing his last body,
Him I call a Brahmin.

401. One who doesn't cling to sense-pleasures –
Like water on a lotus leaf,
Or a mustard seed on a needle's point –
Him I call a Brahmin.

402. One who realizes here
The ending of his own suffering,
Who's laid down the burden, unfettered,
Him I call a Brahmin.

403. One of deep understanding, wise,
Skilled in what is and what is not the way,
Who has reached the supreme goal,
Him I call a Brahmin.

404. One not mixing either
With householders or with homeless ones,
Living houseless, of few desires,
Him I call a Brahmin.

405. One who has laid down the rod
In dealing with beings, moving or still,
Who neither kills nor causes to kill,
Him I call a Brahmin.

406. One who is not hostile among the hostile,
At peace among those who wield the rod,
Unclinging among the clinging,
Him I call a Brahmin.

407. One from whom passion, ill will,
Pride and hypocrisy have been let drop
Like a mustard seed from a needle's point,
Him I call a Brahmin.

408. One who utters speech that isn't rough
But instructive and truthful
So that he offends no one,
Him I call a Brahmin.

409. One who in this world
Takes nothing that is not given,
Whether long or short, tiny or great, fair or foul,
Him I call a Brahmin.

410. One in whom no wishes are found
For this world or the next,
Without longing, unfettered,
Him I call a Brahmin.

411. One in whom no longings are found,
Who, through knowledge, has no doubts,
Plunged into the deathless, not arising again,
Him I call a Brahmin.

412. One who here has gone beyond both good and evil,
Both kinds of clinging,
Sorrowless, stainless, pure,
Him I call a Brahmin.

413. One who is stainless and pure as the moon,
Peaceful and untroubled,
With indulgence and existence exhausted,
Him I call a Brahmin.

414. One who has gone beyond this winding path,
so hard to travel –
Saṃsāra, delusion –
Crossed over, passed beyond, a meditator,
Clear, free from doubt,
Who has attained *nibbāna* without clinging,
Him I call a Brahmin.

415. One who here gives up sense-desires
And wanders homeless,
With sense-desires and existence exhausted,
Him I call a Brahmin.

416. One who here gives up craving
And wanders homeless,
With craving and existence exhausted,
Him I call a Brahmin.

417. One who has given up human attachment
And gone beyond divine attachment,
Unfettered from all attachment,
Him I call a Brahmin.

418. One who has given up both pleasure
and displeasure,
Who's cooled, with no remnant of craving,
A hero who's overcome the whole world,
Him I call a Brahmin.

419. One who knows in every way
The death of beings, and their arising,
Unattached, well gone, awakened,
Him I call a Brahmin.

420. One whose destination
Neither gods nor spirits nor human
beings know,
With defilements exhausted, an Arahat,
Him I call a Brahmin.

421. One who owns nothing – before,
After, or in the middle –
Possessing nothing, without clinging,
Him I call a Brahmin.

422. The bull, the finest, the hero,
The great sage, the conqueror,
Desireless, bathed, awakened,
Him I call a Brahmin.

423. One who knows former abodes,
Sees heavens and hells,
Who has reached the end of births,
Sage perfect in knowledge,
Who has perfected all perfections,
Him I call a Brahmin.

SUMMARY VERSES

1. 'Twins', 'Awareness', 'The Mind',
   'Flowers' and 'Fools', 'The Wise Man',
   'The Arahat' and 'Thousands',
   'Evil' and 'The Rod' – these make ten.

2. 'Old Age', both 'Self' and 'The World',
   'The Buddha', 'Happiness' and 'The Dear',
   'Anger' and 'Rust', 'The Just',
   And the chapter on 'The Path' make twenty.

3. 'Miscellaneous', 'Hells', 'The Elephant',
   'Craving', 'The Monk' and 'The Brahmin':
   These are the twenty-six chapters
   Taught by the Kinsman of the Sun.

Appendix I
Extract from the Gāndhārī Dharmapada

From Chapter 1: The Brahmin

1. You don't become a Brahmin
   By matted locks, by lineage, or by caste:
   If you drive away evils on every side,
   Small ones and great,
   Through driving away evils
   You are called a Brahmin.

2. Fool, what use are your matted locks,
   Your antelope-skin garment?
   There's a mess inside you:
   You clean the outside.

3. The one from whom you can learn the Dharma
   Taught by the Fully Awakened One
   You should honour with reverence
   As a Brahmin honours the sacrificial fire.

4. You don't become a Brahmin by matted locks,
   Nor by the three Vedas nor by traditional
   learning,
   Nor by reverencing the fire,
   Nor by plunging into water.

5. The one who knows his previous abodes,
    Sees heavens and hells,
Who has reached the end of births,
    Is a sage, purified by higher knowledge.

6. By these three knowledges
    You become a Brahmin, a knower of the
        three Vedas:
Endowed with knowledge and conduct
    You're called a Brahmin.

7. Endowed with the three knowledges,
    Calmed, with future births destroyed,
Unattached to the whole world,
    You're called a Brahmin.

8. By asceticism and the holy life,
    Restraint and self-control,
You become a Brahmin.
    This is the highest Brahminhood.

9. Strive, and cut across the stream;
    Drive away sense-pleasures, Brahmin.
Without getting rid of desires
    No sage can attain oneness.

10. Strive, and cut across the stream;
    Drive away sense-pleasures, Brahmin.
Knowing the destruction of conditioned things,
    You'll know the unmade, Brahmin.

11. A Brahmin should not strike a Brahmin,
    Nor unleash his anger against him.
Shame on him who strikes a Brahmin!
    More shame on him who unleashes his anger!

12. After killing mother and father
    And two royal kings
And destroying a kingdom with its tax-gatherers,
    The Brahmin walks unharmed.

13. After first killing the king
    And then an entire assembly,
After killing an enemy with his army,
    The Brahmin walks unharmed.

14. When, among twofold states,
    A Brahmin goes to the other shore,
Then, once he knows,
    All fetters pass away.

15. This is of no small benefit to a Brahmin,
    To have restraint of mind towards things
        that are dear.
The more the mind turns away from these things,
    The more is sorrow calmed.

16. One's called 'Brahmin' for getting rid of evil;
    One's called 'wanderer' for equable conduct;
For getting rid of one's own stain
    One's called 'renouncer'.

17. But I don't call someone a Brahmin
    Because he's born of a Brahmin womb
        or mother:
If he owns anything
    He's just a man who says 'good sir'.
One who owns nothing, without clinging,
    Him I call a Brahmin.

18. One who has laid down the rod
    In dealing with beings, moving or still,
Who neither kills nor causes to kill,
    Him I call a Brahmin.

19. One who in this world
Takes nothing that is not given,
Whether long or short, tiny or great, fair or foul,
Him I call a Brahmin.

20. One who here gives up sense-desires
And wanders homeless,
With the enjoyment of sense-desires exhausted,
Him I call a Brahmin.

21. One who doesn't cling to sense-pleasures –
Like water on a lotus leaf,
Or a mustard seed on a needle's point –
Him I call a Brahmin.

22. One who utters speech that isn't rough
But instructive and truthful
So that he offends no one,
Him I call a Brahmin.

23. The one who does no wrong
Through body, speech or mind,
Restrained in the three ways,
Him I call a Brahmin.

24. One perfectly calmed, ceased,
A gentle speaker, not puffed up,
Who illuminates the meaning and the Dharma,
Him I call a Brahmin.

25. One perfectly calmed, ceased,
A gentle speaker, not puffed up,
Who has reached the supreme goal,
Him I call a Brahmin.

NOTES

Chapter 1 of the Khotan Manuscript of the Gāndhārī Dharmapada has the equivalent title to Pali Dhammapada Chapter 26, 'The Brahmin' (*brammaṇa*), and shares some of the same material. Both seek to redefine the Brahmin, attacking those who claim superiority merely on grounds of birth or traditional Brahmanical practices. The weight given to this topic throughout the Dharmapada literature suggests that this was a topic of great concern for early Buddhists. The Gāndhārī version of the chapter has fifty verses; here I translate the first twenty-five.

In what follows, I have noted where verses in the extract have close equivalents in the Pali Dhammapada. The symbol '=' denotes that, apart from the normal sound-changes between Gāndhārī and Pali, the verses are identical. Where the verses are closely related but not identical, I have marked them as 'equivalent'.

1. For ll. 1–2, cf. Dhammapada 393. For ll. 3–6, cf. Dhammapada 265, but here the pun is on 'Brahmin' (*brammaṇa*) and 'to drive away' (*brah-*).
2. Equivalent to Dhammapada 394.
3. Equivalent to Dhammapada 392.
4. *three Vedas*: In the original usage, the three Vedas are the most ancient part of Hindu scripture, comprising the Ṛgveda, Yajurveda and Sāmaveda, consisting respectively of hymns, ritual formulae, and chants, intended for use as part of the elaborate Brahmanical ritual. In v. 6, below, the concept is reinterpreted in a Buddhist sense.
5. cf. ll. 1–4 of Dhammapada 423.
   higher knowledge: *abhiña* (Pali *abhiññā*).
6. *You become . . . You're called*: Literally, 'One becomes . . . One's called'.
   Endowed with knowledge and conduct: cf. Dhammapada 144 and note.
8. *the holy life*: *brammayirya* – equivalent to Sanskrit *brahmacarya*, Pali *brahmacariya*.
9. For the first two *pādas* cf. Dhammapada 383.
10. Here the 'you' is literal: the Buddha is addressing a particular person.
11. = Dhammapada 389.
12. = Dhammapada 294. For the symbolism, see notes there.

13. Presumably the enemy is Māra, and the 'assembly' and the 'army' his followers, the various defilements of the mind.
14. = Dhammapada 384.
15. Equivalent to Dhammapada 390, and probably representing its earlier (and more comprehensible) form.
16. = Dhammapada 388.
17. = Dhammapada 396.
18. = Dhammapada 405.
19. = Dhammapada 409.
20. *enjoyment of sense-desires*: Or perhaps 'sense-desires and enjoyment'. Equivalent to Dhammapada 415, with *kama-bhoka-parikṣiṇa* in place of *kāma-bhava-parikkhīṇaṃ*.
21. = Dhammapada 401.
22. = Dhammapada 408.
23. = Dhammapada 391.
24. *Pādas* b and c as Dhammapada 363.
25. *Pādas* b and c as Dhammapada 363; *pādas* c and d as Dhammapada 386 and 403.

Appendix II
Extract from the Patna Dharmapada

Chapter 22: The Snake

398. The monk who, like one looking for blossom
on fig trees,
Has found no substance in states of being
Leaves behind this shore and the other shore
As a snake sloughs its old, worn-out skin.

399. The monk who controls passion that's arisen
As you'd treat with antidotes snake-venom
that's spread through the body
Leaves behind this shore and the other shore
As a snake sloughs its old, worn-out skin.

400. The monk who controls ill will that's arisen
As you'd treat with antidotes snake-venom
that's spread through the body
Leaves behind this shore and the other shore
As a snake sloughs its old, worn-out skin.

401. The monk who controls delusion that's arisen
As you'd treat with antidotes snake-venom
that's spread through the body
Leaves behind this shore and the other shore
As a snake sloughs its old, worn-out skin.

402. The monk who controls anger that's arisen
As you'd treat with antidotes snake-venom
that's spread through the body
Leaves behind this shore and the other shore
As a snake sloughs its old, worn-out skin.

403. The monk who controls pride that's arisen
As you'd treat with antidotes snake-venom
that's spread through the body
Leaves behind this shore and the other shore
As a snake sloughs its old, worn-out skin.

404. The monk who has cut off passion completely
As you'd plunge in and pluck a lake-growing
lotus flower
Leaves behind this shore and the other shore
As a snake sloughs its old, worn-out skin.

405. The monk who has cut off ill will completely
As you'd plunge in and pluck a lake-growing
lotus flower
Leaves behind this shore and the other shore
As a snake sloughs its old, worn-out skin.

406. The monk who has cut off delusion completely
As you'd plunge in and pluck a lake-growing
lotus flower
Leaves behind this shore and the other shore
As a snake sloughs its old, worn-out skin.

407. The monk who has cut off anger completely
As you'd plunge in and pluck a lake-growing
lotus flower
Leaves behind this shore and the other shore
As a snake sloughs its old, worn-out skin.

408. The monk who has cut off pride completely
As you'd plunge in and pluck a lake-growing lotus flower
Leaves behind this shore and the other shore
As a snake sloughs its old, worn-out skin.

409. The monk who has cut off passion completely
As you'd cut bonds, fetters of *kuśa* grass,
Leaves behind this shore and the other shore
As a snake sloughs its old, worn-out skin.

410. The monk who has cut off craving completely,
Drying up the swift-flowing river,
Leaves behind this shore and the other shore
As a snake sloughs its old, worn-out skin.

411. The monk who has neither gone too far nor fallen short,
Who has gone beyond this realm of proliferation,
Leaves behind this shore and the other shore
As a snake sloughs its old, worn-out skin.

412. The monk who has neither gone too far nor fallen short,
Who knows all this is a thing of lies, a falsehood,
Leaves behind this shore and the other shore
As a snake sloughs its old, worn-out skin.

413. The monk who has no desires
That can act as causes to bind him to existence
Leaves behind this shore and the other shore
As a snake sloughs its old, worn-out skin.

414. The monk who has no fears,
Whose unwholesome roots have all been dug up,
Leaves behind this shore and the other shore
As a snake sloughs its old, worn-out skin.

NOTES

This is the last chapter of the Patna Dharmapada. Its title is missing in the manuscript, but in view of the refrain (*passim*) and the mention of snake-venom (vv. 399–403), Roth's reconstruction (1980) of the title as *Uraga*, 'Snake', is surely correct.

Verses with his refrain were clearly very popular. Although they are not included in the Pali Dhammapada, another Khuddaka Nikāya text, the Sutta Nipāta, begins with an Uraga Sutta, consisting of seventeen such verses. The Khotan version of the Gāndhārī Dharmapada has ten as part of its second chapter, 'The Monk' (*bhikhu*). The thirteen verses that survive of the London Dharmapada include nine 'snake' verses, probably also from a 'Monk' chapter. The Sanskrit Udānavarga (ed. Bernhard 1965–90) has a set as part of Chapter 32, 'The Monk' (*bhikṣu*), vv. 55–79. Each version has variations and changes of order, but all preserve the same refrain within their different languages.

398. *looking for blossom on fig trees*: Fig trees do not have flowers (or, from a botanical point of view, have very small flowers which are not very recognizable as such).
this shore and the other shore: (Here and throughout the passage) this life and the next.
sloughs: (Here and throughout the passage) word added for clarity.

399–403. *you'd treat*: Words added for clarity.
with antidotes: *oṣadhīhi. Oṣadhi* originally meant 'herb', but came to be used for any kind of medicine or remedy. In this context an antidote to poison is clearly meant.
through the body: Added for clarity. The venom is *visaṭa* (< *visṛta*), 'spread throughout [the body]'.

409. *kuśa*: See note on Pali Dhammapada 70.

411. *realm of proliferation*: 'realm of' added for clarity. *Prapañca* (Pali *papañca*) is the tendency of the mind to create more and more distractions.

414. *unwholesome roots*: Greed (*lobha*), hate (Sanskrit *dveṣa*, Pali/Prakrit *dosa*) and delusion (*moha*), viewed as the roots of all unwholesome conduct.

Appendix III
Extract from the Mahāvastu

The Blessed One went from the hermitage of Uruvilvā Kāśyapa with a great assembly of monks, twelve hundred and fifty in number, to Dharmāraṇya, the place of the hermitage of the Great Ṛṣis. At that time seven hundred long-haired ascetics lived there, each of them a hundred and twenty years of age, all of whom had attained the four meditations and the five higher knowledges, and all of whose wholesome roots were thoroughly ripe and who were in their last existence. The Blessed One went to the place of the hermitage in order to help them.

The Blessed One spoke the 'Thousands' chapter of the Dharmapada to the long-haired ascetics:

1. Better than a thousand sayings
   Made up of useless words
   Is one saying with meaning
   Which calms you to hear it.

2. Better than a thousand verses
   Made up of useless words
   Is one line of verse
   Which calms you to hear it.

3. Though you should conquer in battle
   A hundred thousand men
   You're the finest battle-winner
   If you conquer just one – yourself.

4. Though you should conquer, month by month,
A hundred thousand at a time
You're not worth a sixteenth part
Of confidence in the Buddha.

5. Though you should conquer, month by month,
A hundred thousand at a time
You're not worth a sixteenth part
Of confidence in the Dharma.

6. Though you should conquer, month by month,
A hundred thousand at a time
You're not worth a sixteenth part
Of confidence in the Saṅgha.

7. Though you should conquer, month by month,
A hundred thousand at a time
You're not worth a sixteenth part
Of those who are endowed with morality.

8. Though you should conquer, month by month,
A hundred thousand at a time
You're not worth a sixteenth part
Of those of the well-taught Dharma.

9. Though month after month a fool
Eats food with the tip of a *kuśa*-grass blade
He's not worth a sixteenth part
Of confidence in the Buddha.

10. Though month after month a fool
Eats food with the tip of a *kuśa*-grass blade
He's not worth a sixteenth part
Of confidence in the Dharma.

11. Though month after month a fool
Eats food with the tip of a *kuśa*-grass blade
He's not worth a sixteenth part
Of confidence in the Saṅgha.

12. Though month after month a fool
Eats food with the tip of a *kuśa*-grass blade
He's not worth a sixteenth part
Of those who trust in meditation.

13. Though month after month a fool
Eats food with the tip of a *kuśa*-grass blade
He's not worth a sixteenth part
Of those who are endowed with morality.

14. Though month after month a fool
Eats food with the tip of a *kuśa*-grass blade
He's not worth a sixteenth part
Of those of the well-taught Dharma.

15. You could live a hundred years,
Tend the fire,
Eating leaves, wearing skins,
Practising all kinds of asceticism,

16. But if you were to pay respect to a developed person
Once, just for a moment,
That single worship would be better
And not the hundred-year offering.

17. Whatever sacrifice or offering in the world
One who seeks merit might offer for a year,
All that is not worth a quarter as much
As reverence to those who are upright.

18. Better than living a hundred years
    Ill behaved, unconcentrated,
Is living for one day
    Well behaved, a meditator.

19. Better than living a hundred years
    Lazy, without effort,
Is living for one day
    Steadfastly making effort.

20. Better than living a hundred years
    Not seeing the Buddha's dispensation
Is living for one day
    Seeing the Buddha's dispensation.

21. Better than living a hundred years
    Not seeing the supreme Dharma
Is living for one day
    Seeing the supreme Dharma.

22. Better than living a hundred years
    Not seeing arising and passing away
Is living for one day
    Seeing arising and passing away.

23. Better than living a hundred years
    Not seeing the unfallen state
Is living for one day
    Seeing the unfallen state.

24. Better than living a hundred years
    Not seeing the deathless state
Is living for one day
    Seeing the deathless state.

And they were brought by the Blessed One to a state of mastery of the powers; and they all attained *parinirvāṇa*. The Blessed One performed their funerary rites and built *stūpas* for them.

Then from Dharmāraṇya he came to the Goatherd's Banyan Tree . . .

NOTES

From Mahāvastu Avadāna 3.434–7: 'Dharmapadeṣu sahasravargaḥ' (pp. 581–5 of Basak's edition). An equivalent chapter is also found in the Udānavarga, but called 'Peyālavarga' ('Repetition Chapter') rather than 'Thousands'.

In what follows, I have noted where verses in the extract have close equivalents in the Pali Dhammapada. The symbol '=' denotes that, apart from the normal sound-changes between Sanskrit and Pali, the verses are identical. Where the verses are closely related but not identical, I have marked them as 'equivalent'.

In the Introduction

with a great assembly of monks, twelve hundred and fifty in number: Literally, 'with a great community (*saṅgha*) of monks, with twelve and a half hundred monks', or rather, using the usual curious Sanskrit/Pali idiom, '. . . with hundreds of monks having half [i.e. instead of another whole hundred] as their 13th'. The repetition of *bhikṣu* ('monks'), while natural in the original languages, seems awkward in English.

Dharmāraṇya: The Forest of Dharma.

Great Ṛṣis: Important sages, particularly within the Hindu tradition.

long-haired ascetics: *jaṭila*, those wearing the *jaṭā*, the uncut and uncombed hair still characteristic of many Hindu ascetics, often worn as a topknot or as dreadlocks.

four meditations: *dhyāna* (Pali *jhāna*) – the four (or in some lists five) states attained through the practice of concentration-based meditation. In these states the mind becomes temporarily freed from the hindrances and so receptive to insight and wisdom.

five higher knowledges: *abhijñā* (Pali *abhiññā*) – abilities ('psychic powers') thought to result from the deep practice of concentration: clairvoyance, clairaudience, knowledge of the thoughts of others, recollection of past lives, and the knowledge that puts an end to the defilements (*āsavas*).

wholesome roots: Non-greed (generosity), non-hatred (loving kindness) and non-delusion (wisdom).

in their last existence: At a point when no further births would be needed as a result of *karma/kamma*. The point being made here is that these ancient ascetics have gone as far as possible with concentration-based meditation. They need the jolt of insight that the Buddha can provide in order to attain complete freedom as Arahats.

of the Dharmapada: Literally, 'in the Dharmapadas'.

1. Equivalent to Dhammapada 100.
2. Equivalent to Dhammapada 101.
3. Similar to Dhammapada 103.

4–8. *Though you should conquer . . . You're not worth*: Literally, 'The one who would conquer . . . He is not worth'. The equivalent verses in the Dhammapada and Udānavarga all have the neuter form: '. . . That is not worth . . .'

4. *conquer*: The first half of vv. 4–8, *yo jayeta sahasrāṇāṃ māse māse śataṃ śataṃ*, is clearly a variation on Dhammapada 106, *māse māse sahassena yo yajetha sataṃ samaṃ*, but with a repetition of *śataṃ*, 'hundred', in place of *samaṃ*, 'for a year' (Sanskrit *samāṃ*), and *jayeta* (from *ji*-, 'conquer',) in place of *yajetha* (from *yaj*-, 'sacrifice'). In some Prakrits, forms from *j* and *y* would have been indistinguishable, so we cannot be sure which meaning was the original one. Here I have assumed that 'conquer' was intended, since it carries on the theme from v. 3. Moreover, a group of renouncers such as these *jaṭilas* would not have carried on the rituals (*yajña*) associated with the household life. But there may well be the hint of a pun here. The equivalent sequence in the Udānavarga (24.21–9) has 'sacrifice'.

8. *those of the well-taught Dharma*: *svākhyāta-dharmaṇāṃ* – literally, 'those possessing the well-taught Dharma', or perhaps simply 'of well-taught *dharmas*' (though the preceding item in this list is also a possessive compound referring to persons). In fact it is likely that the expression is a variant of *saṅkhāta-dhammānaṃ* in Dhammapada 70, 'of those who've mastered *dhammas*', where the first element has been misunderstood as *svākhyāta* (Pali *svākkhāta*), 'well-taught', a very common formula in praise of the Buddha's teaching.

9–14. Verse 14 is equivalent to Dhammapada 70: see the note on v. 8, above. There is a similar expanded list at Udānavarga 24.17–20, varying in different editions: Udānavarga 24.17–19 corresponds to vv. 9–12 here, and one version of 24.20 corresponds to v. 14 here (reading *svākhyāta*, as here), while other editions expand the list in varying ways, with virtues such as 'confidence in morality' and 'compassion for beings'. However, in the Udānavarga verses the second half always reads 'That's not worth . . .' rather than 'He's not worth . . .'

15. *wearing skins*: Or 'wearing tree-bark' – either being characteristic of different kinds of ascetics. Verses 15–16 are an expansion of Dhammapada 107.
17. Equivalent to Dhammapada 108.
18. = Dhammapada 110.
19. = Dhammapada 112.
21. = Dhammapada 115.
22. = Dhammapada 113.
24. = Dhammapada 114.

A further expanded version of vv. 18–24 is found at Udānavarga 24.1–15.

Concluding passage

the powers: Faith/confidence, energy/courage, mindfulness, concentration and wisdom.

attained parinirvāṇa: Died as awakened beings, with no need for further rebirth.

stūpas: Sacred mounds housing relics of the Buddha or (as here) of Arahats.

Glossary

Unless otherwise stated, Indian words are initially given in Pali form. Where the Sanskrit form is different, and is likely to be encountered, it is given in brackets after the Pali. Bold type within explanations indicates a cross-reference.

Abhidhamma (Abhidharma) The section of the **Tipiṭaka** concerned with the detailed analysis of psychological states. It is said in the **Theravāda** tradition to have been taught by the **Buddha** on a visit to the **Tusita** heaven, and transmitted by **Sāriputta**. Not all the early **Mainstream Buddhism** schools regarded the Abhidhamma/Abhidharma as canonical.

accharā (*apsaras*) A heavenly nymph, one of the beautiful dancers attending the gods of the **Tāvatiṃsa** heaven.

Ajātasattu (Ajātaśatru) A king of Māgadha in the **Buddha**'s time. When young he killed his father, **Bimbisāra**, in order to seize the throne, and supported **Devadatta** in his attempt to kill the Buddha. He repented and became a powerful supporter of the Buddha, though he could not escape the consequences of his actions (***kamma***).

Ājīvika (also spelled 'Ājīvaka') A member of a religious movement founded around the fifth–fourth century BCE by Makkhali Gosāla, said to have been a contemporary of the **Buddha** and of Mahāvīra, the founder of **Jainism**. The Ājīvikas seem to have rejected the idea of ***kamma*/*karma*** as understood by other groups, and taught that in order to achieve liberation, the individual just had to live out (*ā-jīv-*) his or her own destiny. The Ājīvika religion survived in southern India until at least the fourteenth century CE, but has now disappeared.

anāgāmin 'Non-Returner': one who has attained the third of the **Higher Stages**. He or she has abandoned the five lower fetters (*saṃyojana*), and after death will be reborn in the heaven of the **Pure Abodes**, and attain **Arahatship** there.

Ānanda The **Buddha**'s faithful attendant monk. Because so much of his time was spent in taking care of the Buddha, rather than in **meditation**, he did not become an **Arahat** until after the Buddha's ***parinibbāna***, so at the time at which the commentarial stories are set he is still a **Stream-Enterer**. He had a wonderful memory, and was responsible for handing on the Buddha's teachings now contained in the Sutta Piṭaka: the words 'Thus have I heard' at the start of each **Sutta** are his.

Anāthapiṇḍika (Anāthapiṇḍada) 'Giver of Alms to the Refuge-less' – a wealthy ***seṭṭhi*** and generous layman-supporter of the **Buddha**.

anattā (*anātman*) 'No-self': the Buddhist teaching that there is no unchanging, abiding self (*attā*, Sanskrit *ātman*) within living beings.

anicca (*anitya*) 'Impermanence': the Buddhist teaching that no conditioned thing can remain unchanged, so attachment to such things necessarily entails suffering (***dukkha***).

Arahat (Arhat) 'Worthy One': one who has attained the fourth of the **Higher Stages**, a fully liberated being. Though used also as a title for the **Buddha**, in its specialized sense it refers specifically to one who has attained liberation by following the teaching of a Fully **Awakened** Buddha (whether in that Buddha's lifetime or in after centuries). Cf. **Buddha, Paccekabuddha**.

Arahatship The liberated state of an **Arahat**.

asura ('powerful one') Generally translated as 'demon' or 'titan': a being of comparable powers to the ***devas***, but jealous of and constantly at war with them.

Avīci A hell realm (*niraya*), frequently appearing as an awful warning in the commentarial stories. The etymology is doubtful: it is sometimes explained, not very satisfactorily, as 'waveless', or 'without intermission'; but I wonder if it is an irregular formation from *avāc*, 'downwards', since this realm is pictured as being below the earth.

awakened My preferred English translation of Pali/Sanskrit *buddha*, closer to the original sense than the more conventional 'enlightened'.

bhante 'Blessed one', 'venerable one' – a polite form of address to a monk.

bhikkhu (*bhikṣu*) A fully ordained monk.

bhikkhunī (*bhikṣuṇī*) A fully ordained nun.

Bimbisāra King of Māgadha in the early years of the **Buddha**'s teaching career, and a devout supporter. He was murdered by his son **Ajātasattu**, with the collusion of **Devadatta**.

Bodhisatta (Bodhisattva) A being working towards **Buddha**-hood: either the historical Buddha before his enlightenment, or (especially in **Mahāyāna** Buddhism) one of a multiplicity of such beings.

Brahmā A high deity living in a 'formless' realm, far above such sensuous heavens as the **Tāvatiṃsa**. In Buddhist thought, there are a multiplicity of Brahmās, and their worlds, though very long-lasting, are characterized by impermanence (***anicca***), like everything else in ***saṃsāra***: Buddhist thought has no room for a Creator Deity, like the Brahmā of Hinduism. In the accounts of the life of the **Buddha**, the deity Brahmā Sahampati seems to embody the impulse of universal compassion that inspired the Buddha to undertake his arduous career of travel and teaching, rather than settle for a life of meditative ease.

Brāhmī (Sanskrit) An ancient Indian script, the ancestor of most of the modern Indian scripts and many of those of South East Asia. It was written from left to right. Cf. **Kharoṣṭhī**.

Brahmin (Sanskrit and Pali *brāhmaṇa*) A member of the priestly class, highest in the Hindu social system. For my use of this form of the word, see Introduction, n. 39.

Buddha '**Awakened** One', an enlightened being: (1) A Fully Awakened One (*sammāsambuddha*), capable of teaching the **Dhamma** to countless other beings; in particular (2) the Buddha Gotama (Sanskrit Gautama, also known in Sanskrit as Śākyamuni, the Sage of the Śākyas), regarded as the most recent in the succession of such teachers. His traditional dates are 623–543 BCE, though modern scholars place him up to 150 years later: see Introduction, 'Life of the Buddha'. (3) More broadly, any liberated being, including **Paccekabuddhas** and **Arahats**. A Fully Awakened Buddha rediscovers and teaches the Dhamma in an age when it has been forgotten on earth – though he has received teaching from other Buddhas in previous lives. A Paccekabuddha discovers the Dhamma for himself, without teaching from others: it is said that for that reason he does not have the teaching ability of the Fully Awakened Buddha. An Arahat or Anubuddha, 'Awakened following [a Buddha]', is liberated by teachings received from a Fully Awakened Buddha, either in person or through the tradition established by that Buddha. According to most traditional sources, Fully Awakened Buddhas and Paccekabuddhas are all male, and females aspiring to these states will have to be reborn as males to achieve them; Arahats, however, can be male or female. (4) As the first of the Three **Refuges**, the Buddha represents not only the historical founder of the tradition, but the potential for awakening within all beings.

concentration (*samādhi*) The power of focusing and centring the mind on a chosen object: an important aspect of **meditation**, often paired with **mindfulness**.

conditions, conditioned things My preferred translations of ***saṅkhāras*** (others use 'formations', 'fashionings' or 'volitional forces'), a technical term applied in Buddhist thought to the processes that fashion the physical, mental and emotional states of living beings, and the results of these processes. The terminology reflects the belief that everything in ***saṃsāra*** is subject to conditions: i.e. it comes into being as a result of previous states and processes, and passes away when the conditions that maintain it pass away. Therefore all *saṅkhāras* are subject to impermanence (***anicca***) and incapable of providing permanent satisfaction, hence subject to suffering (***dukkha***). Only ***nibbāna*** is unconditioned (*asaṅkhata*).

cūḷa/cūla/culla 'Small', often used as a title for a junior brother or sister: cf. ***mahā***. The variant forms of the word seem to be more or less interchangeable.

deva ('bright one') Generally translated as 'god': a being in one of the higher realms of rebirth, ranging from the high and rarefied beings generally called **Brahmās**, through powerful deities such as **Sakka** and **Yama**, to nature spirits such as ***yakkhas*** and ***nāgas***.

Devadatta The **Buddha**'s cousin, who tried to take over the community from the Buddha, and even to have him assassinated. He appears as the villain in many of the stories of previous lives of the Buddha.

devatā 'Deity', often used of the more earthy types of ***deva***.

Dhamma (Dharma) (1) The teaching, regarded as perennial truth, discovered and taught by all **Buddhas**: the second of the Three **Refuges**. (2) (With lower case in the text) any natural, perennial truth, e.g. in Dhammapada 3–4; a general term for any mental or physical state, viewed as an instance of such truth, e.g. in Dhammapada 1–2.

dukkha (*duḥkha*) 'Suffering', 'dis-ease', 'unsatisfactoriness': the Buddhist teaching that no permanent satisfaction can be found in any **conditioned thing**.

Eightfold Path (*aṭṭhaṅgika magga*) The path to freedom from suffering: (1) right view (*sammā diṭṭhi*), (2) right thought (*sammā saṅkappa*), (3) right speech (*sammā vācā*), (4) right action (*sammā kammanta*), (5) right livelihood (*sammā ājīva*), (6) right effort (*sammā vāyāma*), (7) right mindfulness (*sammā sati*), (8) right concentration (*sammā samādhi*).

Elder (*thera*, fem. *therī*; Sanskrit *sthavira*, fem. *sthavirī*) A title given to senior monks and nuns; in the Commentary, often, but not always, used of **Arahats**.

Ender, the (Pali/Sanskrit Antaka) A frequent name for **Yama**, the god of Death.

gandhabba (*gandharva*) A minor deity, one of the musicians in the **Tāvatiṃsa** heaven: male counterpart of the nymphs (***accharās***).

garuḍa A mythical solar bird, natural enemy to the ***nāgas***.

gati 'Going', 'bourn', 'destination', a place of rebirth. In the Commentary, one of the realms in which a being who has not become free of ***saṃsāra*** can be reborn, in accordance with previous actions. There are generally said to be six: a being can be reborn among the gods (***devas***), human beings, demons (***asuras***), animals, unsatisfied ghosts (***petas***), or the denizens of a hell realm (*niraya*).

Higher Stages The attainments of those who, through following the **Buddha**'s path, achieve various degrees of freedom from the fetters (***saṃyojana***). The Stream-Enterer (***sotāpanna***) gets rid of the first three fetters; the Once-Returner (***sakadāgāmin***) in addition weakens the fourth and fifth fetters, while the Non-Returner (***anāgāmin***) gets rid of them completely; the **Arahat** gets rid of all the rest. Each of these attainments itself has two stages, the path, *magga* (*mārga*), the moment at which the attainment takes place, and the fruit, *phala*, the transformed state of mind experienced thereafter.

hindrance (*nīvaraṇa*) One of the five hindrances to **meditation**: (1) sense-desire, (2) ill will, (3) sloth and torpor, (4) excitement and depression, and (5) sceptical doubt.

hiri (*hrī*) Generally coupled with *ottappa* (Buddhist Sanskrit *apatrapya/apatrapā*). Both words are notoriously difficult to translate into English: attempts include 'shame and regard for consequences', 'moral shame and moral dread'. *Hiri* is the (inner) quality that prevents us from doing actions that would go against our self-respect, while *ottappa* is the fear of the (external) consequences of doing such actions. In a frequent analogy, if we were to see an iron bar covered with filth at one end and red hot at the other, *hiri* would stop us picking it up by the filthy end, and *ottappa* would stop us picking it up by the red-hot end. Together, *hiri* and *ottappa* are called 'the Guardians of the World'.

iddhi (*ṛddhi*) A psychic attainment or power. The psychic powers attained by the **Buddha** or **Arahat** are described in, for example, Dīgha Nikāya 1.87 (Sutta 2: Sāmaññaphala Sutta):

> He then enjoys different powers: being one, he becomes many – being many, he becomes one; he appears and disappears; he passes through fences, walls and mountains unhindered as if through air; he sinks into

> the ground and emerges from it as if it were water; he walks on the water without breaking the surface as if on land; he flies cross-legged through the sky like a bird with wings; he even touches and strokes with his hand the sun and moon, mighty and powerful as they are; and he travels in the body as far as the Brahmā world. (tr. Walshe 1987: 105)

Lesser kinds of magical powers are also recognized in the Dhammapada Commentary.

impermanence See ***anicca***.

Jains, Jainism The Jain religion – founded by Mahāvīra, 'Great Hero', also known as the Jina, or 'Conqueror' – has much in common with Buddhism. Mahāvīra and the **Buddha** were contemporaries, both practising in the ***samaṇa*** tradition: both rejected theistic explanations of the universe, the authority of the **Vedas**, and much of the Hindu social system. In Pali literature, the Jains are called Nigaṇṭhas ('Those Who are Free from Knots/Ties'), partly perhaps because the monks of one of the two main denominations go naked. (The monks of the other denomination, and all nuns, wear white robes.)

Jātaka Literally, 'Birth'. (1) A story of one of the previous existences of the **Bodhisatta** or **Buddha**-to-be. (2) A collection of such birth-stories, such as that found in the Khuddaka Nikāya of the Pali Canon (though strictly speaking only the verses are regarded as canonical).

jhāna (*dhyāna*) (1) **Meditation**. (2) Specifically, one of a series of four (or in some lists) five stages of meditative experience, based on **concentration**, which purify and transform the mind, freeing it from defilements so that insight and wisdom can arise.

Jīvaka Physician to King **Ajātasattu**, and a supporter of the **Buddha**.

kamma (*karma*) Actions viewed as incurring consequences for the future, in the present life or a future one.

Kassapa (Kaśyapa) The name of various men, including (1) a previous **Buddha**; (2) **Mahā** Kassapa ('Kassapa the Great'), one of the leading **Arahats**, noted for his austere way of life. After the Buddha's ***parinibbāna***, he became the leader of the monastic order, as **Sāriputta** and **Moggallāna** had predeceased the Buddha; (3) **Kumāra Kassapa**, a prince.

khandha (*skandha*) 'Aggregate': one of the five physical and mental components of that which we regard as 'ourselves': *rūpa*, 'form'; *vedanā*, 'feeling'; *saññā* (*sañjñā*), 'perception'; *saṅkhāra* (*saṃskāra*), 'mental creations'; *viññāna* (*vijñāna*), 'consciousness'.

Kharoṣṭhī (Sanskrit) An early script used in north-west India, particularly in Gāndhārī texts. Unlike **Brāhmī**, it has no current descendants. It was written from right to left.

Khattiya (Kṣatriya) The second class in the Hindu social system, that of the warriors and princes: the class from which the future **Buddha** came.

Khemā (Kṣemā) A great **Arahat** and chief of the nuns, renowned for wisdom: the female counterpart of **Sāriputta**.

Kumāra Kassapa Kassapa the Prince (or Youth), adopted grandson of King **Pasenadi**.

Maghavan 'Mighty One': a name of the god **Sakka**.

mahā 'Great', often as a title for an elder sibling (cf. ***cūḷa***), or to distinguish a particularly important holder of a name (e.g. Mahā **Moggallāna**, Mahā **Kassapa** – both often written as one word), especially where the name is a fairly common one.

Mahāyāna 'Great Vehicle': the form of Buddhist practice based on the Bodhisattva (**Bodhisatta**) path; by extension, the Northern School of Buddhism, which emphasizes the Mahāyāna path.

Mainstream Buddhism My preferred term (following Paul Harrison 2005) for the early schools of Buddhism from which the **Mahāyāna** schools broke away.

Māra 'Death-Causer': a renegade deity of high rank who seeks to keep beings imprisoned in ***saṃsāra*** by tempting them, primarily through lust and fear. His three alluring daughters are named in the commentaries as Ragā (from *rāga*, 'Passion') or Rati ('Pleasure'), Arati ('Displeasure', 'Aversion') and Taṇhā ('Craving'). Like all states within *saṃsāra*, the role of Māra is subject to impermanence (***anicca***), and the wrong actions performed by a Māra are liable to bring grievous consequences in subsequent rebirths.

meditation Conventionally used to translate two Buddhist terms, neither of which exactly corresponds to its conventional English meaning: (1) *jhāna*, a particular kind of **concentration**-based practice, and (2) *bhāvanā* ('causing to be', 'bringing into being'), covering all aspects of spiritual development.

mindfulness (*sati*, Sanskrit *smṛti*) Awareness: the quality of being present in the moment rather than letting the mind wander elsewhere – an important aspect of **meditation**, often paired with **concentration**.

Moggallāna (**Maudgalyāyana**) A great **Arahat** (often referred to as Mahā Moggallāna or Mahāmoggallāna – 'Moggallāna the Great') – famous for his psychic powers, and, with **Sāriputta**, one of the two chief monks.

nāga (fem. ***nāginī***) A minor deity or spirit in serpent-like form, generally pictured (in the Indian tradition) as part human, part snake, with one or more cobra hoods and sometimes a snake-like tail. Elsewhere in Asia, *nāgas* often take on a dragon-like appearance. *Nāgas* are never viewed as evil, though like other nature spirits they may be capricious.

nibbāna (*nirvāṇa*) The freedom attained by **Arahats, Paccekabuddhas** and **Buddhas**. During their lifetimes they still experience a remnant of suffering, through the physical body and its attendant ills, but on death (called ***parinibbāna***, because it is different from the deaths of other beings) they attain complete freedom from suffering, and are reborn no more.

no-self See ***anattā***.

Noble As in 'Noble Truths', 'Noble **Eightfold Path**': translation of *ariya* (*ārya*), elsewhere a word with connotations of high birth or social class, but in Buddhist texts used to refer to high attainments and the knowledge and practices that lead to such attainments (see the story of Ariya in the note on v. 270).

Noble Ones Used of **Stream-Enterers, Once-Returners, Non-Returners, Arahats, Paccekabuddhas** and **Buddhas**, it implies experience of the **unconditioned**.

Non-Return The attainment of a Non-Returner (***anāgāmin***). See **Higher Stages**.

Non-Returner See ***anāgāmin***.

Once-Return The attainment of a Once-Returner (***sakadāgāmin***). See **Higher Stages**.

Once-Returner See ***sakadāgāmin***.

Paccekabuddha (Pratyekabuddha) 'Private **Buddha**', 'Individual Buddha': an enlightened being who, unlike the Fully **Awakened** Buddha, is not a world-teacher, and does not found a **Saṅgha**.

pāda 'Foot' or 'quarter', one of the half-lines of traditional Indian verse. Most Dhammapada verses contain four *pādas*; some, such as vv. 1, 2, 7, 8 and 20, have six.

parinibbāna (*parinirvāṇa*) The complete freedom (***nibbāna***) attained by **awakened** beings on death. In the case of the **Buddha** it is often called the Mahāparinibbāna (Mahāparinirvāṇa).

Pasenadi (Prasenajit) King of Kosala, mentioned in the Canon and prominent in the stories of the Dhammapada Commentary.

peta (*preta*) 'One who has passed away/died' – a type of ghost. In the Commentary, a term particularly applied to a being in one of the lower kinds of rebirth who is suffering the results of some serious wrong action.

pipal or **peepal** (Pali *assattha* or *pipphala*, Sanskrit *aśvattha* or *pippala*)

The sacred fig, *Ficus religiosa*. The species of the Bodhi tree, under which the **Bodhisatta** reached awakening (*bodhi*) and became the **Buddha**. The pipal tree has been sacred in the Indian subcontinent from a very early period: its distinctive heart-shaped leaves are depicted on Indus-valley seals of the second millennium BCE.

Pure Abodes (Pali *suddhāvāsa*, Sanskrit *śuddhāvāsa*) One of the heavens of the **Brahmā** gods.

Rains Retreat (*vassa*) Three months of the year, beginning around July, when monks are expected not to wander but to stay in one place. The **Buddha** is said to have given this **Vinaya** rule so that monks would not damage growing crops by walking through the fields during the rainy season. The period is observed as a retreat, with extra time set aside for study and **meditation.**

Refuges, Three (Pali *tisaraṇa*, Sanskrit *triśaraṇa*) **Buddha, Dhamma** and **Saṅgha**, the 'Triple Gem' (*tiratana*, Sanskrit *triratna*) to which Buddhists make their commitment.

sakadāgāmin (*sakṛdāgāmin*) 'Once-Returner': someone who has attained the second of the **Higher Stages**. He or she has abandoned the first three of the fetters (***saṃyojana***) and weakened the next two, and after death will be reborn in this world only once more.

Sakka (Śakra, 'Powerful', but in Sanskrit more commonly known as Indra) Thunderbolt-wielding sky god, ruler of the **Thirty-Three Gods** in the **Tāvatiṃsa** heaven.

sal (Pali *sāla*, Sanskrit *śāla*) A tall forest tree (*Shorea robusta*) found throughout South and South East Asia: the species of tree under which both the birth and the ***parinibbāna*** of the **Buddha** took place.

samaṇa (*śramaṇa*) Literally, 'striver': a wandering spiritual seeker, practising outside the conventional stages of life, often paired (and contrasted) with the Brāhmaṇa (**Brahmin**). In the Dhammapada, it is used more or less as a synonym for ***bhikkhu***. Possibly the origin of the word 'shaman': see Introduction, n. 80.

samatha (*śamatha*) Calm, especially of a way of **meditation** based on developing wholesome states of **concentration** (***jhāna***). With ***vipassanā***, one of the two basic forms of meditation in the Buddhist tradition.

saṃsāra The **conditioned** universe in which beings die and are reborn. All realms, from the highest heavens to the lowest hells, are part of *saṃsāra*, and all are liable to their own particular kinds of **suffering**. Only those who attain ***nibbāna*** become free of it.

saṃyojana 'Fetter', one of ten fetters binding us to rebirth: (1) *sakkāya-diṭṭhi*, views identifying various things (body, personality etc.) as 'self'; (2) *vicikicchā*, sceptical doubt; (3) *sīlabbata-parāmāsa*, attachment to precepts and rituals; (4) *kāma-rāga*, sense-desire; (5) *vyāpāda*, ill will; (6) *rūpa-rāga*, desire for form; (7) *arūpa-rāga*, desire for the formless; (8) *māna*, conceit; (9) *uddhacca*, restlessness; and (10) *avijjā*, ignorance. Fetters are left behind at each of the four **Higher Stages.**

Saṅgha The Community, with a number of shades of meaning. (1) Any of the four communities of the followers of the **Buddha**: those of monks (*bhikkhu-saṅgha*), nuns (*bhikkhunī-saṅgha*), laymen (*upāsaka-saṅgha*) and laywomen (*upāsikā-saṅgha*). (2) In common usage, often used by itself to refer to the *bhikkhu-saṅgha*. (3) The Buddhist community as a whole (probably a modern usage). (4) As the third of the **Refuges**, the community of all those beings who have attained the **Higher Stages** and serve as an example and inspiration to all Buddhists.

saṅkhāra (*saṃskāra*) The process of conditioning and anything created by **conditions**; specifically, (conditioned) mental states, viewed as a component of what is generally experienced as 'self' (***khandha***).

Sāriputta (Śāriputra/Śāliputra/Śāradvatīputra) The chief **Arahat**, nicknamed 'the General of the **Dhamma**' (*dhammasenāpati*), famous for his wisdom and knowledge of the **Abhidhamma**, but also for his kindness in training novice monks. Curiously, unlike other great Arahats such as **Moggallāna** and **Kassapa**, he never seems to be referred to with a **Mahā** ('Great') in front of his name: perhaps he was considered so unmistakable that it was not felt necessary.

Satipaṭṭhāna Sutta '**Sutta** on the Setting Up of **Mindfulness**': a discourse on practising **meditation** through observing the body, feelings etc. (Majjhima Nikāya 1.55–68 (Sutta 10)).

sāvaka (***śrāvaka***) Disciple (literally 'hearer'), a committed follower of the **Buddha**, especially one who has attained one of the **Higher Stages.**

seṭṭhi (*śreṣṭhin*) Translated in the notes as 'banker', the *seṭṭhi* is a prominent figure in the Dhammapada Commentary, with **Anāthapiṇḍika** as the supreme example. There is some controversy about the role of the *seṭṭhi*: was he a wealthy merchant, a moneylender, the head of a guild, or a royal appointee? The descriptions in the texts seem to combine aspects of all these, and we find the word variously translated as 'treasurer', 'guildmaster', or even 'millionaire'. In the Dhammapada Commentary, the *seṭṭhi* appears at times to have a magical power over money, as a result of acts of generosity in previous lives. (See Fišer 1954; Fick 1920: 257–66.)

signs, three The characteristics of all existence in ***saṃsāra***: ***anicca*** (impermanence), ***dukkha*** (suffering) and ***anattā*** (no-self). Contemplation of these signs leads to insight.

sotāpanna (*śrotrāpanna*) 'Stream-Enterer' or 'Stream-Winner': one who has abandoned the first three fetters (***saṃyojana***), and is irrevocably destined to liberation in, at most, seven lives.

Śrāvakayāna (Sanskrit) 'Vehicle of the Disciples [cf. ***sāvaka***]', i.e. of the **Arahats** and those who have attained the other **Higher Stages**. When used to denote non-**Mahāyāna** Buddhism, it is a politer term than 'Hīnayāna' ('Lesser Vehicle'), but still not entirely satisfactory as a description of early **Mainstream Buddhism**, or of modern-day practice in the **Theravāda** tradition.

Stream-Enterer See ***sotāpanna***.

Stream-Entry The attainment of a Stream-Enterer (***sotāpanna***). See **Higher Stages**. Burlingame (1921: *passim*) somewhat distractingly uses the expression 'Conversion' for this stage.

suffering See ***dukkha***.

sukha 'Happiness', 'bliss': linguistically, the opposite of ***dukkha***. Buddhism does not deny the possibility of happiness, but points out that all forms of happiness dependent on **conditioned things** are subject to impermanence (***anicca***) and alloyed with *dukkha*. (Even rebirth in a heavenly realm will end eventually, leading to grief.) Only the freedom of ***nibbāna*** brings true happiness. (See Dhammapada Chapter 15, especially vv. 197–205.)

Sutta (Sūtra) A teaching of the **Buddha** in narrative or dialogue form.

Tantra 'Loom', 'framework', 'treatise': (1) the name of certain texts, both Hindu and Buddhist; (2) the teachings embodied in these texts: a way of spiritual practice that seeks to use the body and its drives as a means to liberation by transforming, rather than rejecting, them. It is viewed as a rapid but dangerous path, characterized by transgressive rituals, which are practised in reality (in 'left-handed' forms of Tantra), or symbolically (in 'right-handed' forms). Tantra (of the right-handed kind) plays a powerful role in **Vajrayāna** Buddhism, and its influence is pervasive in the art and ritual of Tibetan Buddhism.

Tathāgata 'Thus-gone', a title used for Fully **Awakened Buddhas**. The meaning has been debated, but it probably suggests 'one who has gone by the same path as all the Buddhas of the past'.

Tāvatiṃsa (Trāyastriṃśa) '[Heaven] of the **Thirty-Three**': the realm ruled by **Sakka**, a place of great beauty and pleasure, where nymphs (***accharā***) and celestial musicians (***gandhabba***) attend those who have performed acts of merit. In the Buddhist view, this is a fairly lowly heaven, in comparison with, for example, the **Brahmā** realms: but in any case, all heavens, like everything else in ***saṃsāra***, are impermanent.

Theravāda (Sthaviravāda) 'Doctrine of the **Elders**', the Buddhism of present-day Sri Lanka and South East Asia, based on the early **Mainstream Buddhism** tradition.

Thirty-Three Gods Deities of a similar kind to the Olympian gods of classical myth: gods of sun, moon, fire, wind etc., living in the **Tāvatiṃsa** heaven.

Tipiṭaka (Tripiṭaka) 'Three Baskets', the Buddhist canonical scriptures, consisting of **Vinaya**, **Sutta** and **Abhidhamma** collections.

Tissa (Tiṣya) A fairly common name for men, including several monks, in the commentarial stories.

Tusita (Tuṣita) 'Joyful [heaven]', where future **Buddhas** are said to live just before their final birth on earth. According to **Theravāda** tradition, the Buddha's mother, who died after giving birth to him, was reborn here, and he visited her there one year for the **Rains Retreat**, teaching the **Abhidhamma** for the first time to her and the other deities.

udāna An inspired utterance of the **Buddha** (or of one of his followers, endorsed by him), often in verse; also used of a collection of such utterances.

Udena (Udayana) A king of Kosambī (Kauśāmbī).

unconditioned, the (Pali *asaṅkhata,* Sanskrit *asaṃskṛta*) ***Nibbāna***, as being free from **conditions** (*saṅkhāras*)

uposatha (*upavasatha*) Literally, 'fast': the full moon, new moon and two half-moon days of each month, when the monastic community meet together and laypeople often visit monasteries and devote the day to spiritual practice.

Uppalavaṇṇā (Utpalavarṇā) A great **Arahat** and, with **Khemā**, one of the two chief nuns. Skilled in psychic powers, she is the female counterpart of **Moggallāna**.

Vajrayāna (Sanskrit) 'Vehicle of the Diamond/Thunderbolt': the Tantric form of Buddhism (cf. **Tantra**), influential in the Tibetan tradition.

Veda The most ancient scriptures of South Asia. Their authority, basic to the Hindu tradition, was rejected by the Buddhists and **Jains**.

Vinaya The disciplinary code for Buddhist monks and nuns, and the collection of scriptures (see **Tipiṭaka**) dealing with it.

vipassanā (Buddhist Sanskrit *vipaśyanā*) Insight, especially of a way of **meditation**, based on observing the changes in body and mind rather than seeking to control them. With *samatha*, one of the two basic forms of meditation in Buddhism.

Visākhā (Viśākhā) A great laywoman-supporter of the **Buddha**, famous for her wealth, generosity and good sense. (A layman called Visākha – with a short final 'a' – is also mentioned, in the story accompanying v. 421.)

yakkha (fem. *yakkhinī*) (*yakṣa*, fem. *yakṣī/yakṣiṇī*) A nature spirit, often associated with trees. In stories, the females are often portrayed as man-eaters, in every sense of the word.

Yama God of Death, also known as the Ender (Antaka).

Yoga Literally 'application', 'yoke', 'union', from *yuj-*, 'to join', 'to yoke', 'to apply oneself'. In Asian religions, any way of spiritual practice, not necessarily one involving particular physical postures. In the Dhammapada, it seems to refer either to the Buddhist path in general or specifically to the practice of **meditation.**

Notes

In this section, I have used the overall numbering of the verses (rather than chapter + verse numbering) as the means of keying the notes. For each verse or group of verses, any explanatory notes are followed by a very brief retelling of the commentarial stories from the Dhammapadaṭṭhakathā. Many of these stories, particularly those concerning leading followers of the Buddha, are based on material from the Pali Canon: further information about the sources can be found in the *Dictionary of Pāli Proper Names* (Malalasekhara 1937–8), available in its online version at <http://www.palikanon.com/english/pali_names/dic_idx.html>. On matters connected with meditation and spiritual attainments, an excellent source is Sarah Shaw's *Buddhist Meditation* (Shaw 2006a), which draws extensively on the canonical and commentarial literature of the Theravāda tradition.

CHAPTER I
TWINS

1. *mental states*: *dhamma* – see Glossary.
made of mind: *manomayā*; K. R. Norman (1997: 1, 61) takes as 'made by mind'. All traditions apart from the Pali Dhammapada have *manojavā*, 'swift as mind' (or forms corresponding to that).
Suffering: *dukkha*.
of the ox: i.e. that draws the cart.

STORY: A blind monk who is an Arahat unknowingly crushes insects under his feet as he walks. Because there is no intention to kill, he commits no offence. The Buddha explains the action in a past life that caused the monk to lose his sight. (For a fuller account of the commentarial stories on this verse, see the section on Commentaries in the Introduction.)

2. *mental states . . . made of mind*: See comments on v. 1.
Happiness: *sukha*.

STORY: A miser's young son dies because his father is too mean to spend money on a doctor. As he dies, the boy mentally takes refuge in the Buddha, and is reborn in a heavenly realm. Appearing to his former father in his divine form, he causes him to mend his ways. (See also the section on Commentaries in the Introduction for more on this verse.)

3–4. *does not cease . . . ceases completely*: *na sammati . . . upasammati*. The latter implies a complete end, with reference to *upasama* = *nibbāna*.

STORY: This concerns a stubborn monk, Tissa the Fat, who harbours resentment against other monks who do not treat him with the deference which he thinks he deserves. Tissa is a common name in the commentaries, and it is not always possible to determine which stories relate to the same person, but the Tissa of the present story seems to be one who later became an Arahat. (For the Buddha's teaching to him, see Shaw 2006a: 53–6.)

5. *here*: i.e. in this world.
By freedom from hatred: *averena*, 'by non-hatred'. In Pali, such negative expressions are stronger than in English, though there is some debate about the exact shade of meaning here. Some translators think it means 'the opposite of hatred', i.e. 'loving kindness'; the equivalent passage in the Udāna (14.11) has *kṣāntyā*, 'by patience', implying the simple refusal to respond to hatred with hatred (Fišer 1979).
This is a perennial truth: *esa dhammo sanantano*, here in the sense of a fact that is always (and naturally) true, without the connotations of a universal religion implied in modern Hindu uses of *sanātana dharma*.

STORY: This concerns a quest for vengeance pursued over many lives. A man takes two wives, marrying the junior wife when the senior proves unable to have children. When the junior wife becomes pregnant, the senior, fearing to lose her own status within the household, gives her drugs to bring about a miscarriage. She does this twice more, but, the third time, the junior wife herself dies along with the baby. Her dying wish is to devour children of the senior wife, and she is reborn as a cat. When the husband finds out what has happened, he batters the senior wife.

She dies, and is reborn as a hen. The cat that was the junior wife eats her eggs. The hen is then reborn as a leopardess, and the cat as a doe, and the cycle of revenge continues. Finally the senior wife is reborn as a human woman and the junior wife as a child-eating *yakkhinī*, who tries to attack her baby.

Fleeing from the *yakkhinī*, the woman rushes into the monastery where the Buddha is staying, and lays the baby at his feet. Because of the Buddha's power, the *yakkhinī* is unable to follow her there until he himself sends for her. He speaks to the *yakkhinī* about the need to end hatred, uttering the present verse. She attains Stream-Entry. Encouraged by the Buddha, the woman hands the baby to the *yakkhinī*, who kisses and caresses him and gives him back unharmed. But the *yakkhinī*, no longer a child-eater, is now worried about how she is going to get enough to eat. The Buddha instructs the woman to take the *yakkhinī* home, install her in a shrine in the village, and bring her offerings of food. Through her prophecies, the *yakkhinī* brings great good fortune to the woman, who becomes wealthy and respected, and takes the opportunity to make regular offerings to the monks.

6. *we must control ourselves*: *yamāmase*, probably a first-person-plural imperative form from *yam-*, 'to control', 'to restrain'. Others take it as a denominative from Yama, the name of the god of Death, so that the sentence would mean, 'Others here do not understand that we must die.'

STORY: The Commentary retells the story, found in the Vinaya of the Pali Canon (Mahā Vagga 5.1–5) of the Buddha's sojourn in the Pārileyyaka Forest, where he is attended by an elephant (also called Pārileyyaka).

At a monastery in Kosambi, 500 monks fall out. The matter begins with a small infraction of the Vinaya, but, as the accusations fly and no one will apologize, the situation gets progressively worse until the monastery splits into two factions. Three times the Buddha himself tries to reconcile them, but the monks pay no attention. Eventually the Buddha decides to leave them, and goes off alone to the forest. The elephant, who has also grown tired of living with the herd, comes to attend him, keeping predators away, bringing him water when he needs it, and carrying his bowl and robe when he goes on alms-round. In the commentarial version, a monkey, too, comes to offer honey to the Buddha. When the Buddha accepts it, the monkey is so delighted that he leaps from branch to branch; when a branch breaks, and he falls, he is reborn as a deity in the Tāvatiṃsa heaven. (The scene of the Buddha attended by these two animals is a popular one in Buddhist art, particularly in Thailand.)

Meanwhile the quarrelsome monks are having an uncomfortable time of it, since the laypeople no longer wish to support them. At the end of the Rains Retreat, when they are free to travel, Ānanda visits the Buddha to request him to come back to Kosambi. (When he expresses concern as to the hardships the Buddha must have experienced, alone in the forest, the Buddha reassures him with vv. 328–30.)

The Buddha leaves, parting with the elephant at the point where the animal might have been in danger from human beings if he had followed him. The elephant dies of a broken heart, but because of his faith in the Buddha is reborn in the Tāvatiṃsa heaven.

When the Buddha arrives back at Kosambi, he once more speaks to the monks about the importance of restraint and reconciliation and speaks the verse. Understanding, the monks attain Stream-Entry.

7–8. *the fair . . . the foul*: *subha . . . asubha*, probably used here in a technical sense. If a person constantly dwells on the attractive aspects of the body, his or her sense-desire will grow stronger. *Asubha* meditation is designed to break this attachment: as in the story, the meditator contemplates a dead body, and watches the various stages of change and decay in it. (This is not regarded as a suitable subject for all meditators, and would normally be attempted only on the advice of a skilled teacher: see Shaw 2006a: 101–8.)
Māra: The tempter, who seeks to bind beings to the world – see Glossary.
ill-rooted: Literally, 'weak' (*dubbala*).

STORY: Two brothers, Mahākāḷa and Cūlakāḷa (Great and Small Kāḷa, 'Black'), formerly merchants, become monks. Mahākāḷa achieves Arahatship, through contemplating a corpse in a cremation ground, but Cūlakāḷa goes on thinking about his former married life. When the monks pay a visit to their home town, Cūlakāḷa is sent ahead. He is seized by his two former wives and made to disrobe and return to the household life. The Buddha then sends Mahākāḷa. Other monks have misgivings about this, in view of what has happened to the younger brother, but the Buddha reassures them with the verses. Mahākāḷa is unaffected by the blandishments of *his* former wives, even though there are eight of them, not just two.

9–10. There is an untranslatable pun here on the words *kasāva*, 'stain', 'impurity', and *kāsāva*, the monk's robe, dyed in various natural shades of yellow, orange, ochre or brown.

STORY: This concerns an occasion when Devadatta's followers give him a robe, offered by a benefactor, that should have been given to Sāriputta. The Buddha tells the story of a previous life, when an elephant-hunter put on a monk's robe to trick the elephants into approaching him. The hunter was Devadatta, while the leader of the elephants, who saw through the trick and reproached the hunter, was the future Buddha.

11–12. *Those who imagine value where there's none, / And don't see value where there's value*: Literally, 'Those imagining value in the valueless, / And seeing valuelessness in value [*sāra*, "genuine worth"]'. Similarly with the opposite in v. 12.
Dwellers in the realm of wrong thought . . . right thought: *micchā-saṅkappa-gocarā . . . sammā-saṅkappa-gocarā*: 'having wrong/right thought as their range/scope' – with a clear reference to the second element of the Eightfold Path, *sammā-saṅkappa*, 'right thought' or 'right intention'.

STORY: The Commentary here summarizes the traditional account of the Buddha's search for awakening, and the attainment of Arahatship by his leading followers.

Many aeons in the past, a young Brahmin ascetic called Sumedha ('Wise') encounters a Fully Awakened Buddha, Dīpaṅkara ('Light-Maker'). He feels great reverence towards him, and forms a profound wish to attain what Dīpaṅkara has attained. Seeing him, Dīpaṅkara recognizes his qualities and foretells that Sumedha will one day become a Fully Awakened Buddha by the name of Gotama. From that time on, through many thousands of years and the eras of twenty-four Buddhas from Dīpaṅkara on, Sumedha works towards developing the qualities of a Buddha. After thousands of rebirths, the Bodhisatta who had been Sumedha is reborn in the Tusita heaven, where all Buddhas-to-be spend the life before the last.

When the time comes for him to be reborn, the Bodhisatta chooses as his family the royal household of the Sākiyas. He is brought up with every possible comfort and luxury; but when he is twenty-nine years old, he sees, on three successive days, three heavenly messengers – an old man, a sick man and a corpse – and he becomes aware of the suffering of all existence. On the fourth day, as he ponders a way to become free from suffering, he sees a fourth heavenly messenger, a man who has left the household life and become a monk, and he himself determines to do the same. Receiving word that a son, Rāhula, has been born to him, he understands that if he does not go now he will never be able to go at all. Aided by his charioteer Channa and a multitude of deities, he escapes from the palace by night, cuts off his hair, puts on an ochre robe, and embarks on the life of a wandering holy man.

He spends the next six years in search of the path to freedom from suffering (see the Introduction, 'Life of the Buddha'), studying first with the meditation teachers Āḷāra and Uddaka, and then with five monks practising strict asceticism. At last he sits under the Bodhi tree, determined to find his goal. In the course of the night he is assailed by temptation, in the form of the renegade deity Māra, his ferocious armies and his voluptuous daughters, symbolizing all the defilements of the mind; but he refuses to give up the quest, and attains the goal.

The Buddha, as he now is, spends seven weeks at Bodh Gayā, pondering the implications of the knowledge that he has attained. He wonders whether to teach it to others, experiencing misgivings as to whether anyone will be able to understand it. But the deity Brahmā Sahampati, who oversees ten thousand worlds, requests him on behalf of all beings to teach the Dhamma, and he assents. Looking around the world for people who will understand his teaching, the Buddha sees that Āḷāra and Uddaka are both dead, but the five monks who attended him through his period of asceticism are still alive, and capable of understanding his teaching. He goes to them at Isipatana, near Varanasi, where he gives his first teaching. First Koṇḍañña and then the other four understand, and attain Arahatship. Other followers join them and follow the Buddha's teaching. Soon there are sixty-one Arahats in the world, and the Buddha sends them out in all directions to teach others.

The Commentary now tells of two Brahmin youths from wealthy families, great friends, named Upatissa and Kolita. They live happily until they go together to a festival which lasts several days. To begin with they enjoy all the entertainment on offer, laughing when everyone else laughs, weeping when everyone else weeps, and giving alms when everyone else gives alms. But it then occurs to each of them separately that in a hundred years' time all these people will be dead, and they laugh, weep and give alms no more.

Noticing the change in one another, they find that both have had the same experience, and they decide to leave the household life and seek the way to the deathless. They become followers of a holy man called Sañjaya, but in a few days they have learned all that he knows and are still dissatisfied. So they travel India, trying to find a teacher who can help them achieve their quest. They make a pact that whichever of them first attains the deathless is to find and tell the other.

At Rājagaha, Upatissa meets the Elder Assaji, one of the five who heard the Buddha's first teaching. Upatissa recognizes that Assaji has a quality that he has not seen before. He seeks a meeting with him, and engages him in discussion. Assaji speaks to him one of the most famous summaries of the Buddha's teaching:

> Of all things (*dhamma*) that come from a cause,
> The Tathāgata has taught the cause

at which point Upatissa attains Stream-Entry. Assaji completes the verse:

> And the cessation, too,
> The Great Wanderer* has spoken.

But at this point Upatissa does not progress any further in the higher attainments.

Overjoyed to learn from Assaji that a Buddha has appeared in the world, Upatissa seeks out his friend Kolita. He speaks the same verse to him, on which he too attains Stream-Entry. They determine to go together to see the Buddha, but before they do they will visit their first teacher, Sañjaya, and invite him to come with them. However, Sañjaya is too attached to his reputation and status and refuses to go.

The two friends go to the Buddha, who ordains them as monks. Through his teaching, both attain Arahatship. But since then Upatissa has generally been known as Sāriputta, and Kolita as Moggallāna. (These are 'metronymic' names, taken from their mothers – a common ancient Indian custom. Upatissa is the son of Rūpasārī ('Sārī the Beautiful' – see the story for v. 400), and Moggallāna of a woman named Moggallī.) And as Sāriputta and Moggallāna they were named by the Buddha as his two chief monks.

*Mahāsamaṇa – see Glossary under *mahā* and *samaṇa*.

Verse 12 is taken to refer to the attainment of the great Arahats; v. 11 to Sañjaya, who refused the opportunity to follow the Buddha.

13–14. STORY: The Commentary retells the very popular story of Nanda, the Buddha's cousin, who is lured by the Buddha into becoming a monk when he has just married the most beautiful woman in the country. Nanda is discontented as a monk, and constantly misses his bride. Eventually the Buddha shows him a heavenly realm full of 500 celestial nymphs (*accharā*), in comparison with whom his bride appears ugly. He tells Nanda that if he perseveres in the monastic life he will win these nymphs. Nanda applies himself to the practice with vigour, and eventually achieves Arahatship. Having no longer any desire for women or nymphs, he releases the Buddha from his promise. The Buddha speaks these verses, and tells a story of a previous birth when Nanda was controlled through his sexual desire, when the future Buddha was a merchant and Nanda his donkey, who desired a mate.

15. *Seeing his own action was defiled*: 'Seeing the defilement of his own action'.

STORY: This tells of Cunda, a butcher. He makes his living by fattening pigs, slaughtering them in cruel ways, and selling the meat; and he never has a generous or compassionate thought. In his last illness he sees a vision of the Avīci hell that awaits him. In his terror, he begins to behave like a pig, grunting and crawling on all fours, to the horror of his family. After seven days of this, he dies and is reborn in the Avīci hell.

16. *Seeing his own action was pure*: 'Seeing the purity of his own action'.

STORY: A pious layman lives well and generously, and encourages his family to do the same. As he lies dying, monks chant the Satipaṭṭhāna Sutta (Majjhima Nikāya 1.56–83: Sutta 10), which teaches how to practise meditation through mindfulness, successively, of body, feelings, mind and *dhammas*. (For a translation and discussion, see Shaw 2006a: 76–85.) The man suddenly cries, 'Wait!' His family are appalled, thinking that he is afraid of death; but, as the Buddha later explains, he is in fact addressing the gods who have come to escort him to a heavenly realm, since he wishes to hear the rest of the Sutta before he goes.

17. *a bad place*: *duggati*, a bad *gati* (see Glossary), i.e. birth in a hell realm, the animal realm, or the realm of the *petas* (hungry ghosts).

STORY: The long Commentary on this verse retells the story of Devadatta and his evil deeds. He is ordained as a monk along with five other princes of the Sākiya clan (including Ānanda and Anuruddha) and their barber Upāli, all of whom become great Elders. Devadatta gains psychic powers (*iddhi* – see Glossary), but without any of the higher attainments. He becomes jealous of the Buddha and the great Arahats. He plots to oust the Buddha as leader of the Order, and even tries to have him assassinated. The Buddha never loses patience with him. Eventually, when Devadatta has caused a schism in the Order, he is swallowed by the earth* and is reborn in the Avīci hell.

18. *He rejoices here*: As often in the Dhammapada, masculine terms are intended to be understood in an inclusive sense, as shown by the fact that the commentarial story refers to a woman (or in this case a girl).
a good place: *suggati*, a good *gati* (cf. note 17) – birth in a heaven or the human realm. (The form *suggatiṃ* replaces the expected *sugatiṃ* for metrical reasons: see K. R. Norman 1997: 65.)

STORY: The generous banker Anāthapiṇḍika has three daughters, and places each in turn in charge of giving alms to the monks: first Mahāsubhaddā, then Cullasubhaddā, and then, when these are both married, Sumanādevī. Sumanādevī attains the state of Once-Return, but falls ill and is unable to eat. She sends for her father, but as she lies dying she calls him 'youngest brother', leading those around to speculate that her mind is wandering. But the Buddha explains that she uses these words because she has reached a higher state than her father, who is just a Stream-Enterer. She has been reborn in the Tusita (Joyful) heaven.

Burlingame (1921: I, 242–4), followed it seems by Malalasekhara (1937–8: II, 1243–4), has misunderstood this story, taking it that Sumanādevī has refused food out of grief because she is unmarried, when her sisters are married, and has fallen ill as a result. He has over-interpreted the word *kumārikā*, 'young

*This is regarded as the inevitable result of committing a great crime against a Buddha or an Arahat (cf. the stories for vv. 69, 128, 176, 363): the Buddha or the Arahat has not caused it to happen.

girl', 'maiden', assuming it to mean specifically 'virgin', 'unmarried woman', and taking it as the reason for her distress. In fact she has given up eating *because* she is ill, and has sent for her father because she is still a young girl. (My thanks to L. S. Cousins for pointing this out.) A Once-Returner would not suffer from grief or disappointment at her lot, since she would already have let go of the ill will that gives rise to such feelings. As Anāthapiṇḍika says to the Buddha, '*Bhante*, here my daughter went about among her relatives rejoicing, and now that she's gone from here she has been reborn in the place of rejoicing.' The Buddha replies with the Dhammapada verse.

19–20. *scripture*: *sahitaṃ*, accusative of *sahitā*, equivalent to Sanskrit *saṃhitā*, which is generally used of the Vedic literature.

If you go from dhamma to dhamma: *dhammassa hoti anudhammacārī* – '[If one] is practising *anudhamma* of the *dhamma*'. An obscure expression, often translated simply as 'If one acts in accordance with Dhamma'. *Anudhamma* could mean 'subsidiary *dhamma*' or 'following-*dhamma*'. But the most likely sense here seems to be that of progressively following the Buddhist path.

wanderer's life: *sāmañña*, the condition of a *samaṇa* (see Glossary).

STORY: Two friends become monks. One learns the Tipiṭaka by heart, while the other, who is not so good at studying, devotes himself to meditation. The learned monk looks down on the unlearned one, but when both are questioned by the Buddha it turns out that the latter has attained Arahatship, while the former just knows the theory.

CHAPTER 2
AWARENESS

The Pali word translated here as 'awareness' is *appamāda*, the opposite of *pamāda*, 'intoxication', 'carelessness', 'unawareness'. As often in Pali, the negative suffix has a stronger force than in English, and *appamāda* is one of the most important qualities for a Buddhist to develop: that of constant mindfulness. The pair form one of the most important oppositions in Buddhist literature. Other commonly found translations are 'heedfulness' and 'heedlessness' and 'diligence' and 'negligence'. In v. 309, I have translated the related adjective *pamatta* as 'reckless'.

21–3. *peace of yoga*: *yoga-kkhema* – a compound word that seems to change its meaning over the course of Pali literature (and Sanskrit literature, where it appears as *yogakṣema*). Sometimes it is taken as a *dvandva* compound, '*yoga* and *khema*' (e.g. 'getting and enjoyment'), and sometimes as a *tatpuruṣa*, with various possible relationships between the two: 'the *khema* of *yoga*', 'the *khema* from *yoga*' etc. Unfortunately, both the individual words vary greatly in their meanings. I have taken it as the peace (*khema*) reached through practice (*yoga*). K. R. Norman (1997: 4, 67) takes it as 'rest from exertion'; Carter and Palihawadana (1987: 112) as 'freedom from bonds'.

STORY: A cycle of stories concerns the adventures of King Udena (or Udayana) and his wives Vāsuladattā, the chief queen, Sāmāvatī, the daughter of a banker (*seṭṭhi* – see Glossary), and Māgandiyā, a Brahmin woman. Sāmāvatī and her maids are devoted followers of the Buddha, having heard his teaching reported by a hunchbacked slave woman called Khujjuttarā, who first hears him teach when sent out to buy flowers for the queen, and attains Stream-Entry. Sāmāvatī notices a change in Khujjuttarā when she starts to bring twice as many flowers back as before. Previously, it appears, she used to keep half the flower money for herself, but now she spends it all on flowers. Far from being angry, Sāmāvatī continues to send Khujjuttarā to hear the Buddha's teaching and to report to them what she has heard. (Khujjuttarā becomes the laywoman most skilled in teaching the Dhamma.)

Māgandiyā, in contrast, hates the Buddha, because he rejected her when her father offered her to him in marriage – see the story for vv. 179–80. She tries to stir up the mob against him (see the story for vv. 320–22). She also tries to poison the king's mind against Sāmāvatī, making it appear that she is plotting against him. This fails, and indeed the king joins Sāmāvatī in taking refuge in the Buddha.

Finally, Māgandiyā has Sāmāvatī and her maids burned to death in their house. At the point of death, all of them meditate on loving kindness, and are reborn in higher states. When the king finds out the truth about what has happened, he has Māgandiyā and her accomplices put to death.

The Buddha speaks the verses as a comment on the contrasting fates of Sāmāvatī and Māgandiyā.

24. STORY: In a time of plague, a layman called Kumbhaghosaka leaves his native city and lives as a hired hand, despite having a secret store of treasure. After a number of adventures, he becomes the banker (*seṭṭhi*) of King Bimbisāra and marries the king's daughter. The Buddha praises his wisdom with this verse.

25. STORY: Two brothers, Mahāpanthaka and Cūḷapanthaka (or Cullapanthaka), 'Big Wayman and Little Wayman', become monks. Mahāpanthaka is quick to learn, and soon attains Arahatship. Cūḷapanthaka is slow, and his brother turns him out of the monastery. To help Cūḷapanthaka, the Buddha gives him a clean cloth as a meditation object. Rubbing the cloth, he sees how it gradually becomes dirty; realizing impermanence, he attains Arahatship. He then becomes a great scholar of the Tipiṭaka.

26–7. *guards . . . as the finest treasure*: *dhanaṃ seṭṭhaṃ va rakkhati*. In the equivalent verse (4.10), the Udānavarga has 'guards . . . as the banker [guards] his wealth' (*dhanaṃ śreṣṭhīva rakṣati*).

STORY: It is a Fools' Holiday in Sāvatthi – seven days given over to coarse behaviour and rude language. (The 'fools' keeping the holiday would smear themselves with ashes and cow dung and hang about in doorways uttering crude remarks until people gave them money to go away.) While it goes on, the Buddha's followers arrange for him to receive food outside the city. When it is over, they tell him about the unpleasant time they have had over the last seven days, and he speaks the verses.

28. STORY: The Buddha observes the Elder Kassapa contemplating the coming into existence and passing away of beings in *saṃsāra*. He remarks that, as a Fully Awakened Buddha, he himself sees far more of this even than a great Arahat like Kassapa. He causes a likeness of himself to appear before Kassapa and utter this verse.

29. *The wise one goes, leaving them behind / As a swift horse leaves a weak horse behind*: Literally, 'The wise one goes, having left [the unaware etc.] as a swift horse a weak horse.' The equivalent in the Udāna (19.4) appears to be corrupt, as it seems to have the other horse winning.

STORY: This concerns a diligent monk and a lazy monk. The diligent monk works hard at his meditation practice; the lazy monk wastes time, while accusing his colleague of laziness. The diligent one attains Arahatship.

30. *Maghavan*: Sakka, king of the Thirty-Three Gods.

STORY: The Buddha explains that in a previous life Sakka was a prince called Mahāli. He attained the rank of Sakka by keeping seven observances: supporting his parents; supporting his elders; using courteous and friendly speech; avoiding divisive speech; avoiding avarice (i.e. practising generosity); being truthful; and overcoming anger. The splendid state of Sakka and his wives, and his victories over the *asuras*, are described.

31. *fetters*: *saṃyojana* – see Glossary.

STORY: A monk cannot make progress with his meditation subject, and goes to visit the Buddha to request a new one. On the way, he sees a forest fire burning up everything before it, and resolves to progress in the same way. The Buddha sends a likeness of himself to appear before him and speak the verse, and the monk attains Arahatship.

32. STORY: A monk called Nigama Tissa lives in a small town (*nigama*), and is content with the alms he receives there, never going to the neighbouring city of Sāvatthi to receive alms from wealthy donors such as Anāthapiṇḍika. He is praised for his frugality in eating.

CHAPTER 3
THE MIND

33–4. *As the fletcher makes straight the arrow*: cf. v. 80.
out of its watery home: *oka-m-okata*, taking the first *oka* as equivalent to *ogha*, 'flood', hence 'its home, the water' – cf. the notes to v. 91 (K. R. Norman 1997: 6, 69–70; Carter and Palihawadana 1987: 122).

STORY: A monk called Meghiya refuses to stay with the Buddha when requested, but insists on going alone to a mango grove, where he thinks he will be able to meditate better. He is unable to calm his mind there, and, beset by distractions, realizes his error and returns to the Buddha. Learning his lesson, Meghiya attains Stream-Entry.

This story comes from the Canon – Aṅguttara 4.354–8 and Udāna 34–7; for a translation and discussion, see Shaw 2006a: 24–8.

35. STORY: A laywoman (referred to only as 'Mātika's mother', her son being the village headman) supports a group of sixty monks. Impressed by their behaviour, she asks them to teach her meditation, and soon attains the state of Non-Return, together with the ability to read minds. She then realizes that the monks – her 'sons' – have not yet attained this state: they have the capacity, as well as suitable lodgings and good companions, but they are not receiving the right kind of food to support their practice. Using her insight, she provides them with excellent food which helps to nourish their practice, and all attain Arahatship. Another monk, who has heard about the laywoman's good food, goes to her village. Every time he wishes for a particular thing, Mātika's mother provides it, and he soon realizes that she can read his thoughts. Fearing what she will do to him if he ever has an evil thought, he leaves and goes back to the Buddha.

However, the Buddha tells him that that laywoman's village is precisely where he ought to be, in order to learn how to control his thoughts: he speaks the verse, and sends him back there. Guarding his thoughts and sustained by the wholesome food provided by Mātika's mother, the monk attains Arahatship. Recollecting to see whether she has supported him in previous lives too, the monk discovers that in fact in ninety-nine of a hundred previous lives she has been an unfaithful wife of his who conspired with other men to cause his death. He thinks, 'What wicked deeds this laywoman has done!'

Perceiving his thought, Mātika's mother herself recollects and realizes that in a hundredth previous life as his wife she had spared him. She telepathically urges him to remember that life too. Filled with joy and gratitude for her support, the monk gives up every trace of clinging to existence and attains *parinibbāna*.

36. STORY: A monk becomes dissatisfied with the teaching he receives, since his teacher and preceptor are specialists in the Vinaya and the Abhidhamma respectively, and neither teaches him the way to become free from suffering. Feeling trapped by their constant emphasis on the rules, the monk gives up his practice and thinks of disrobing. He becomes very ill. When his teacher hears of this, he takes him to the Buddha, who instructs him in the one thing necessary in order to take care of all the rest: the way to guard his mind.

37. STORY: A young monk attends an older one, his uncle. While fanning him, the younger monk feels resentment and his mind starts to wander. He thinks about returning to the household life, marrying, and having a son. In the course of the daydream, he and his wife have an argument about who should carry the child on a journey. Refusing to let her husband have him, the wife insists on carrying the boy, but, growing weary, lets him fall under the wheels of a cart. Meaning to strike the imaginary wife, the young monk hits his uncle on the head with the fan. In shame, he tries to run away from the monastery, but is caught and taken to the Buddha, who counsels him with the verse.

The idea of the would-be meditator who becomes lost in daydream (or sometimes the illusory power of a deity) until he performs some foolish and violent act becomes a recurrent theme in Indian folklore.

38–9. STORY: A man who is unable to settle keeps going backwards and forwards between the monastic and the household life. The seventh time he goes back to the household life he sees his wife asleep, dribbling and snoring, and the sight reminds him of a corpse. Recollecting impermanence and suffering, he returns to the monastery. The monks are naturally somewhat doubtful about how long he is likely to stay, but this time he attains Arahatship. When he tells the monks that he has no longer any desire for the household life, they disbelieve him, but the Buddha confirms his claim, speaking these verses.

40. *like a pot*: According to the Commentary, as fragile as a pot.
territory: *jita*, originally '[that which has been] conquered', but in Pali it has taken on the regular meaning of 'empire' or 'territory'.
without resting: Following K. R. Norman (1997: 6). The Commentary takes *anivesana* as 'without remnant of clinging'.

STORY: Five hundred monks who spend the Rains Retreat in a pleasant grove are harassed by the deities who live in the place, who send uncanny sights and afflict them with ailments to try to drive them away. The Buddha gives them a weapon to deal with these beings: the Mettā Sutta, a famous chant on the development of loving kindness towards all beings (Sutta Nipāta 143–52) – translated in many places: for translation and discussion see e.g. Shaw 2006a: 166–7.

41. STORY: A monk called Tissa becomes very ill with boils, which eat into his flesh and even into his bones, causing them to break. No medicine can help him, and so disgusting is his state that his fellow monks will have nothing to do with him. The Buddha visits his monastery and sets an example by himself heating water, cleaning the monk, and washing his robes. Once Tissa has been made comfortable, the Buddha teaches him with this verse. Tissa attains Arahatship and dies, entering *parinibbāna*.

The Buddha explains that in a previous birth Tissa was a bird-catcher, who broke the legs and wings of the birds he had caught to stop them flying away. However, he eventually saw the error of his ways and offered food to an Arahat, with the wish that he too might attain the same state.

42. STORY: The Buddha visits the herdsman Nanda to give him a teaching, and Nanda attains Stream-Entry. Nanda accompanies the Buddha on his way, but after bidding him farewell and leaving his presence he is accidentally killed by a hunter's arrow. The monks remark that, if the Buddha had not come to Nanda on that occasion, Nanda would not have been killed. The Buddha tells them that, whether he had come or not, Nanda would not have escaped death. But, we are told, the monks did not ask the Buddha what Nanda had done in a previous life, so the reason for his sudden death remains unexplained.

43. *What mother or father cannot do*: As K. R. Norman points out (1997: 71), we would expect a parallel to v. 42, 'Whatever mother or father can do', but the change in wording, if there has been one, took place early, since it has also happened in the equivalent Udāna verse (31.10).

STORY: The commentarial story is somewhat reminiscent of the Greek myth of Tiresias. Soreyya, a banker's son, who is married with two sons, sees the great Arahat Kaccāyana and feels desire for him because of his radiant golden body. As a result, Soreyya immediately turns into a woman, Soreyyā. Embarrassed, Soreyyā dares not return home, but travels to another town, where she marries a man and has two more sons. Years later, after meeting the Arahat again and confessing her earlier fault to him, she again becomes a man and ordains as a monk. People often ask the monk Soreyya which pair of sons he loves better, those he fathered or those he mothered, and he always replies that the ones he mothered are dearer to him than the ones he fathered. But later, when he has attained Arahatship, he says instead that he does not feel attachment for any beings.

CHAPTER 4
FLOWERS

44–5. These verses seem to suggest a half-pun on *vijessati*, 'will conquer', a derivative of *ji-*, 'conquer', and *pacessati*, 'will pluck', a derivative of *ci-*, 'pick'. Some manuscripts actually have *vicessati*, 'Who will discern this earth . . . ?', 'The Learner will discern this earth . . .', from *vi-ci-*, another derivative of *ci-*. In some Prakrits the verbs *ci-* and *ji-* would have been been identical in form, making the pun a full one.
word of Dhamma: *dhammapada*.
a skilled one: A florist or garland-maker.
The Learner: *sekkha*, generally used of a follower of the Buddhist path who has reached one of the stages from Stream-Entry to Non-Return, but not yet attained Arahatship.

STORY: The Buddha overhears some monks talking about the qualities of different kinds of soil that they have seen on their journey. He points out that it is more important to cleanse the soil of the heart.

46. *foam . . . mirage*: There seems to be a reference here to Saṃyutta Nikāya 3.142, in which the five *khandhas* (see Glossary) are compared to things that are empty and unreal: *rūpa*, 'form', to a mass of foam on water; *vedanā*, 'feeling', to a bubble; *saññā*, 'perception', to a mirage; *saṅkhāra*, 'mental creations', to a banana tree (which is hollow within); and *viññāna*, 'consciousness', to a magical trick.
nature: *dhamma*.

STORY: A monk has difficulty with the meditation object given to him by the Buddha, and determines to go and see him to ask for another one. On the way, he sees first a mirage, and then a rainstorm that causes bubbles to rise up and burst along a terrace. He understands that 'self' is just as unreal and transitory as the mirage and the bubbles. The Buddha sends a likeness of himself to him to speak the verse, and the monk attains Arahatship.

47. STORY: The Commentary has a long story of rivalry between princes of the Sākiya clan. Viḍūḍabha is the son of a king by the daughter of a slave woman, and feels himself slighted by his more aristocratic relatives. He takes bloody vengeance on them, but on the way home he himself and his retinue are swept away and drowned by a river in flood. The monks wonder why the innocent followers perished along with the prince. The Buddha explains that, although they have done nothing to deserve it in the present life, in a previous life they had poisoned the river, killing large numbers of fish.

48. STORY: That of Patipūjikā ('Husband-Worshipper'). A god called Mālabhārin ('Garland-Bearer') is enjoying himself with a thousand nymphs (*accharā*) in the Tāvatiṃsa heaven. One of the nymphs, who is sitting in a tree picking blossoms to make garlands for him, suddenly disappears. She is reborn in the human world, where she grows up, marries, and has four children; but she never forgets her divine husband. She becomes a devoted Buddhist laywoman, and every time she performs an act of merit she makes a wish to be reborn with Mālabhārin (hence her nickname). Suddenly she becomes ill, dies, and is reborn in the Tāvatiṃsa heaven, where the other nymphs are still making garlands. Mālabhārin greets her with the cry 'We haven't seen you since morning! Where have you been?' When he hears her story, and learns how short human life is, Mālabhārin wants to know whether human beings spend their lives in meritorious actions. He is quite shocked to learn the answer.

Back in the human realm, the monks themselves are shocked by the sudden death of Patipūjikā, who had given them alms that very morning. The Buddha speaks the stanza to remind them of the briefness of earthly existence.

49. *In the village . . . nectar*: The right attitude for a monk going into a village for alms.
Flower, colour or scent: K. R. Norman (1997: 8, 73) takes *pupphaṃ vaṇṇa-gandhaṃ* as an unusual compound, broken to avoid running over the caesura in the line of verse, in which case it would mean 'the colour and scent of a flower'.

STORY: The miser Kosiya and his wife do not wish to offer alms to the Buddha and the monks, so they prepare their meal in an upstairs room where they think no one will see them. This does not prevent the Elder Moggallāna, famous for his psychic powers, from standing outside the window. Kosiya then tells his wife to cook a very small pancake to offer in alms to Moggallāna, but each time she tries to do this the pancake destined for him becomes enormous. In the end, they offer the whole basketful to Moggallāna, who teaches them about generosity. Rather than simply accept the food for himself, Moggallāna brings Kosiya and his wife to offer their alms to the Buddha and 500 monks.

The Buddha, too, gives a teaching on generosity, and Kosiya and his wife attain Stream-Entry. The Buddha speaks the verse in praise of Moggallāna, encouraging the other monks to be like him.

50. STORY: The Ājīvika ascetic Pāṭhika seeks to undermine a laywoman's attempts to offer alms to the Buddha: among other tricks, he tries to mislead the Buddha about the route to her house. When the Buddha finds his way there in spite of his efforts, Pāṭhika behaves so rudely that the laywoman is too upset to concentrate on the Buddha's teaching. The Buddha speaks the verse to her to encourage her not to mind Pāṭhika's behaviour, but to pay attention to her own conduct.

51–2. STORY: While the layman Chattapāṇi, a Once-Returner, is sitting listening to the Buddha, King Pasenadi also comes to visit. Since the Buddha is sitting down, Chattapāṇi does not get up. Pasenadi is angry, until the Buddha calms him by talking of Chattapāṇi's good qualities. Another day, Pasenadi sees Chattapāṇi passing his palace, and sends for him. Now Chattapāṇi prostrates himself before Pasenadi and pays him every respect. Pasenadi wants to know why Chattapāṇi did not stand up for him on the previous occasion. Chattapāṇi points out that, if one were in the presence of a king of kings, and a subject king were to arrive, it would be insulting to the king of kings if one were to stand up for the subject king.

Pasenadi is impressed, and invites Chattapāṇi to teach the Dhamma in the women's quarters of his palace. But Chattapāṇi says that it would be improper for him, as a layman, to do this, and recommends that the king ask the Buddha to send a monk. (There would have been no obstacle to a layman's giving a Dhamma teaching: the problem is the question of his visiting the women's quarters. Clearly Chattapāṇi does not wish to give Pasenadi any cause for suspicion, particularly in view of their previous misunderstanding.)

The Buddha sends Ānanda, who teaches the Dhamma to King Pasenadi's two wives and their attendants. Mallikā learns and practises what she has heard, while Vāsabhakhattiyā does not. The Buddha speaks the verses on the different attitudes of the two queens.

53. STORY: This concerns the early life and marriage of the great laywoman Visākhā, known for her beauty, generosity and good sense. The story culminates in her donating a monastery to the Saṅgha. When it is complete, she walks around the monastery, accompanied by her children, grandchildren and great-grand-children, and appears to be singing. In view of her usual extremely proper behaviour, the monks are shocked; however, the Buddha explains that she is not singing, but uttering an *udāna*, full of joy that her wish to make this great donation has been fulfilled. He explains that she originally conceived this wish hundreds of thousands of aeons before, in the times of the earlier Buddhas Padumuttara and Kassapa. He speaks the verse in praise of Visākhā.

54–5. *tagara*: The plant *Tabernaemontana coronaria*, whose roots were ground to make a fragrant powder.

STORY: Ānanda asks the Buddha whether there is any kind of perfume that can be wafted against the wind. The Buddha describes the qualities of the man or woman who takes refuge in the Buddha, Dhamma and Saṅgha.

56. STORY: The Elder Kassapa refuses alms from 500 nymphs (*accharā*), wives of the god Sakka, because he wishes to accept alms from someone who is very poor. But Sakka and one of his ladies disguise themselves as an impoverished weaver-couple and give alms. The fragrance of the food they offer fills the city.

57. STORY: A monk called Godhika makes great efforts, and almost reaches the point of attaining Arahatship; however, because of illness, he keeps falling away from it. He determines to free himself by cutting his own throat. As he dies, he attains Arahatship and enters *nibbāna*. Māra looks for him, but cannot find him, and the Buddha utters the verse.

The story is a canonical one, from the Saṃyutta Nikāya (1.120f.): the Commentary on that (SA 1.144f.) explains that the chief monks tried to dissuade Godhika from this course, and that the Buddha tried to reach him but arrived too late. It was through controlling his pain and meditating at the point of death that

Godhika attained Arahatship. The texts are very careful not to give any sort of encouragement to suicide, which is normally considered to bring kammic consequences as serious as those of any other kind of killing.

58–9. STORY: The (not apparently very edifying) story of two laymen, Sirigutta and Garahadinna, respectively the followers of the Buddha and of the Nigaṇṭhas (Jains). Garahadinna maintains that the Nigaṇṭhas know everything, past, present and future, while Sirigutta claims the same for the Buddha. Each tries to prove his point by inviting the other's teacher or teachers for alms, and setting up a booby trap for them to fall into. The ascetics are caught, but the Buddha is not: indeed, some dishes that Garahadinna had deliberately left empty are found to be full of delicious alms-food for the Buddha and his monks. Garahadinna is profoundly moved and pays homage to the Buddha, inviting him to speak the traditional words of thanks in the form of a Dhamma talk, at the end of which both Sirigutta and Garahadinna attain Stream-Entry.

CHAPTER 5
FOOLS

60. *league*: Representing the Pali *yojana*, derived from the distance that can be ploughed by an ox-team in one day. It appears to have varied between about 4.5 and 9 miles (7.2 and 14.4 km) – see Rau 1959: 162–3.

STORY: The Commentary has a complex sequence of stories, pointing out the perils of adultery, and praising the wisdom of a good wife. King Pasenadi conceives a desire for the wife of a poor man, and seeks a pretext to get rid of her husband. He makes him his servant, and sets him a difficult task: to bring him red earth and blue and white lotuses from a river a *yojana* away, and be back with them by the time the king goes to bathe in the evening. Not only is this a long journey on foot, but the river is inhabited by *nāgas*. Not daring to stop to eat before he goes, the man takes his lunch of curry and rice with him in a basket. On his way he gives a portion of the food to a traveller, and when he reaches the river he throws in some rice for the *nāgas*. He offers to give the merit of these good actions to the *nāgas* in return for their red earth and blue and white lotuses. The *nāga* king appears in the form of an old man and gives him what he needs, and the man returns to the palace with the earth and flowers. However, Pasenadi, seeking to frustrate him, has had the doors locked early. The man leaves the gifts at the palace door, calling all to witness that he has obeyed the king's command. He then takes refuge for the night in the monastery where the Buddha is staying.

Meanwhile, Pasenadi has a sleepless night, disturbed by strange and terrible sounds. In the morning he consults his household priest, who claims that they are sounds of ill omen, whose effects he should avert by sacrificing hundreds of living beings, including human boys and girls. Pasenadi's wife, Mallikā, becoming aware of the preparations for the sacrifice, tells her husband that he is a fool for thinking that a man can save his own life through the death of another. She persuades him instead to go with her to visit the Buddha.

When they are in his presence, the king is too full of fear to speak, so Mallikā tells the Buddha about the unearthly sounds. The Buddha explains that these are the sounds made by four beings in a hell realm, who are suffering the consequences of lives spent committing adultery by being boiled for aeons in a giant kettle. King Pasenadi takes the point, and silently makes up his mind never again to set his heart on another man's wife.

The king now knows how long the night is; the poor man knows how long a *yojana* is; and the adulterers know how long *saṃsāra* is – in confirmation of which the Buddha speaks the verse. The king sets free the poor man and all the chosen sacrificial victims, who praise Queen Mallikā for saving their lives. The Buddha tells the story of a previous life in which Mallikā saved the lives of herself, a hundred kings and a hundred princes.

61. *steadfastly*: K. R. Norman (1997: 10, 76) takes *daḷhaṃ* as 'certainly'.
with fools: Taking *bāle* as a rare form of the instrumental plural. Alternatively, taking it as locative singular, 'in a fool'.

STORY: The Elder Kassapa has a novice who persistently misbehaves, resents correction, and eventually burns down his master's hut. The Buddha consoles Kassapa by speaking the verse. He tells the story of a previous life, in which a foolish monkey destroys the nest of a wise *siṅgila* (apparently a mythical horned bird): the novice was the monkey, and Kassapa the bird.

62. STORY: Ānanda the Banker (*seṭṭhi*) is a miser. He passes on some of his wealth to his son, Mūlasiri, but keeps the bulk of it hidden. He dies suddenly, and is reborn in a Caṇḍāla ('untouchable') family, as a deformed child who seems to bring bad luck on those around him. Even his mother, reduced to begging, eventually sends him away to beg by himself.

He finds his way into Mūlasiri's house, where the sight of him frightens the children, and the servants throw him out. But the Buddha comes by, and sends for Mūlasiri. He tells the former Ānanda the Banker to point out to his son where he formerly hid his treasure.

63. STORY: Two friends are part of a crowd that has gathered to listen to the Dhamma. One of them listens and attains Stream-Entry, while the other steals a purse. The thief has food to eat that night, while the Stream-Enterer has nothing. The thief and his wife make fun of the Stream-Enterer, saying that he is too wise for his own good. The Stream-Enterer thinks about the thief, 'At least this man, in his folly, doesn't think he is wise.'

64. *dhammas*: Or 'the Dhamma', but here *dhammaṃ* seems to be used in a plural sense. Similarly with *rasaṃ*: 'flavours' or 'flavour'.

STORY: The Elder Udāyi fancies himself as wise, and likes to sit in the teacher's seat. However, when there he proves unable to answer the most elementary questions.

65. STORY: Thirty men are in a forest looking for a woman (presumably for sexual purposes). However, instead they meet the Buddha, who ordains them with the words, 'Come, monks!' They work hard at practising the Buddha's teaching, and quickly attain Arahatship. When other monks remark on the speed of their attainment, he speaks the verse.

66. STORY: Suppabuddha ('Well-Awakened') suffers from leprosy. He hears the Buddha's teaching and attains Stream-Entry. He wishes to speak to the Buddha about it, but, not daring to force his way through the crowd that is there, he decides to go and see him at the monastery later on.

While he is on his way there, the god Sakka decides to tempt him. He offers him enormous wealth to deny his faith in the Buddha, Dhamma and Saṅgha, but Suppabuddha rejects the offer with scorn. Sakka reports his experience to the Buddha, who confirms that it would not be possible to prevail upon a Stream-Enterer like Suppabuddha to deny his faith.

Suppabuddha himself then goes to see the Buddha, who welcomes him in a friendly way. But, after he leaves, Suppabuddha is killed by a cow, and afterwards is reborn in the heaven of the Thirty-Three Gods. The Buddha recounts the wrong actions in past lives which led to his dying in this way and to his having contracted leprosy. The verse is a comment on these actions.

67. *working-out*: *vipāka*, literally, 'ripening', the result of previous action (*kamma*).

STORY: A farmer who finds a stolen purse on his land is arrested and wrongly accused of theft. He calls on the Buddha, who knows what really happened, and is set free. Presumably the farmer's trouble is thought to be the result of wrong actions in a previous life, but this is not explicitly stated.

68. *working-out*: See the note on v. 67.

STORY: King Bimbisāra's gardener, Sumana, offers to the Buddha the flowers intended for the king. Such is his joy that he does not mind whether the king kills or banishes him for his action. The flowers hover round the Buddha all day, following him like a moving canopy. The king does not punish Sumana, but rewards him lavishly, and the Buddha foretells that one day the gardener will become a Paccekabuddha called Sumana. (Sumana means 'Good Mind', but also suggests *sumanā*, 'jasmine'.)

69. STORY: The canonical story of the great Arahat Uppalavaṇṇā. The daughter of a wealthy merchant, she is so beautiful that many kings and princes desire to marry her. (Her name means 'Having the Complexion of the [Dark-Blue] Water Lily'.) Not wishing to offend any of these great men, her father asks her to become a nun – which happens to be her own dearest wish, cultivated through many lives. She soon attains Arahatship through meditation while gazing at the flame of a lamp.

One night, while living in a hut in a forest, she is raped by a suitor from her earlier life. Afterwards, as a result of his crime against an awakened being, her attacker is swallowed up by the earth, and is reborn in the Avīci hell (cf. the story for v. 17). It is in relation to this man's behaviour and subsequent fate that the Buddha speaks the verse.

Some people, discussing Uppalavaṇṇā's misadventure, begin to speculate that perhaps Arahats are not free of sense-desire. The Buddha corrects them, speaking Dhammapada v. 401. He also makes a rule that, in future, nuns should not live alone in the forest, and the king provides them with accommodation within the city.

70. *kusa*: A grass (Sanskrit *kuśa*) used in Vedic rituals. It is regarded as sacred, but has very sharp blades.
Of those who've mastered dhammas: *saṅkhāta-dhammānaṃ* – i.e. by investigating them in insight meditation.
This verse is closely paralleled in a Jain text, the Uttarajjhayaṇa Sutta (9.44): see Roth 1976.

STORY: Jambuka, an Ājīvika ascetic, pretends to live on next to nothing, but is secretly surviving by eating his own excrement. The Buddha understands what is really happening, visits him, and explains to him the reason for his current degraded state – a series of coarse insults offered to an Arahat in the time of the Buddha Kassapa. The Buddha gives Jambuka a garment. Then Jambuka listens to the Buddha's teaching, attains Arahatship, and ordains as a monk. When his lay followers come to visit him, he now directs them to the Buddha, as his master. The Buddha points out that, even if Jambuka were genuinely to abstain from food, as he previously pretended to do, this ascetic practice would not be worth a sixteenth part of the feeling of remorse that had led him to change his ways.

71. *curdles*: Added for clarity. Following Patna Dharmapada 107 and Udānavarga 9.17, K. R. Norman (1997: 11, 79) takes *muccati* as representing *mucchati* (< *mūrcchati*), 'coagulates', 'goes off'. The Pali Commentary takes *sajju-khīraṃ* as a compound, 'that day's milk', 'fresh milk', so that the first two lines of the verse would then mean, 'For an evil deed that is done, / Like fresh milk, does not ripen [at once]'. However, the alternative versions both have it as two separate words (*sajjaṃ chīraṃ*, PDhp 107; *sadyaḥ kṣīraṃ*, Uv 9.17), giving Norman's reading, which I have followed here.

STORY: Two stories about ghosts (*petas*) seen by the Elders Moggallāna and Lakkhaṇa. When they report what they have seen to the Buddha, he explains the reason for the beings' rebirth in this form. (1) A crow steals food brought by villagers for the

Buddha Kassapa. It is reborn in the Avīci hell, and afterwards as a gigantic ghostly crow. (2) A farmer, angry because people visiting a Paccekabuddha have trampled his fields, destroys the holy man's hut. He too is reborn in the Avīci hell, and afterwards as a ghostly snake.

72. *reputation for knowledge*: *ñattaṃ*, probably equivalent to Buddhist Hybrid Sanskrit *jñātra* (K. R. Norman 1997: 11, 80).
causes his head to split [or *'fall'*]: The Commentary interprets 'head' as a synonym for 'wisdom': see Carter and Palihawadana 1987: 156. However, in ancient Indian literature we find a persistent belief that a person's head could split (or fall off) through overweening arrogance. (It is described as happening to the sage Vidagdha Śākalya in the Bṛhadāraṇyaka Upaniṣad, III.9.26 (Roebuck 2000: 69; 2003: 59).)

STORY: Another tale of a ghost seen by the Elders Moggallāna and Lakkhaṇa. A disabled man has great skill in throwing stones, using it to cut the leaves of a banyan tree into amusing shapes and so earn a living. An apprentice learns the craft from him, but uses it to kill a Paccekabuddha. Finding out what has happened, the local people, who loved the Paccekabuddha, beat the apprentice to death. He is reborn first in the Avīci hell, and afterwards as a 'sledgehammer ghost': a figure, three-quarters of a league in height, being repeatedly battered on the head by burning sledgehammers.

73–4. *respect among bad people*: Taking *asataṃ* as genitive plural, following K. R. Norman (1997: 11, 80) and the Patna Dharmapada 178. The Commentary takes it as accusative singular: 'undue respect'.
renouncers: *pabbajitā*, those who have 'gone forth'.
Let me be in charge / Of everything: Literally, 'Let it be controlled by me in everything.'

STORY: A proud monk called Sudhamma feels slighted by the layman Citta because the latter pays attention to another monk who is a Once-Returner. He behaves badly to Citta, but eventually the Buddha prevails upon him to apologize. He repents his rudeness and attains Arahatship. Citta visits the Buddha, who praises him with v. 303.

75. Reminiscent of Kaṭha Upaniṣad II.1ff., which, interestingly in view of the commentarial story, concerns a young boy choosing

between wealth and the spiritual path (tr. Roebuck 2000: 318; 2003: 277):

> The better is one thing, the pleasanter another:
> Both bind a man, to different ends.
> Of the two, it is well for the one who chooses the better.
> The one who chooses the pleasanter fails of his end.
>
> . . . .
>
> These two are far apart, disparate,
> Ignorance and what is called wisdom . . .

STORY: Tissa, a seven-year-old novice, attains Arahatship. When the monks remark on the immensely wealthy background that the boy has renounced, the Buddha speaks the verse.

CHAPTER 6
THE WISE MAN

76. *such a one*: *tādisaṃ*. In the Dhammapada, *tādisa*, '[one/s] like that', seems always to be used as a term of respect – cf. vv. 196, 208.

STORY: A poor Brahmin called Rādha lives at a monastery and works for the monks. Despite his attentiveness, they are not willing to admit him to the Order. But Sāriputta, remembering a kindness on the part of Rādha, ordains him and takes him on his alms-round. Rādha is attentive in following Sāriputta's instructions, and Sāriputta is grateful for his help.

77. *then*: Word added for clarity.

STORY: A group of monks behave badly, breaking all sorts of Vinaya rules. The Buddha tells Sāriputta and Moggallāna to admonish them. Some listen and reform, others voluntarily return to the household life, while the hardest cases are expelled from the Order.

78. STORY: The Elder Channa repeatedly insults Sāriputta and Moggallāna. After the Buddha's death, when punished by being boycotted by the Order, he repents and soon attains Arahatship.

79. *Dhamma-drinker*: There is a pun here on *pīti* (< Sanskrit *pīti*), 'drinking', and *pīti* (< Sanskrit *prīti*), 'joy': 'Dhamma-drinker'/

'One who takes joy in the Dhamma'. The commentator takes it purely in the former sense, while the Udānavarga, PDhp and GDhp all have *prīti*: see K. R. Norman 1997: 82.

STORY: A king and queen, Kappina and Anojā, become followers of the Buddha, and they and all their entourage are ordained as monks and nuns. All attain Arahatship. Kappina is heard wandering around the monastery exclaiming, 'Oh, happiness! Oh, happiness!' Some hearers think he is referring to his previous life as a monarch, but the Buddha explains that he is referring to the peace of *nibbāna*.

80. *shape*: Literally, 'bend' – cf. v. 145.

STORY: Paṇḍita Dāraka ('Little Boy Wiseman') is a seven-year-old novice. One day he accompanies Sāriputta into a village on the alms-round, carrying the Elder's robe and bowl. On the way, he sees a drainage ditch directing the course of water, fletchers making arrows, and carpenters making chariot wheels. Seeing that even inanimate objects are capable of being led or shaped, he is inspired to strive for Arahatship.

Paṇḍita Dāraka hands the Elder's robe and bowl back to him, and asks him to bring food for him too. Sāriputta is not offended by the novice's behaviour, but sends him back to the monastery as he wishes. As the boy meditates, the sun and moon stand still. The Buddha becomes aware that Sāriputta is returning with food for the boy, so, to prevent him from interrupting the boy's meditation, he detains him by asking him four tricky questions about food. While Sāriputta is answering them, the novice attains Arahatship. The Buddha then utters this verse.

81. STORY: The Arahat Elder Lakuṇṭaka Bhaddiya – said elsewhere to have been a very tiny man – is teased and tormented by novices and others, but remains unperturbed. (For more on this Elder, see the stories for vv. 260–61, 294–5.)

82. *Dhamma teachings*: *dhammāni* – an odd usage if it simply means '*dhammas*', since it seems to be neuter instead of the expected masculine. K. R. Norman (1997: 83) takes it as an Eastern form of the masculine. I take it as a derivative (equivalent to Sanskrit *dhārmyāṇi*) meaning 'things connected with the Dhamma'.

STORY: A girl called Kāṇā resents Buddhist monks because her mother gave away to some monks the food that the girl was meant to take to her future husband's house, so the marriage that had been arranged for her fell through. However, when she actually hears the Buddha's teaching, she becomes calm and generous towards the monks. She is rewarded by the king, who adopts her as his daughter and arranges her marriage to a kind and wealthy nobleman.

The Buddha speaks the verse referring to Kāṇā's change from the sadness in her past to the peace of her present state.

83. *go everywhere*: Reading *vajanti*, 'they go'; variant, *cajanti*, 'they renounce', giving '. . . practise renunciation everywhere' – the reading that seems to be followed by the Commentary.
boast: Or possibly 'chatter'/'cause to chatter' (*lapayanti*) – see Carter and Palihawadana 1987: 167–8; K. R. Norman 1997: 83.
from desire for sensual things: Taking *kāma-kāmā* as an ablative singular – literally, 'from desire for desires (i.e. sense-pleasures)'. Some take it as a nominative plural agreeing with 'the good' – 'desiring desires'.
excitement or depression: *uccāvacaṃ* (literally 'up-and-down-ness') – a common pairing which refers to one of the hindrances to meditation, the tendency of the mind to excessive highs and lows. (See 'hindrance' in Glossary.) K. R. Norman (1997: 12, 83) translates *uccāvacaṃ* as 'variation'.

STORY: This concerns the contrasting behaviour of monks and others during a period of famine.

84. *injustice*: *adhamma*.
just: *dhammika*.

STORY: A layman wishes to become a monk, but his wife puts him off, first until she gives birth to the child she is expecting, then until the child is able to walk, then until the child is of age. At this point the layman decides that he does not care about her permission, and gets ordained anyway, after which he achieves Arahatship. Eventually the son and wife too are ordained, and they too attain Arahatship.

The message of the story seems to be that one should not desire worldly satisfactions at all, whereas that of the verse seems to be primarily that one should not seek them through improper means.

85–6. STORY: The residents of a street in Sāvatthi get together to give alms, and spend a whole night listening to the Dhamma. But some are overcome by desire or ill will and wander away, while others fall prey to lethargy and fall asleep. None of them manages to listen all night through.

87–9. *states*: *dhammas* (taking *dhammaṃ* as accusative plural).
enlightenment factors: Often listed as seven: mindfulness (*sati*), investigation of *dhammas* (*dhammavicaya*), effort/courage (*viriya*), joy (*pīti*), calming (*passaddhi*), concentration (*samādhi*) and equipoise (*upekkhā*).
have attained nibbāna: *parinibbutā*, 'are fully liberated' – participle form from the same verb as *parinibbāna*.

STORY: A brief account of the Buddha's teaching to a group of fifty monks who visit him at Jetavana, at the end of the Rains Retreat.

CHAPTER 7
THE ARAHAT

90. STORY: When Devadatta attempts to kill the Buddha by dropping a rock on him, the rock splits and passes the Buddha by, but a splinter injures his foot. The physician Jīvaka dresses the wound, but is unable to return at the appointed time to remove the bandage. He is extremely troubled, fearing that the Buddha will experience pain as a result. The Buddha, perceiving his thought at a distance, asks Ānanda to remove the dressing, and all is well. When Jīvaka returns, he tells the Buddha of his worry, and the Buddha speaks the verse in reply.

91. *geese*: The *haṃsa* is not a 'swan', as in Carter and Palihawadana 1987: 174–5, but a goose, greatly admired in ancient Indian literature for the strength and beauty of its flight. Specifically, it probably refers to the bar-headed goose (*Anser indicus*), a bird that is remarkable for both the height and the speed of its flight on its migrations over the Himalayas between India and Tibet. (For a discussion of the goose in Indian art and literature, see Vogel 1962.)
any kind of home: *okamokaṃ*. A variant reading is *okam oghaṃ*, 'their watery home', 'their home, the water' – cf. v. 34. This agrees with the Udāna reading (17.1). For the geese, this would

apply to the pools where they have been living before migration; for the mindful, it would mean the flood of *saṃsāra* (K. R. Norman 1997: 14, 85–6). Carter and Palihawadana (1987: 174) translate the line as 'One shelter after another they leave,' but offer the alternative of 'Home they abandon, the flood.'

STORY: Other monks misunderstand the actions of the Elder Kassapa, thinking that they stem from attachment to particular households of lay supporters. The Buddha explains that Kassapa is not attached to the households, but is obeying the Buddha's instructions. Kassapa is as free as the (migrating) goose in the verse.

92. STORY: The monk Belaṭṭhasīsa, intent on spending time in meditation, stores food overnight to avoid going on an alms-round every day. The Buddha, on hearing of this, makes a Vinaya rule against it. But he declares that Belaṭṭhasīsa himself has not done wrong, because the rule had not yet been given, and also because he had stored only a modest amount of boiled rice.

93. STORY: When the Elder Anuruddha's robes are worn out, a goddess called Jālinī, who was his wife in a previous existence, leaves celestial cloth in a rubbish heap so that he will find it. The Buddha and the chief Elders sew the cloth into robes. Meanwhile, the goddess inspires villagers to bring them all sumptuous food. When some monks express disapproval, believing that Anuruddha had asked his supporters for these gifts, the Buddha puts them right with the verse.

94. *calm*: *samatha*, the concentration aspect of meditation.

STORY: Sakka himself comes to do honour to the great Arahat Kaccāyana. When some other monks are offended that he has done this only for Kaccāyana, and not all the Elders, the Buddha speaks the verse in praise of Kaccāyana.

95. *royal pillar*: *indakhīla*, the main pillar before the gate of a town.

Like the earth . . . royal pillar: The Commentary points out that the earth doesn't mind whether pure things, like garlands of flowers, or impure ones, like urine and excrement, are thrown on it; and similarly the pillar in front of the town gate doesn't mind whether people hang offerings on it or little boys relieve themselves against it.

no more wanderings in saṃsāra: Literally, 'no more *saṃsāras* [i.e. rebirths in this world or that]'.

STORY: A monk fancies himself injured by Sāriputta, and works up a tremendous head of resentment against him. But, when he sees the forbearance of the Elder, he repents. The Buddha speaks the verse in praise of Sāriputta.

96. STORY: A seven-year-old novice, attending upon an Elder, loses an eye when it is accidentally caught by the handle of the Elder's fan. Far from being angry, the boy attempts to conceal his injury, and when it is found out he reassures the Elder, saying that it was neither the Elder's fault nor his own, but that of the round of existence.

97. *That man who's faithless . . . brave fellow indeed*: *assaddho akataññū ca sandhicchedo ca yo naro / hatāvakāso vantāso sa ve uttamaporiso.* An elaborate sequence of puns, whose most obvious meanings are all disparaging, but which on reflection reveal a set of meanings that express praise. For example *sandhiccheda* means 'burglar', but the context here shows that it is also to be taken in its literal sense as 'breaker/cutter of links'. Full understanding of the double meanings seems to have been lost in the Pali commentarial tradition, but remembered in the Chinese commentaries on the Sanskrit version (Hara 1992).

Here, meaning (1) is the bad, and (2) the good sense:

faithless/desireless: *assaddha.* (1) Without faith (*saddhā*) in its usual sense of confidence in the Buddha's path. It can also refer to the quality that causes a person to practise generosity, so *a-ssaddha* would then mean 'miserly'. (2) More rarely, *saddhā* can mean 'desire' (confidence in the wrong things?), so I have taken *assaddha* in its laudatory sense as meaning 'free from desire'. Some translators have taken *assaddha* in its laudatory sense to mean 'not credulous'; however, there is little evidence that in ancient times *saddhā* was ever regarded as equivalent to credulity, since 'faith' in the Buddhist tradition has never meant 'believing in' dogmas etc. In the story below, Sāriputta is complimented not on lack of excessive credulity, but on the fact that, as one who has experienced attainments for himself, he no longer needs *saddhā* (K. R. Norman 1979).

Ungrateful/Who knows the unmade: *akataññū.* (1) *a-kataññū*, 'ungrateful' (< 'not (*a-*) knowing (*ññū*) what has been done (*kata*) [for him]'). (2) *akata-ññū*, 'knowing (*ññū*) the unmade (*akata* [= *nibbāna*])' (cf. v. 383). Ingratitude is regarded with particular disapproval in Buddhism, and this pun is a fairly common one.

burglar/breaker of links: *sandhiccheda*. (1) 'Breaker of links', i.e. 'burglar' (one who broke his way through the partition walls (probably of wood or clay) in ancient Indian homes). (2) 'Breaker of the links' that bound him to existence.

Who's blown his chances/Who's gone beyond chances: *hatāvakāsa*, 'having destroyed opportunity'. (1) Having destroyed his chances of performing good actions. (2) Having destroyed occasions for quarrels, or, perhaps, having destroyed occasions for good and bad *kamma* to arise – the interpretation I have followed here.

an eater of forbidden food/who's got rid of desire: *vantāsa* – *vanta* + *āsa*. (1) An eater (*āsa*) of that which is vomited (*vanta*) – i.e. leftover food, regarded as unclean. (2) One who has vomited out (*vanta*) hope or expectation (*āsā*).

brave fellow/fine person: *uttamaporisa*, taken by most translators as equivalent to *uttama purisa* (Sanskrit *uttama puruṣa*), 'topmost man/person'; but, as Hara (1992) has pointed out, it is more likely to mean 'possessing the highest manliness/courage' (Sanskrit *uttamapauruṣa*), which is appropriate either to (1) a daring criminal or (2) an Arahat who has made the supreme effort to attain liberation.

STORY: The Buddha praises Sāriputta, who relies not on belief but on experience to know the truth of his teaching.

The Pali Commentary does not address the fact that the most obvious meaning of the words is disparaging or even criminal. Perhaps in an earlier version of the story the Buddha was being deliberately provocative by describing the great Elder in terms that would normally be applied to a bandit chief – cf. the startling words applied to Lakuṇṭaka Bhaddiya, notes to vv. 294–5.

98. *What a lovely place it is*: *taṃ bhūmiṃ rāmaṇeyyakaṃ*, following K. R. Norman (1997: 14, 88), who takes the odd syntax here as a split compound (cf. the note on v. 49), equivalent to *taṃ bhūmi-rāmaṇeyyakaṃ*, literally, 'that is a loveliness of a place'. His interpretation is supported by PDhp 245, which has *taṃ bhomaṃ rāmaṇīyakaṃ*, 'that is earthly delightfulness'. Probably there is an underlying sense of 'that [i.e. the presence of Arahats] is what makes a place lovely'.

STORY: When the Buddha goes to visit Revata, the youngest brother of Sāriputta, Revata by his psychic power (*iddhi*) creates a wonderful residence for the Buddha in the forest. Monks who have seen that residence find the forest a wonderful place. However, two old monks who get lost in the same forest see it as merely a wilderness of thorny acacia trees. The Buddha explains the different perceptions people have of the forest, but points out that to an Arahat it does not matter what kind of forest it is.

99. *Where folk find no delight*: 'Folk' meaning 'worldly folk'.
sensual things: Literally, 'desires', as in v. 83.

STORY: A monk is trying to meditate in the forest. A courtesan has arranged to meet a client there, and when he fails to turn up she turns her charms on the monk, who becomes distracted. The Buddha, at a distance, becomes aware of what is going on, and sends a likeness of himself to the monk, through which he teaches him and speaks this verse. The monk attains Arahatship.

CHAPTER 8
THOUSANDS

'Thousands' sequences seem to have been popular, as they occur in all known versions of the Dharmapada literature, though not always under that title. Verses of the same type occur also in Jain and Hindu texts: see Roth 1976. In my translation, I have adapted the syntax of the verses to convey what I feel to be a similarly proverbial feeling in English: see my comments on individual verses.

100. *Better than a thousand sayings . . . Is one word of meaning*: Literally, 'If [there are] a thousand sayings . . . better [is] one word of meaning . . .'
word: *pada*, 'word' or 'saying'.
Which calms you to hear it: Literally, 'Hearing which, one is calmed'.

STORY: An executioner, who has just retired after killing hundreds of criminals, gives alms to Sāriputta. During Sāriputta's talk after the meal, the executioner's mind is distracted by the thought of his former bloody actions. The Elder reminds him that he did not originally undertake the post at his own will, but only because he had been ordered to do so by the king. The man's mind then becomes calm, and he is able to profit by Sāriputta's teaching. Later that day he is killed by a *yakkhinī* in the form of a cow, and is reborn in the Tusita heaven. When asked where the former executioner has been reborn, the Buddha utters the words:

On hearing the well-spoken word,
He who killed thieves in the city
Gained patience in accordance with that
And rejoices, having gone to heaven.

The monks express surprise that a man who had performed cruel acts for fifty-five years should attain such a state after hearing only a small amount of teaching. The Buddha explains that the Dhamma should not be thought of as little or much, and he speaks the Dhammapada verse.

101. *Better than a thousand verses . . . Is one word of verse*: Literally, 'If [there are] a thousand verses . . . better [is] one word of verse . . . '
Which calms you to hear it: As in v. 100.

STORY: A man called Bāhiya loses everything in a shipwreck, so on reaching the shore he makes himself a garment from tree-bark. Since ascetics often wore such garb, he is taken for a holy man, and people address him as 'Arahat'. He starts to wonder if he really *is* an Arahat. A deity who meditated with him in an earlier life sees his danger, and encourages him to go and see the Buddha, who teaches him and offers to ordain him once he has equipped himself with robes and bowl. While he is trying to find them, he is killed by a *yakkhinī* in the form of a cow. The Buddha reveals that Bāhiya has attained Arahatship, after hearing just a few short words of teaching.

102–3. *Better than speaking a hundred verses . . . Is one word of meaning*: Literally, 'Though someone might speak a hundred verses . . . better [is] one word of *Dhamma* (*dhammapada*) . . . '
Which calms you to hear it: As in v. 100.
you . . . yourself: Literally, 'one . . . oneself' – and similarly in the following verses.
There is a close parallel in Jain literature to v. 103, Uttarajjhayaṇa Sutta 9.34: see Roth 1976.

STORY: Kuṇḍalakesī ('Curly-Haired' – also known elsewhere as Bhaddā) is the beautiful sixteen-year-old daughter of a wealthy merchant of Rājagaha, and her parents try to keep her secluded from men in order to find a suitable husband for her. But one day she looks out of the window and sees a captured bandit being brought back to the city in chains, and instantly falls in love with him. She refuses all food until her parents agree to make this man her husband. Her father bribes an official to save the bandit from execution (and execute somebody else), and the bandit and Kuṇḍalakesī are married.

Kuṇḍalakesī does everything possible to win her husband's heart; but he has not really changed, and soon forms a plan to kill her and steal her jewels. He pretends to be troubled because he has a vow to fulfil: when he was facing execution, he says, he swore, if he were saved, to make a sumptuous offering to the deity of Robbers' Cliff, the execution place, where robbers are thrown down to their deaths. So Kuṇḍalakesī prepares the offerings, dresses in her finest garments and jewellery, and accompanies her husband, alone, to the top of Robbers' Cliff.

When they get there, he tells her to take off her jewels, as he is going to kill her. Her pleas fail to melt his heart, so she decides to rely on quick thinking. She begs permission to embrace him before she dies; and as she does so, she gets behind him, gives him a shove, and pushes him off the cliff. The deity of the place salutes her for her wisdom, but she is troubled. She dares not return to her parents, so she becomes a nun with the Nigaṇṭhas (Jains). A skilled disputant, she wanders India, challenging anyone to debate with her. If a householder beats her in debate, she will become his servant; if a renunciant does so, she will join his Order.

No one is able to defeat her, until one day she arrives at Sāvatthi when Sāriputta is there. He answers all her questions, but she cannot answer his. She asks to become his follower; but he takes her to the Buddha, who has her ordained as a nun. In a short time she becomes an Arahat with great powers, the quickest in understanding of all the nuns. The monks discuss the fact that Kuṇḍalakesī has become an Arahat after very little teaching; and that she has come to them after fighting a bandit* and defeating him. So the Buddha speaks the two verses.

*It is noteworthy that her exploit is viewed in these terms, and never as the killing of a husband. Presumably it was felt that, because of his actions, the bandit had forfeited this status; however, this suggests a different view of marriage from that of many Hindu texts, where a woman is encouraged to be devoted to her husband, however badly he treats her.

104–5. *Better to conquer yourself*: Literally, 'A better conquest is self' – see K. R. Norman 1997: 89.
spirit: *gandhabba* – see Glossary.

STORY: A Brahmin asks the Buddha whether he knows about both winning and losing, and asks him about losing. The Buddha speaks of things that lead to loss. He then asks the man the reason for his interest in the topic, and the Brahmin reveals that he is a professional gambler. Sometimes he wins, and sometimes the other man wins. The Buddha says that such victories are trivial, and speaks the verse on the nature of the truest kind of victory.

106. *offerings*: Word added for clarity. The Commentary takes it as 'a thousand pieces of money'.

STORY: The uncle of Sāriputta – who comes from a Brahmin family – thinks he will win rebirth in the world of Brahmā by sacrificing every month with a thousand pieces of money. Sāriputta takes him to the Buddha, who points out that it would be better for the man if he were to offer a spoonful of boiled rice to Sāriputta.

107. STORY: As for v. 106, but told about Sāriputta's nephew.

108. *All that is not worth a quarter as much / As reverence to those who are upright*: Literally, 'All that does not go to a quarter, better is reverence to the straight-goers.'

STORY: As for v. 106, but told about a friend of Sāriputta.

109. A verse that is frequently recited in blessing after the giving of alms to monks. As was noted by Fausbøll (1855: 289), it is an almost exact translation of v. 2.121 of the Mānavadharmaśāstra, 'The Laws of Manu', an important Hindu text in Sanskrit dated to the late centuries BCE, except that in that text the four things said to increase are 'life-span, knowledge, fame and strength'.

STORY: According to a prediction, a boy is fated to be killed at an early age by a *yakkha* called Avaruddhaka; however, the Buddha recites protective chants for him, benign deities gather round, and Avaruddhaka is unable to touch him. The boy survives, and there is a new prediction: that he will live to 120 years of age. When the monks later discuss the things that might cause an increase in life-span, the Buddha speaks the verse.

110. *Better than living a hundred years . . . a meditator*: Literally, 'One who might live a hundred years . . . better [for him is] one day's life [when he is] well behaved, a meditator.'

STORY: The seven-year-old novice Saṃkicca is a remarkable child who is in his last life and ripe for Arahatship. He joins a group of forest monks. The leader of a gang of 500 bandits demands one of the monks to use as a human sacrifice. Though each of the monks volunteers to go, Saṃkicca insists, and is taken to the bandits' camp. The bandit leader proves miraculously unable to kill him, and he and his followers all become monks, followers of Saṃkicca. Commenting on the contrast between the present and past lives of these monks, the Buddha speaks the verse.

111. For the syntax, see the notes on v. 110.

STORY: The Elder Khāṇu Koṇḍañña sits so still in meditation in the forest that one night a gang of 500 bandits mistake him for a tree-stump (*khāṇu*, hence his name) and prop their bags of loot round him. In the morning, seeing him there, they think he is a spirit and start to run away. The Elder reassures them; they apologize, and ask him to ordain them as monks. The Buddha speaks the verse, as in v. 110.

112. For the syntax, see the notes on v. 110.

STORY: The Elder Sappadāsa ('Having a Snake as his Slave') becomes discontented as a monk, but does not wish to return to the lay life, so decides to commit suicide. He puts a snake into a jar, and tries to make it bite him, but it refuses. Then he decides to cut his throat with a razor, but just as the razor is resting against his throat he recollects his conduct since he joined the Order and realizes that it has been without fault. Filled with joy, he goes on to develop insight and attains Arahatship.

When he tells his fellow monks what has happened, they refuse to believe that anyone could have attained Arahatship in such a short time; they also wonder why the snake refused to bite him. The Buddha explains that the snake was Sappadāsa's slave in a previous life. Speaking the verse, he confirms that it is possible to achieve Arahatship in such a short time.

113. For the syntax, see the notes on v. 110.
arising and passing away: i.e. of beings.

STORY: Paṭācārā, born into a wealthy family of Sāvatthi, is kept in seclusion (cf. the story of Kuṇḍalakesī for vv. 102–3), but she falls in love with a servant boy and runs away with him. They live hard-working lives together in a village. When Paṭācārā becomes pregnant, she wishes to see her parents, according to custom, despite her husband's fear that they will ill-treat him; however, she gives birth to a son on the way, and returns to the village without seeing them.

A second time she becomes pregnant, and tries to see her parents, taking her husband and child with her. On the way, during a terrible storm, she goes into labour. Her husband goes to find brushwood to make a shelter for her, but is bitten by a snake and dies. Paṭācārā has the baby in the open. Thinking her husband has abandoned her, she continues towards her parents' house, carrying the baby on her hip and holding the other child by the hand. Finding her husband's body by the roadside, she blames herself for what has happened to him.

Eventually she reaches a river. She is too weak to carry both children, so she first takes the baby across, then goes back for the older child. But, while she is crossing, a bird of prey sees the baby and carries it off, thinking that it is a piece of meat. As she tries to shout at the bird to scare it away, the other child thinks she is calling him, runs into the river, and is swept away.

Paṭācārā carries on to Sāvatthi, hoping to find her parents, but there learns that the very same storm in which she suffered has blown down the family house, killing her mother, father and brother: they have only just been cremated. On hearing this final piece of news, Paṭācārā goes mad, and runs around the city naked, lamenting for her family. Some people call her a crazy woman, and throw things at her.

She comes to the Jetavana monastery, where the Buddha is staying. His followers try to keep her away from him, but he tells them to admit her. When she comes near to him, he tells her, 'Sister, regain mindfulness,' and she comes back to her senses. A man gives her his cloak, and she puts it on and prostrates herself before the Buddha. She begs him to be her refuge, and tells him her terrible story. He agrees to be her refuge, and tells her not to be troubled. Just as today, he explains, throughout her wanderings in *saṃsāra* she has shed tears over sons and other loved ones:

> More than the water in the four oceans
>   Is the vast expanse of tears,
> The grief of a man, touched by suffering.
>   Why then, lady, are you unaware?

As he speaks, her grief becomes less, and he reminds her (with Dhammapada vv. 288–9) that family cannot be a refuge at the time of death. She attains Stream-Entry, and asks to be ordained as a nun.

One day, as she pours out water to wash her feet, she sees that some streams run a little way, and disappear; some run a little further, and some further yet. It reminds her that some beings die in childhood, some in the prime of life, and some in old age. The Buddha sends a likeness of himself to stand before her and teach her, uttering the present verse. She attains Arahatship.

114. For the syntax, see the notes on v. 110.
the deathless state: *nibbāna*.

STORY: That of Kisā Gotamī and the mustard seed – perhaps the best-known of all Buddhist stories. Kisā Gotamī ('Gotamī the Lean'), from a poor background, marries a wealthy merchant's son. When she bears him a boy child, her happiness seems complete; but the boy dies as soon as he is able to walk. Unable to accept that he is dead, Kisā Gotamī wanders from house to house, carrying the child and asking for medicine to cure him, until a wise man sends her to the Buddha.

The Buddha tells her that he can cure the child if she brings him a pinch of mustard seed, but it has to be from a house where no one has died. As she searches from house to house, she realizes that there is no house where no one has died: the living are few, and the dead are many. She leaves the child's body in the forest, and returns to the Buddha. He teaches her with Dhammapada v. 287 – on which Kisā Gotamī attains Stream-Entry, and is ordained as a nun.

One night, seeing the flames of a lamp flaring up and flickering out, she contemplates impermanence. The Buddha sends a likeness of himself before her, to teach her and speak this verse, and she attains Arahatship.

115. For the syntax, see the notes on v. 110.

STORY: A wealthy laywoman, Bahuputtikā ('She Who has Many Children'), has seven sons and seven daughters, all of them married and doing well. When her husband dies, her sons keep trying to persuade her to give up her property to them, promising that they will look after her. But when she finally does so, her daughters-in-law treat her with contempt. Tiring of this, she leaves them and becomes a nun. As she has entered the Order in old age, she feels that she has to make an extra effort, and sits all night in meditation. The Buddha sends his likeness to her, and speaks the verse, and Bahuputtikā becomes an Arahat.

CHAPTER 9

EVIL

116. *what is right*: *kalyāṇa*, 'the pure', 'the meritorious', 'the good'. *good*: *puñña*.

STORY: Ekasāṭaka ('He Who has One Robe'), a poor Brahmin, and his wife have only one outer garment between them. They take it in turns to wear it, and go to hear the Buddha. One night, however, the Brahmin feels a strong urge to offer the garment to the Buddha, and, after struggling all night with selfish thoughts, he lays it at the Buddha's feet, crying out three times, 'I have won!' King Pasenadi is present, and on learning what the Brahmin has done he is so impressed that he gives him more clothes, which again Ekasāṭaka offers to the Buddha. In the end, Pasenadi rewards the Brahmin with four of everything (elephants, horses, thousands of coins, wives, female slaves, and villages). The Buddha tells the monks that if Ekasāṭaka had made the donation in the first watch, he would have received sixteen of everything; if in the middle watch, eight of everything; but as he did not give until the last watch he received only four of everything.

117. *painful*: *dukkha*.

STORY: A monk, discontented with the rule of celibacy, gets into the habit of masturbating – an offence requiring confession to the Order. The Buddha rebukes him with the verse.

118. *pleasant*: *sukha*.

STORY: A young woman who is parching corn (similar to making popcorn) in a field sees the Elder Kassapa the Great. Delighted, she offers him some of the corn and asks to share in the Dhamma that he has seen. Shortly afterwards she is bitten by a snake and dies; but, as she is still full of the joy of giving, she is reborn in the heaven of the Thirty-Three Gods as the goddess Lājā ('Parched Corn'). In her divine form, she comes back to clean Kassapa's cell and put out everything he needs, just as a novice monk would do.

When Kassapa finds her there, he fiercely rebukes her, and she is very upset. The Buddha explains to her that the Elder was right to maintain the rules regarding the contact between monks and women, but it is also understandable that she should wish to repeat the works of merit that have brought her such happiness.

119–20. *evil action . . . good action*: 'action' added for clarity.

STORY: The wealthy banker Anāthapiṇḍika falls on hard times, and loses his wealth. He continues to donate to the Buddha and the monks out of what he has. A deity* of his household tries to persuade him to give up making offerings in order to save what he has left. Because of this wrong advice, Anāthapiṇḍika evicts the deity from his household, and he/she can find nowhere else to stay. The deity approaches a succession of higher-ranking deities for help, without success, until Sakka advises him/her to perform an act to make amends to Anāthapiṇḍika, and then to ask his pardon.

The deity disguises him/herself as Anāthapiṇḍika's steward, approaches the banker's debtors, and recovers the money they owe him. He/she also finds him some hidden treasure without an owner, and so restores the banker to his former wealth. Finally the deity approaches Anāthapiṇḍika and begs his pardon.

121. STORY: A monk is in the habit of leaving his requisites lying about. He leaves his bed and chair outside, where they are liable to be destroyed by sun, rain and insects. When rebuked about it, he maintains that this is merely a trivial fault, and that very little damage has been done. The Buddha points out that this is not a useful way to think: a vessel left outside may not be filled by the first drop of rain, but if it stands out in rainfall after rainfall it will eventually be filled.

122. *good*: *puñña*.

STORY: A layman hears from the Buddha that it is good both to give and to urge others to give, so he invites the Buddha and his monks for a meal the next day, and asks all his fellow villagers to

*Burlingame (1921: II, 268–71) translates *devatā*, 'deity', as 'goddess'; but, though the word is grammatically feminine, it is used of any deity when the sex is not particularly important. Contrast the being in the previous story, who is specifically a *devadhītā* (literally, 'daughter of the gods') because her sex is relevant to the story.

join him in giving. A wealthy but somewhat stingy banker is angry that the layman has involved others in this way. The banker takes tiny amounts of food, such as he can hold between three fingers, and puts them in the offering-dish. (Because of this, he receives the nickname Biḷālapādaka – 'Cat's Foot'.) The layman puts together all the offerings from other people, but places the banker's offerings apart. He then puts grains from the banker's offerings into the other, more sumptuous, dishes. The banker thinks that the layman is planning to expose his meanness in front of everyone, so he hides a knife in his clothes, meaning to kill the layman before he can say anything about it. But the layman simply requests blessings on all those who have given, including the banker. Stricken by remorse, the banker confesses the whole story to the Buddha. The Buddha says that no good deed is a trifling matter, and speaks the verse. Biḷālapādaka attains Stream-Entry.

123. *evil actions*: 'actions' added for clarity.

STORY: A merchant called Mahādhana ('Great Wealth') abandons a planned journey because he has heard that 500 bandits are planning to plunder his caravan. A group of monks report this to the Buddha, and he speaks the verse. The monks attain Stream-Entry.

124. *for one who does not do evil*: 'evil' added for clarity.

STORY: A rich man's daughter falls in love with a hunter called Kukkuṭamitta ('Friend of Dogs' or 'Having Dogs as Friends') and follows him back into the forest. They marry, and she bears him seven sons. One day, when all the sons are grown up and married, the Buddha comes to the forest where Kukkuṭamitta and his sons hunt, and leaves his footprint near one of Kukkuṭamitta's nets. Kukkuṭamitta catches nothing that day, and when he sees the Buddha he blames him for it and wants to kill him. He aims his bow, but can neither shoot nor let it go. When his sons come looking for him, they too become fixed there like statues. When they do not return home, Kukkuṭamitta's wife goes looking for them, accompanied by her daughters-in-law.

Seeing the Buddha there, with the men pointing their arrows at him, Kukkuṭamitta's wife cries out, 'Don't kill my father! Don't kill my father!' The men take her words literally, thinking the Buddha is their father-in-law and grandfather, and at once have a change of heart towards him. The Buddha allows them to lower their bows, and they ask his pardon. He teaches the Dhamma to them, and Kukkuṭamitta with his seven sons and seven daughters-in-law attains Stream-Entry and gives up the taking of life.

Afterwards, discussing the event with Ānanda, the Buddha reveals that, while the rest of the family had attained Stream-Entry that day, Kukkuṭamitta's wife was a Stream-Enterer already, having reached that state while still a girl (not Arahatship, as Burlingame mistakenly has it (1921: II, 279)).

The monks are surprised that a girl who was a Stream-Enterer had married a hunter. Stream-Enterers do not take life; yet, every day, Kukkuṭamitta's wife had brought him his bow, arrows and nets, which he had used for precisely this purpose. The Buddha explains that she had acted not with the intention of taking life, but simply with the intention of doing her husband's bidding.

125. STORY: A hunter called Koka meets a monk in the forest and blames him for his lack of success in hunting. Koka sets his dogs on the monk, who climbs a tree. Koka shoots the monk in the feet, and in his agony the monk lets his outer robe fall off. It lands on the hunter, whose dogs mistake him for the monk and devour him. The monk is greatly troubled, fearing that he himself has caused the hunter's death. The Buddha reassures him, and tells the story of a previous birth in which Koka had tried to kill someone else and suffered death himself in the same way.

126. *Some find a womb*: i.e. are reborn as human beings or animals. *Those who go well*: *sugatino*, perhaps a pun, suggesting as it does both those who behave well and those who have a good rebirth (*gati*).

STORY: A jeweller and his wife regularly offer alms-food to an Elder called Tissa. One day, while the Elder is there, the jeweller receives a messenger from King Pasenadi, bringing a ruby to be cut and polished. When the jeweller is not looking, the family's pet crane swallows the ruby, thinking it is a piece of meat. The jeweller accuses the Elder of stealing the jewel, and, despite the remonstrances of his wife, he tortures and beats the monk. While so doing, he also strikes and kills the crane, which is nearby.

Once the crane is dead, the monk can reveal that it has eaten the jewel, which is then found in its crop. (He would not say anything before, to protect the bird from the jeweller.) The jeweller repents, and begs the monk for forgiveness, which he grants.

Soon after, the monk dies as the result of the ill treatment he has received. Being an Arahat, he attains *nibbāna*. The crane is reborn in the womb of the jeweller's wife. When the jeweller's wife dies, she is reborn in a heavenly world, because of her kind thoughts towards the monk. The jeweller is reborn in a hell world.

127. STORY: Three groups of monks, on their way to visit the Buddha, witness or experience disturbing events. They ask the Buddha for explanations. (1) A thatched roof catches fire, and some of the burning thatch flies up into the air. A crow, flying past, is caught by it and burned to death. (2) A woman, thought to be a bringer of bad luck at sea, is thrown overboard and drowns. (3) Seven monks are trapped in a cavern when a rock falls in front of it. No one can remove it, but on the seventh day it rolls away by itself.

In each case, the Buddha offers an explanation. (1) The crow was formerly a farmer, who burned to death an ox that would not do what he wanted it to. As a result, he had suffered this fate in his last seven existences. (2) The woman had formerly drowned a dog, which had annoyed her by persistently following her. (It had been her husband in a yet earlier life, and had not lost its affection for her.) She had therefore suffered death by drowning in her last hundred existences. (3) The monks had been cowherd boys who had kept a lizard trapped without food. However, in the end they had let it go. They had suffered a similar fate in their last fourteen existences.

128. STORY: Suppabuddha, the Buddha's uncle and former father-in-law, resents him for abandoning his daughter – and perhaps also on behalf of his son, Devadatta. He repeatedly insults the Buddha by standing drinking in the street, and blocking his path to the houses where he has been invited for alms: a serious offence. The Buddha turns back without saying anything, but he smiles. When Ānanda asks him why, the Buddha tells him that, as a result of his offence, in seven days' time, while standing on the ground floor of his palace, Suppabuddha will be swallowed by the earth (cf. the story for v. 17). When a spy reports this back to Suppabuddha, he makes up his mind to prove the Buddha wrong. He goes to live on the top floor of his palace, and has the stairs removed. He has two strong men stationed at each door, with orders to prevent him from going down, whatever might happen. Hearing of these precautions, the Buddha comments that

there is nowhere that Suppabuddha can go to avoid his fate, and he speaks the verse.

On the seventh day, the royal charger breaks loose on the ground floor of the palace. Suppabuddha, hearing the commotion, makes a move to go down to it, since he alone knows how to quiet the horse. At that moment the doors swing open, the stairs reappear, and the strong men posted at the door seize Suppabuddha by the neck and throw him down. This happens again on every floor. When he reaches the ground floor, the earth opens and swallows him up, and he is reborn in the Avīci hell.

CHAPTER 10
THE ROD

Daṇḍa – literally, 'rod', 'stick' – is also widely used figuratively in senses such as 'punishment', 'violence'. Some previous translators of the Dhammapada have translated it in this chapter as 'violence'. I have kept to the more literal translation, since the word is used in the chapter in the literal (v. 135) as well as the figurative senses. I did not think that readers would have any difficulty in understanding this usage, since figurative expressions such as 'the big stick' are also common in English.

129–30. *All beings*: 'beings' inserted for clarity.
Seeing their likeness to yourself, / You should neither kill nor cause to kill: Literally, 'Making [one]self the simile [i.e. comparing them with oneself], one should neither kill nor cause to kill.'

STORY: The Commentary clearly takes the latter clause in the sense of 'neither strike nor cause to strike', which is also possible. The stories concern groups of monks who (v. 129) fall out over lodgings and come to blows or (v. 130) fall out over lodgings and make threatening gestures to one another.

131–2. Verse 131 is closely paralleled in Hindu literature in the Laws of Manu (Mānavadharmaśāstra V.45 – cf. v. 109 above) and the Mahābhārata (XIII.5568) – see Müller 1881: 37.
hereafter: *pecca* – literally, 'having passed on', 'having died'.

STORY: The Buddha finds some boys tormenting a snake with a stick, and gives them this teaching.

133–4. Verse 133 is paralleled by Mahābhārata XII.4056 – see Müller 1881: 37.
painful: *dukkha*.
You don't let yourself make a noise: Literally, 'You don't cause yourself to utter [a sound].' In vv. 133–4 the 'you' is a genuine second-person singular, not the indefinite 'one'.

STORY: This concerns a dispute between monks. One of them is followed around by the figure of a woman, and so is accused of breaking his vows. In fact the apparition is rooted in his behaviour in a previous life, when he was a goddess who jealously tried to come between two monks who were close to one another. Through the verses, the Buddha advises him not to quarrel with the other monks any more.

135. *Drives . . . End*: There seems to be a pun here on *pāj-*, 'drive [cattle]', and *pāj-*, 'end' (< *pāc*) – see K. R. Norman 1997: 95.

STORY: A group of 500 women are observing a fast-day. When Visākhā asks them why they are doing it, the older ones say that they desire to be reborn in a heavenly world; the middle-aged ones seek to be freed from the power of their co-wives;* the young ones want children; while the single girls want husbands. None of them is actually seeking freedom from rebirth. When Visākhā reports this to the Buddha, he speaks the verse.

136. *He does not understand*: i.e. that his life will soon be ended by Death.

STORY: Moggallāna and Lakkhaṇa see a ghost (*peta*) in the form of a large snake, its body surrounded by flames (cf. the stories for vv. 71, 72). The Buddha reveals that the being was reborn in that state because in the time of the Buddha Kassapa he was a thief who bore a grudge against a banker who had spotted him attempting a robbery. He persecuted the banker, attacking his cattle, and eventually burning down a dwelling-place that the banker was planning to offer to the Buddha Kassapa, so adding to the seriousness of the crime.

137–40. *who do no harm*: Literally, 'who do little harm'.

**sapattivāsā*. Burlingame (1921: II, 300) interprets their reply as 'from the power of our husbands', from the variant reading *sapati*, 'one's own husband', in place of *sapatti*, 'co-wife'.

STORY: The Commentary retells the story of the death of Moggallāna. Paid by rival ascetics, bandits attack Moggallāna and leave him for dead. Though all his bones are broken, by the power of meditation the great Arahat manages to hold himself firm, and soars through the air to pay his respects to the Buddha before he dies. At the Buddha's invitation, he teaches and performs various miracles, following which he dies, attaining *parinibbāna*. His murderers – both the rival ascetics and the bandits – are caught by King Ajātasattu and burned to death.

The monks are troubled that Moggallāna the Great has met an undeserved end. The Buddha explains that, though this is true as regards the present life, in a previous existence Moggallāna was a son who beat his old blind parents to death, pretending to be an attacking band of robbers. (The Jātaka version differs: in this, hearing his parents pleading with the supposed bandits for their son's life, he eventually relented – Jātaka 522, 125–6.) As a result, he suffered in a hell realm for a very long time, and afterwards met with a similar death in a hundred existences. So both he and the rival ascetics had in fact suffered the consequences of previous actions.

The idea that the great Arahat Moggallāna had had a dark past in previous existences goes back to the Canon. In Majjhima Nikāya 1.332–8 (Sutta 50: the Māratajjanīya, or 'Warning to Māra', Sutta), Māra attempts to possess Moggallāna, but the great Arahat recognizes and expels him. Moggallāna tells him how he himself had been the Māra of a previous age of the world, named Dūsi, 'Corrupter'. He had tempted laypeople to attack the followers of the Buddha Kakusandha, as a result of which he had suffered in hell realms (graphically described) for a long time. The Māra of the present age was the son of Māra Dūsi's sister Kāḷī, so Moggallāna can speak to him as his uncle. He uses his own experience to warn him in vivid terms of the danger of attacking someone like him.

141. *Can purify*: 'Can' inserted for clarity.

STORY: A monk, formerly a rich man, who has hung on to too many possessions is rebuked by the Buddha. Angrily, he removes all his garments but one and stands like that in the middle of the assembly. The Buddha rebukes him for his immodesty, telling a story of the monk's past life when, despite being a *yakkha* with a taste for human flesh, he had kept his modesty.

The Commentary seems to have interpreted the verse as being primarily about immodesty. In the verse itself, however, the practice of going naked is viewed as an extreme form of asceticism, not as immodesty. Ascetic practices performed without meaning are contrasted in the following verse with household practices carried out by one with true understanding. Perhaps naked ascetics were not such a common sight in fifth-century-CE Sri Lanka as they must have been in India in the late centuries BCE.

142. *Even though you wear fine clothes*: Literally, 'If [one is] adorned' – i.e. wearing the jewellery and adornments of a layperson.
living the holy life: *brahmacārin*, often technically meaning 'celibate', but sometimes, as here, referring more generally to one who practises the spiritual life.
wanderer: *samaṇa*.

STORY: A royal minister called Santati returns to Kosala after putting down a rebellion on the borders. The people of Kosala are extremely grateful to him, and King Pasenadi provides him with every luxury, including a beautiful court dancer to dance and sing for him. Santati spends seven days indulging in pleasures and getting very drunk. He then mounts the royal elephant and heads towards the bathing place on the river. On the way he meets the Buddha, who is walking to the city on his alms-round. Santati, seated on the elephant and dressed with royal ornaments, retains enough awareness to bow his head to the Buddha. The Buddha smiles. When Ānanda asks him the reason, he explains that, that very day, and adorned as he is, Santati will attain Arahatship and afterwards pass into *nibbāna*. Naturally, seeing the state the young man is in, many of those present are incredulous.

Santati goes back to the palace and gets ready for yet more indulgence. The beautiful dancer appears and begins to perform. She has fasted for seven days, to try to make her performance even more graceful, and as she dances she suddenly dies, struck down perhaps by a heart attack: 'knife-like pains arose in her belly and as it were cut the flesh of her heart asunder' (Burlingame 1921: II, 313). Santati, instantly sober, is overcome by terrible grief. He realizes that only the Buddha can help him now, and goes to see him. The Buddha explains that this is not the first time that Santati has wept over this woman: more than the water in the four oceans is the volume of tears that he has shed for her in countless lives. Santati attains Arahatship and dies, entering *parinibbāna*.

143–4. Some editions place the first two *pādas* of v. 144 (the first two lines in the translation) at the end of v. 143, so that v. 144 begins with 'By faith, morality and effort'.

honour: *hiri* – see Glossary.

avoids blame: K. R. Norman (1997: 20, 96) has 'thinks little of blame', reading *appabodhati* for *apabodhati*. However, I think the mention of *hiri* gives support to the traditional interpretation.

swift: *saṃvegin*, 'possessed of urgency'.

Endowed with knowledge and conduct: Words often used in praise of the Buddha.

this suffering, great though it is: Literally, 'this not-small (*anappakaṃ*) suffering (*dukkha*)', but the position of *anappakaṃ*, at the end of the verse and after the verb, seems to emphasize it.

STORY: A man who owns only one ragged cloth becomes a monk, and receives offerings of robes and food from the laypeople. Whenever he becomes discontented with the monastic life, he goes and contemplates his old ragged cloth. He calls it 'visiting his teacher'. In time he attains Arahatship, and no longer needs to do this.

145. As v. 80, but with *subbatā* ('those who are true to their vows') for *paṇḍitā*.

STORY: That of a boy novice called Sukha, very similar to that of Paṇḍita Dāraka accompanying v. 80.

CHAPTER 11

OLD AGE

146. *the world*: Added for clarity.

STORY: Some women companions of Visākhā get drunk, and laugh and dance in the presence of the Buddha when they should be listening to his teaching. A deity from Māra's host tries to take the opportunity to possess them, but is driven away by the Buddha, who sends out a dark-blue ray and plunges the place into darkness. He then sends forth a bright ray of light, as though a thousand moons had risen at once. Terrified, the women come to their senses, and are established in the Buddha's teaching.

147. *with many imaginings*: *bahusaṅkappaṃ*. It is not clear whether

the imaginings are those of the person whose body it is or of others. If the latter, Carter and Palihawadana's translation, 'highly fancied', is very much to the point (1987: 215).

STORY: A monk falls desperately in love with Sirimā, a beautiful courtesan who has become a devoted follower of the Buddha and a generous supporter of the monks. (For her earlier life, see the story for v. 223.) Sirimā is suddenly taken ill and dies. The Buddha requests the king that her body should be left unburned for four days, with a guard to make sure that it is not eaten by birds and animals. At the end of that time the Buddha calls everyone together, including the enamoured monk. He arranges for a drummer to announce that the body is for sale, first for large sums of money, then for increasingly smaller sums, until it is offered for nothing. When Sirimā was alive, men would pay enormous sums of money just to spend a night with her; but no one wants her body now that she is dead. The monk, understanding the impermanence of the body, attains Stream-Entry.

148. STORY: A 120-year-old nun donates all her food to a monk, for three days in succession. On the third day she trips and falls over, and the Buddha speaks this verse.

149. STORY: Some monks, who have a high opinion of their own attainments, are sent off to meditate in the cremation ground. But when they see some corpses that have started to decay they feel revulsion, while when they see others that are still undecayed they feel desire. They then realize that they are not yet rid of the defilements. The Buddha sends a likeness of himself to appear before them and utter this verse.

150. *A city made of bones*: i.e. the body.
old age and death, / Pride and hypocrisy: The equivalent verses in GDhp (284) and Uv (16.23) have 'passion and ill will' in place of 'old age and death' – Brough 1962: 263. 'PDhp. has no equivalent verse' – Carter and Palihawadana 1987: 460.

STORY: The Buddha's half-sister, Nandā, who is renowned for her beauty, is ordained as a nun. Hearing that her brother disparages beauty, she avoids hearing him teach. When she is eventually prevailed upon to hear him, he causes to appear before her the figure of a beautiful girl, about sixteen years old, who, even as Nandā watches, grows to old age, becomes ill, and eventually dies. Seeing this, Nandā begins to understand impermanence and suffering. The Buddha speaks verses on the nature of the body, and she attains Stream-Entry. He then encourages her to meditate on emptiness, speaking the Dhammapada verse, and she attains Arahatship.

151. STORY: While Mallikā, the wife of King Pasenadi, is bathing, her pet dog comes in and tries to have sex with her. Apparently she is amused, and does not try to stop him. When the king happens to see this and questions her about it, she does not acknowledge what has happened, but concocts an elaborate lie so that her husband does not believe the evidence of his own eyes.

At the time of her death, instead of remembering all the good actions she has done in her life, Mallikā remembers this one wrong act (primarily the deceit against her husband, rather than the possible sexual misdemeanour), and is reborn in the Avīci hell, where she has to stay for seven days. The king, who adored her, goes to visit the Buddha every day, meaning to ask him where his late wife has been reborn. Each day, the Buddha engages him in such fascinating conversation that he forgets to ask.

On the eighth day, when Mallikā has once more been reborn, the Buddha allows Pasenadi to remember his question, and reveals that she is now in the Tusita heaven. Pasenadi speaks of his grief at his loss, and the Buddha comforts him with the verse.

152. STORY: The Elder Lāḷudāyi always says the wrong thing: when invited to chant at a funeral, he chants cheerful verses; while at festive occasions, he chants funeral verses. The Buddha tells the story of a previous birth in which Lāḷudāyi had also said the wrong thing. (Lāḷudāyi (probably meaning 'Udāyi the Chatterer') may or may not be the same as the Udāyi in the stories for vv. 64 and 241, since there was also a learned Arahat called Lāḷudāyi.)

153–4. *I wandered . . . A journey of many births*: Literally, 'I ran through a *saṃsāra* of many births' (*aneka-jāti-saṃsāraṃ sandhāvissaṃ*).

without respite: Following K. R. Norman 1997: 22, 153. The commentarial reading takes *anibbisaṃ* as 'not finding', i.e. in vain. The Udānavarga (31.6) has *punaḥ punaḥ*, 'again and again', as at the end of the last line of the same verse.

The house-builder: Māra.
house: Body.
The mind, freed from conditioned things: *visaṅkhāra-gataṃ cittaṃ* – 'the mind (*citta*), which has gone beyond the *saṅkhāras* [see Glossary]'. *Citta*, generally translated as 'mind', covers all aspects of consciousness, including much of what would be called 'heart' in English.

STORY: Some of the central verses of Buddhism, these are the words of triumph spoken by the Buddha when he has achieved enlightenment under the Bodhi tree.

155–6. *holy life*: *brahmacariya*, perhaps in the sense of 'celibacy'.
wealth: Presumably spiritual wealth, merit. In the story it refers to both spiritual and worldly goods.
like wasted arrows: *cāpātikhīṇā va*, literally, according to the Commentary, 'as though shot from a bow'; but *ati-khī-* seems to have connotations of waste (*khī-*) and of over-shooting (*ati*). Rhys Davids and Stede (1972, 18 – under *atikhīṇa*) suggest '[shot] from a broken bow'. In any case, the comparison is with the arrows, lying wasted on the ground, not with the person or animal who has been shot.

STORY: Mahādhana ('Great Wealth'), a banker's son, is born with every material advantage: 'eighty crores' (800 million) of treasure. His parents, thinking that he will never have to earn a living, do not trouble to have him taught anything but the arts of playing an instrument and singing. He is married to the daughter of another banker: she too has access to 'eighty crores' of treasure, and has learned nothing but how to sing and dance. When their parents are dead, they live at first in great luxury, but Mahādhana falls in with bad company and becomes addicted to alcohol. He spends all his money, and then his wife's money, until the couple are reduced to begging. One day the Buddha sees them in this state and smiles.

When Ānanda asks the reason, the Buddha explains what he was thinking: that this was a wealthy banker's son, who had squandered two fortunes. If, in his prime, he had devoted himself to business, he could have become the principal banker in the city; or, if he had become a monk, he would have attained Arahatship, and his wife would have attained the state of Non-Return. If he had similarly applied himself in middle life, he could have become the second banker of the city; or, if he had become a monk, he would have attained Non-Return and his wife Once-Return. If he had made such a commitment in old age, he could have become the third banker of the city; or, if he had become a monk, he would have attained Once-Return and his wife Stream-Entry. As it is, he has squandered his chances in both the material and the spiritual realms, and is left like a heron in a dried-up pond.

CHAPTER 12
SELF

157. *the three watches*: Divisions of the night; but in the story it is taken as referring to the three periods of life.

STORY: A group of stories about a prince called Bodhi:

(i) A story reminiscent of that of Daedalus in Greek myth. Prince Bodhi has engaged a builder (name not given) to create a wonderful palace for him. Anxious that no other ruler should have one like it, he determines to kill or mutilate the builder on completion. The builder hears of this, and, pretending that there is still work to do on the palace, insists he has to work in seclusion, with only his wife bringing him food. He then builds a flying *garuḍa* bird. When it is ready, he tells his wife to sell all their possessions for gold, and to bring their children to him. Together, they make their escape in the *garuḍa* bird.

(ii) When the palace is complete, Prince Bodhi invites the Buddha to receive alms in a sumptuous room. He has the floor spread with costly carpets, thinking, 'If I am destined to have a son or daughter, the Teacher will step on these carpets.' But the Buddha will not enter the room until the carpets have been rolled up and taken away, for Prince Bodhi is destined not to father any children.

(iii) The explanation of Prince Bodhi's childlessness. In a previous birth, he and his wife were shipwrecked on an island with a colony of birds. They survived by living on first the eggs, then the young of the birds, without a moment's remorse.

When the Buddha explains all this, and speaks the verse, Prince Bodhi attains Stream-Entry.

158. *defiled*: The Commentary takes this as 'wearied', another possible meaning.

STORY: A greedy monk offers to help in the proper apportioning of donations between two younger monks. He chooses the best items for himself. The Buddha tells the story of a previous life, in which the two young monks were otters, who were arguing over a fish they had caught. They appealed to a jackal (the greedy monk) to act as judge between them. He allotted the head to one otter and the tail to another, and kept the body for himself.

159. *tame others*: 'others' added for clarity.

STORY: The Elder Padhānika Tissa and 500 monks whom he is supposed to be supervising receive a meditation object from the Buddha, and go off to practise. Padhānika Tissa expects the monks to stay awake throughout the three watches of the night. They become too tired to achieve anything, while he himself sleeps.

When they report their experience to the Buddha, he recounts a Jātaka story in which Padhānika Tissa had been a cock who crowed at the wrong times, and ended up having his neck wrung.

160. *protector*: *nātha*, often translated as 'lord'. However, it has a strong connotation of a person to whom one goes for refuge.

STORY: A woman becomes a nun without knowing that she is pregnant. When it starts to show, Devadatta and his followers accuse her of having broken her vow of celibacy, and wish to expel her from the Order. The Buddha instructs the Elder Upāli, expert in the Vinaya, to find out the truth of the matter. Upāli asks Visākhā, with her vast experience as a mother and grandmother, to take the nun to a private place and examine her. She realizes that the nun's pregnancy is so advanced that she must have conceived before she was ordained. She has done nothing wrong, and can remain as a nun.

In due time she gives birth to a splendid boy, who is at first brought up by the nuns. When King Pasenadi finds out about this arrangement, he thinks it unsuitable, and takes the boy home for his daughters to bring up, giving him the name Kumāra Kassapa ('Kassapa the Prince'). But, when he is old enough to find out the story of his birth, Kumāra Kassapa himself wishes to be ordained as a monk. He is, and in time attains Arahatship.

However, the nun, his mother, has never got over her separation from him, and continues to weep for her loss. When at last she meets Kumāra Kassapa, she is overcome with maternal feeling, runs up to him, flings herself at his feet, and then tries to embrace him: all behaviour unsuitable to those who are trying to live the monastic life. Kumāra Kassapa reproaches her with words that are apparently harsh, but in reality intended to help her to overcome this excessive attachment. Shocked, she herself then attains Arahatship.

Some monks, discussing the matter, remark that, if Devadatta had had his way, neither Kumāra Kassapa nor his mother would have attained Arahatship; but the Buddha had proved a true refuge to them. The Buddha, however, tells them that one must be one's own refuge.

161. *thunderbolt*: *vajira*, believed to be made of diamond, and so harder than all other stones.
gemstone: Literally, 'a gem made of stone'.

STORY: Mahākāla, a layman Stream-Enterer who has spent all night listening to the Buddha's teaching, is wrongly accused of robbery and beaten to death. The monks are shocked at this injustice. However, the Buddha explains that, though it is unjust as regards the present life, in a previous existence Mahākāla was a soldier who framed a man for theft in order to get hold of his beautiful wife.

162. *māluvā creeper*: 'creeper' added for clarity. The identity of the *māluvā* is uncertain, but clearly it is a creeper which begins as a small plant, but eventually strangles and kills the tree that supports it – possibly *Bauhinia vahlii* (Singh 1978).

STORY: The Commentary recounts in brief the canonical story of Devadatta's attempt to assassinate the Buddha. The Buddha then tells of a previous life in which Devadatta had tried to kill him. When he speaks the verse, many of those listening attain Stream-Entry.

163. *Things that are wrong and bad for you*: Literally, 'Wrong [things] and [things that are] disadvantageous [for one]', but I assume that the same actions are referred to in each case.

STORY: The Commentary recounts in brief the canonical story of Devadatta's attempt to cause schism in the Order. Devadatta tries to impose a more ascetic regime on the monks, and some recently ordained monks are impressed and follow him. When Ānanda tells the Buddha what is happening, he speaks the verse to warn of the seriousness of what Devadatta is doing. He sends Sāriputta and Moggallāna to the monks who had followed Devadatta, and most of them return to the Buddha.

164. *bamboo*: *kaṭṭhaka* (< Sanskrit *kaṇṭaka*), the spiny bamboo, which flowers only once in about thirty years, and then dies (K. R. Norman 1997: 104; Rau 1959: 169).

STORY: The Elder Kāla so enjoys having the support of an elderly laywoman that he tries to prevent her from hearing teaching from the Buddha himself. When this fails, Kāla tries to persuade the Buddha that she is not intelligent enough to understand the higher aspects of the Dhamma, and should be taught only basic matters such as generosity and morality. Understanding Kāla's motives, the Buddha speaks the verse, and the laywoman attains Stream-Entry.

165. *individual matters*: 'matters' added for clarity.

STORY: Cūḷakāla – like Mahākāla in the story for v. 161 – is wrongly accused of robbery. However, he is saved by some maids on their way to fetch water, who have seen what really happened. (Burlingame (1921: II, 365) has 'courtezans, on their way to the bathing-place on the river', but the Pali just has *kumbhadāsiyo udakatittham gacchamānā* – literally, 'water-pot-slaves [fem.] going to the water-crossing-place' – which suggests that they are simply collecting the day's water for their households.)

166. STORY: The Buddha announces that in four months he will pass away in *parinibbāna*. Many monks who have not yet attained Stream-Entry are grieved, and will not leave the Buddha's side. However, the Elder Attadattha ('Self-Benefit') determines to attain Arahatship while the Buddha is still alive. He goes away by himself to meditate, for which he is criticized by the other monks, who think he cannot love the Buddha as much as they do. However, the Buddha praises Attadattha, saying that others should follow his example. He speaks the verse, and Attadattha attains Arahatship.

CHAPTER 13
THE WORLD

167. *attached to the world*: Literally, 'one who increases/fosters the world(s)'.

STORY: A granddaughter of Visākhā teases a young monk by calling him *chinnasīsa*, 'cut-head'. He is offended, though his

Elder says that it is no offence to a monk to say that he has cut off his hair. However, as the Buddha points out to Visākhā, on this occasion it was clearly meant in a disparaging way.

The young monk is pleased that the Buddha has understood him, as neither his Elder nor Visākhā apparently had. The Buddha, pointing out that it is never right to be unaware, speaks the verse, and the young monk attains Stream-Entry.

168–9. *You should stand up, be aware*: Literally, 'One should stand up, not be unaware' – see the introduction to the notes on Chapter 2. *In this world and the next*: Literally, 'In this world and the other'.

STORY: After his enlightenment, the Buddha returns to his own city, Kapilavatthu. His father, King Suddhodana, is very offended when, instead of going straight to the family home, his son goes from house to house for alms. The king says that this is not the way of their lineage. The Buddha replies that it is the way of *his* lineage, the countless thousands of Buddhas of the past. He speaks the verses, on the importance of keeping the proper practice, and Suddhodana attains Stream-Entry.

170. For the imagery of the verse, cf. v. 46, which could almost be an expansion of this one in a different (and longer) metre.

STORY: A story similar to that for v. 46, but told of a group of 500 monks.

171. STORY: That of Prince Abhaya, which resembles that of Santati (see the story for v. 142).

172. *afterwards becomes aware*: Literally, 'afterwards is not unaware'.

STORY: The monk Sammuñjani ('Broom') spends his whole time sweeping the monastery. He disapproves of the Elder Revata, who spends a great deal of time in meditation. Revata tells Sammuñjani how to spend his time more profitably, with times set aside for meditation and study, as well as a certain amount of sweeping. Sammuñjani does as instructed, and soon attains Arahatship. When the monks complain about the (relatively) unswept state of the monastery, the Buddha speaks the verse in praise of Sammuñjani.

173. *Whoever has done an evil deed / But covers it with a virtuous*

one / Illuminates: The Pali structure does not seem to allow direct translation into English: literally, 'Of whom the evil deed done [before] is covered by a virtuous [deed], that one illuminates . . . '
virtuous: *kusala*, 'skilful', 'wholesome'.

STORY: The famous tale (somewhat expanded from the version known from the Canon) of Aṅgulimāla ('Finger Garland'), a murderous bandit who became a monk and an Arahat.

Aṅgulimāla is born a Brahmin, the son of King Pasenadi's chaplain. When he is a student, the other students are jealous of him and persuade their teacher that he is having an affair with the teacher's wife – a very serious crime. Instead of killing him directly, the teacher asks him to kill a thousand people and bring him a finger from each. Aṅgulimāla becomes a much-feared bandit, wearing a garland of fingers. When he needs only one more finger to make up the thousand, the Buddha realizes that, if he does not intervene, Aṅgulimāla will kill his own mother, an act with enormous kammic consequences, so he decides to meet him himself instead.

When Aṅgulimāla sees the figure of a monk ahead of him, he determines to kill him, and begins to chase him; but, though he seems to be running fast and the monk is not moving, he cannot catch him. Aṅgulimāla shouts, 'Stop!' The Buddha replies, 'I have stopped: you are the one who has not stopped.' Aṅgulimāla understands, throws away his weapon, and asks to be admitted to the Order. When the king and his troops come looking for the dangerous bandit, instead they find a monk, living peacefully at the Buddha's monastery. Aṅgulimāla works hard at his practice, and soon attains Arahatship.

One day, when on his alms-round, Aṅgulimāla is hit with stones and mortally wounded. Encouraged by the Buddha, he bears his suffering with patience, understanding that he is experiencing the consequences of past evil actions that would otherwise have led to prolonged suffering in hell realms, and he dies peacefully. Other monks ask the Buddha where he has been reborn, since he has killed so many people. The Buddha speaks the verse, pointing out that the wrong that Aṅgulimāla did in the past has been overwhelmed by the good that he has done since he became a monk.

174. *the rare one*: Literally, 'few', but in the singular. The idea is that such persons are as rare as birds which get free from a bird-catcher's net.

STORY: When the Buddha visits Āḷavi, he speaks of the importance of meditating on death, so that when our end comes we will not be overcome by fear. Only one of his hearers takes any notice of this – the sixteen-year-old daughter (name not given) of a weaver, who practises this meditation day and night for three years. At the end of that time, the Buddha returns to Āḷavi. The girl longs to see him again; but, before she can go to the meeting, she has to refill a shuttle with thread to take to her father's workshop, so she turns up late. The Buddha, who has come this way specifically to see her, sits silent until she appears, on her way to the workshop. When she arrives, he asks her four questions. He asks, 'Girl, where have you come from?' She replies, 'I don't know, *bhante*.' He asks, 'Where are you going?' She replies, 'I don't know, *bhante*.' He asks, 'Do you not know?' She replies, 'I know, *bhante*.' He asks, 'Do you know?' She replies, 'I don't know, *bhante*.' The other citizens are offended by her words, and accuse her of talking nonsense: when he asked her where she came from, she should have said, 'From the weaver's house,' and when he asked where she was going, she should have said, 'To the weaver's workshop.'

The Buddha silences the crowd, and asks her why she answered as she did. She explains that when he asked her where she was coming from, of course he knew that she came from the weaver's house, so he must have meant something else. She took it to mean, 'Where did you come from when you were born here?', so replied, 'I don't know.' When he asked her where she was going, he knew that she was going to the weaver's workshop, so he must have meant something else. She took it to mean, 'Where are you going when you leave the present existence?', so replied, 'I don't know.' When he asked, 'Do you not know?', she knew that he meant, 'Do you not know that you must die?', so replied, 'I know.' When he asked, 'Do you know?', she knew that he meant, 'Do you know when you will die?', so replied, 'I don't know.' The Buddha acclaims her answers and speaks the verse. She attains Stream-Entry.

The girl then goes to the weaver's workshop, where, not realizing that her father is asleep, she makes to hand him the shuttle of thread. He is startled awake, and accidentally knocks the beam of the loom into his daughter's chest. She dies, and is reborn in the Tusita heaven. The father, distraught, goes to the Buddha for consolation. He ordains as a monk, and soon attains Arahatship.

175. *Geese go by the sun's path; / Mages go through the sky*: *haṃsādiccapathe yanti ākāse yanti iddhiyā*. There has been considerable argument about how this verse is to be understood. Most translators have taken *iddhiyā* in *pāda* b as the instrumental of *iddhi*: 'by psychic power'. The question then is whether the subject is still the geese ('Geese go by the sun's path; / By psychic power they go through the sky') or whether it refers to an indefinite 'they': 'By psychic power [folk] go through the sky', which seems to be how the Commentary takes it. (It might even refer back, in sense if not in grammar, to the rare individual who escapes the net of *saṃsāra* in v. 174.) However, I have preferred to take *iddhiyā* as a nominative plural of **iddhiya*: '[person] of psychic power', equivalent to *iddhika* (which is known to Rhys Davids and Stede (1972: 121), though apparently only on the end of compounds, e.g. *mahiddhika*, 'of great psychic power'). This then makes *pāda* b balance a in the manner characteristic of Dhammapada verse. Versions of the verse in other Dharmapadas show a degree of variation that suggests that it was early seen as problematic; however, this can be explained if **iddhiya* was otherwise unknown, since *iddhiyā* as the instrumental of *iddhi* would have been in common use.
Geese: See v. 91 and note.
Mages: See my comments above. Psychic powers, including such abilities as walking on water and flying through the air (see Glossary under *iddhi*), were thought to be the province not just of those who cultivated them as an end in themselves, but also of Arahats and indeed of the Buddha himself, who acquired them as a side effect of their meditational attainments. The commentarial story seems to take *pāda* b as referring to the psychic abilities of Arahats; however, it is possible that the poet was thinking primarily of those with less exalted aims, so that in *pāda* a we have 'geese' and in *pāda* b 'sorcerers' or 'shamans' both contrasted with the higher attainments of 'the wise' (or 'the steadfast' – *dhīrā*) in *pādas* c and d – a typical Dhammapada sequence.

STORY: Thirty monks visit the Buddha to hear his teaching, as a result of which they all attain Arahatship. Ānanda, waiting outside the Buddha's room, sees them go in but not go out again. When he asks the reason, the Buddha explains that, now that they have attained Arahatship, they have attained psychic powers, and have gone out flying through space. The Buddha then utters the verse.

176. Another slightly problematic verse. The question is, what is the force of *ekaṃ dhammaṃ atītassa*? K. R. Norman (1997: 26) takes it as referring to the (upper-case) Dhamma: 'There is no evil which cannot be done by a creature who has transgressed the unique law, speaks falsely, has abandoned the other world.' I think it means one (lower-case) *dhamma*, the precept against wrong speech (whose terminology the verse quotes). The Commentary, which glosses *ekaṃ dhammaṃ* as *saccaṃ*, 'truth', seems to back this interpretation. The same verse is also found in another Khuddaka Nikāya text, the Itivuttaka (1.25), where again the point is made that, of all the precepts, if a person breaks the one against wrong speech, there is no wrong that he won't do.
just one dhamma: 'just' added for clarity.

STORY: Ciñcā Māṇavikā is engaged by rival ascetics to discredit the Buddha. She goes through an elaborate performance, first pretending to visit his dwelling at unseemly hours, then wrapping a lump of wood under her clothes to make her look pregnant, and even beating her hands and feet to make them appear swollen. Finally, she appears before the Buddha in an assembly and reproaches him for not making any provision for the birth of the child she is carrying. The Buddha says, 'Sister, only you and I know which of us is telling the truth.' Becoming aware of the situation, Sakka and other gods take the form of mice and nibble the cords holding Ciñcā's 'bump' in place. It falls off, revealing the truth and cutting off her toes. Once she leaves the Buddha's presence, the earth swallows her and she is reborn in the Avīci hell (cf. the story for v. 17).

177. *sharing the joy*: *anumodamāno*, 'rejoicing at another's good action', the state of mind known as *anumodanā*, which is thought to be particularly wholesome, inspiring people to undertake good actions themselves.

STORY: King Pasenadi and Queen Mallikā, at the suggestion of the queen, organize a stupendous gift-giving ceremony in honour of the Buddha and 500 monks. Among other details, each of the monks is to be attended by an elephant, bearing a parasol in its trunk. Unfortunately, there are only 499 trained elephants; the only others available are rogue elephants, which might be dangerous to the monks. However, the queen points out that a rogue elephant can safely be employed to attend on Aṅgulimāla (see the story for v. 173): one is put in place for this purpose, and in his presence it becomes completely peaceful.

The king and queen bestow Incomparable Gifts, in an occasion that is said to happen just once in the lifetime of every Fully Awakened Buddha. Two of the king's ministers are present: Juṇha, who feels joy at the king's overwhelming generosity, and Kāla, who disapproves, taking it for extravagance. Understanding their thoughts, the Buddha realizes that he if gives a teaching equal to the gifts, Juṇha will attain Stream-Entry, but Kāla's head will split into seven pieces (see the notes on v. 72); so, out of compassion for Kāla, he gives a talk only four verses long, and returns to the monastery. Fearing that the Buddha is angry with him, the king goes to the monastery with a retinue that includes the two ministers. The Buddha explains his actions. The king points out to Kāla that he gave only what was his own to give, and banishes him from the kingdom. He rewards Juṇha by giving the kingdom to him for seven days, so that he too can bestow alms on the Buddha. The Buddha speaks the verse, and Juṇha attains Stream-Entry.

178. *all the worlds*: Or 'the whole world' (*sabbaloka*).

STORY: Anāthapiṇḍika has a son, Kāla, who is something of a disappointment to him, since he shows no sign of wanting to visit the Buddha or hear his teaching. So Anāthapiṇḍika offers to pay him a hundred pieces of money if he goes to the monastery for the *uposatha* day. He goes, but spends most of his time there asleep. Next day, Anāthapiṇḍika offers him another thousand if he learns a single verse of the teaching. The Buddha arranges that Kāla will keep misunderstanding the verse, so that the young man will stay on and listen to more and more verses. Kāla stays and listens, and attains Stream-Entry. When his father comes, Kāla is now embarrassed and tries to refuse the money. The Buddha says that Kāla has attained something that is worth more than the rank of a Universal Monarch, or rebirth in the world of the gods or the world of Brahmā – in token of which he speaks the verse.

CHAPTER 14
THE BUDDHA

In this chapter, the word 'Buddha' (literally, 'Awakened') seems sometimes to be used specifically of Fully Awakened Ones, and sometimes of awakened beings, such as Arahats, in general.

179–80. STORY: A Brahmin couple have a daughter called Māgandiyā, so beautiful that they cannot find a man they consider good enough for her. Seeing the fine form of the Buddha, the man wishes to bestow his daughter on him, despite the objection of his wife, who has seen the Buddha's footprint and realizes that it bears the marks of one who has gone beyond desire.

When the Brahmin makes the offer of his daughter, the Buddha tells how, before attaining enlightenment, he rejected the daughters of Māra, speaking these verses to them. He tells the couple that he felt no desire for the wonderful golden bodies of Māra's daughters: in comparison, Māgandiyā's body is just a mass of physical impurities like a corpse, on which he would not even wipe his foot. The Brahmin and his wife attain the state of Non-Return, and afterwards join the Order and attain Arahatship. However, it is clear from the commentary on vv. 21–3 that Māgandiyā is mortally offended, and that this leads to her hatred of the Buddha and his followers.

A verse closely similar to v. 179 is found also in a Mahāyāna text, the Mahāvastu. Here the Buddha speaks it to messengers sent by his father, Śuddhodana (= Suddhodana), with instructions to bring him back to the palace (Mahāvastu 3.91).

181. STORY: The Buddha performs a spectacular miracle by means of his psychic powers, walking in the sky and issuing fire and water from his body. Afterwards he spends the Rains Retreat in the heaven of the Thirty-Three Gods, teaching the Abhidhamma to the deities there (including the one who in a previous life had been his mother, Māyādevī). At the end of the three months, he returns to earth attended by a huge following of *devas* and Brahmās, the latter having come down from even higher realms to hear him.

182. STORY: During the time of the Buddha Kassapa, a young monk, while climbing into a boat, grabs an *eraka* plant ('typha grass') and breaks off a single leaf – a breach of the Vinaya, since monks should not damage vegetation. At the time, he dismisses this as a trivial matter, and never gets round to confessing the fault. But on his deathbed he remembers it and is filled with remorse; so, instead of being reborn as a human being, he becomes a king of the *nāgas*, Erakapatta ('Eraka-Leaf'), living in the river Gaṅgā. Knowing that it is going to be a very long time before another Buddha appears, he determines that he will not miss the opportunity again.

Eventually Erakapatta has a daughter, a beautiful *nāginī*. Twice a month, on full-moon and new-moon days, the *nāga* king lies on the surface of the water, sets his daughter on his great cobra-hood, and gets her to dance and sing. The song is a series of riddles to which only a Buddha will know the answer:

> What sort of ruler is a king?
> What sort of king is ruled by passion?
> How can one be free of passion?
> How does one come to be called a fool?

If anyone answers the riddles correctly, he will receive the *nāga* princess's hand in marriage – and great wealth besides, for, if someone can answer, it will mean that another Buddha has appeared in the world.

When eventually the present Buddha appears, he becomes aware that a young Brahmin called Uttara is going to Erakapatta to try to answer the riddles. He speaks to Uttara, and tells him what to sing in answer to the *nāga* princess's questions:

> The ruler of the six doors [of the senses] is a king.
> One who indulges is ruled by passion.
> By not indulging, one becomes free of passion.
> Because of indulging, one is called a fool.

The Buddha then tells Uttara what the *nāga* princess will sing in reply:

> By what is the fool carried off?
> How does the wise man dispel it?
> How does one find the peace of *yoga*?*
> Riddle me this, as I ask you.

Uttara is then to reply:

> The fool is carried off by the flood.
> The wise man dispels it through practice (*yoga*).
> When freed from all bonds (*yoga*)
> One finds the peace of *yoga*.†

*'How does one become a *yoga-kkhemin* [a possessor of *yoga-kkhema*: see the note on vv. 21–3]?'

†'One becomes a *yoga-kkhemin*.'

Uttara follows the Buddha's instructions, attains Stream-Entry, and goes on to win the *nāga* maiden's hand. Erakapatta now goes to see the Buddha: on meeting him, he weeps, lamenting how easily he fell from the human state, and how long he has been living an animal existence, deprived of the Buddha's teaching. The Buddha speaks the verse, and 84,000 beings achieve understanding of the Dhamma. We are told that the *nāga* king would have achieved Stream-Entry that day if it had not been for his animal nature: as it is, he has to wait until his next birth.

183–5. *Not to do any evil*: Verse 183 is a famous summary of 'the teaching of the Buddhas' – i.e. not just of the historical Buddha, but of all his predecessors and those to come. For possible Jain parallels, see Watanabe 1994.
true wanderer: *samaṇa* – 'true' added for clarity.
These three verses are found also at Dīgha Nikāya 2.49 (Sutta 14, the Mahāpadāna Sutta, 3.26–8), where they occur in a different order (184, 183, 185), spoken by the previous Buddha, Vipassin – see e.g. Walshe 1987: 219. An equivalent verse to v. 184, in Buddhist Hybrid Sanskrit, is also found in a Dīrghāgama text of the Sarvāstivāda school recently discovered in northern Turkestan: see Fukita 2003: 156, ll. 21–4. Here too it is spoken by the Buddha Vipaśyin (= Vipassin).

STORY: Ānanda asks the Buddha what teaching the Buddhas of the past gave on *uposatha* days. The Buddha says that all spoke the very same verses – the three that are given here.

186–7. STORY: A discontented monk receives a legacy of one hundred pieces of money, and is tempted to return to the household life. The Buddha makes him count it out into piles for the things he will need: food and drink, a plough, bullocks to pull it, and farming tools. In this way the monk discovers that a hundred pieces will not be nearly enough. The Buddha points out that the great world-ruling monarchs of the past, who had the power to cause rains of jewels to fall from the sky, still died with their desires unsatisfied.

188–92. These verses, like vv. 183–5, summarize central teachings of Buddhism.

STORY: A Brahmin teacher called Aggidatta encourages his followers to take refuge in forests, groves and trees. The Buddha determines to teach them what is really meant by a safe refuge, and sends Moggallāna to them. Instead of a normal dwelling, Aggidatta's followers lodge Moggallāna in a hut that is home to a dangerous fire-breathing *nāga*. In the morning, when the followers go to see what has happened to him, they find that, through his psychic powers, he has subdued the *nāga*, who is holding his hood over the Elder's head as a sign of respect. The Buddha arrives and teaches Aggidatta and his followers that mountains, forests etc. are not true refuges: the Buddha, Dhamma and Saṅgha are the true refuges, through which one can gain release from suffering. He speaks the verses. Aggidatta and his followers attain Arahatship, and are ordained as Buddhist monks.

193. *He's not born just anywhere*: Literally, 'He's not born everywhere.'
that steadfast one: The commentator here takes *dhīra* in the sense of its homonym 'wise', but, as K. R. Norman points out (1997: 110), PDhp 79, GDhp 173 and Uv 30.27 all have forms from *vīra*, 'hero'.

STORY: The Elder Ānanda, reflecting that the finest elephants, horses and bullocks are born only among the descendants of certain famous beasts, asks the Buddha whether the greatest of men can be born in any family, or only in certain lineages. The Buddha replies that they are born only in Khattiya (Kṣatriya) and Brahmin families. Traditionally, Buddhas are said to be born only in such families, though Arahats can be from any social background.

194. STORY: Five hundred monks dispute what is the pleasantest thing in the world, some naming rulership, some love, and some good food. The Buddha points out that all these in fact belong to the realm of suffering: truly happy are the arising of a Buddha, the hearing of the Dhamma, and harmony among the Saṅgha.

195–6. *If you honour*: Literally, 'The one who honours'.
ones like that: *tādise* – cf. the note on v. 76.
To be measured by anyone – so great it is: Or perhaps 'To be measured as "so much" by anyone'. Carter and Palihawadana (1987: 251) have 'Of one worshiping [*sic*] such as them, / Calmed ones who fear nothing, / The merit cannot be quantified / By anyone saying "It is of this extent."'

STORY: The Buddha stays at a shrine. A Brahmin visits, but pays respects only to the shrine, not to the Buddha. The Buddha praises him for doing so, and causes the shrine of the Buddha Kassapa to appear on the spot. He speaks the verses, and the Brahmin attains Stream-Entry.

CHAPTER 15
HAPPINESS

197–9. *Ah, how happily we live*: *susukhaṃ vata jīvāma* – *susukhaṃ jīvāma* means 'very happily we live', but *vata* turns a statement into a fervent exclamation. *Jīvāma* and *viharāma* ('we dwell' in l. 3) could equally be imperatives: 'let us live!' and 'let us dwell!'

Carefree . . . careworn: Those who are *anussuka* or *ussuka*, free of or full of care and anxiety.

STORY: A war is about to break out between the Sākiyas and Koliyas, relatives of the Buddha's father and mother respectively. The Buddha goes up to the armies to find out the cause of the conflict, but no one can remember, not even the commanders: the quarrel has taken on a momentum of its own. Finally one of the slaves recollects that the quarrel originated in a dispute over the irrigation rights to a river.

The Buddha points out to the warring parties that water is of little value, whereas the lives of the warriors are beyond price. He speaks the verses, contrasting his way of life with that of the combatants.

200. *Radiant Gods*: *devā ābhassarā*, a class of beings from the high Brahmā heavens.

Verse 9.12 of the Jain Uttarajjhayaṇa Sutta resembles this one in its first two *pādas* – Roth (1976: 166–9) quotes a translation by Hermann Jacobi: 'Happy are we, happy live we who call nothing our own; when Mithilā is on fire, nothing is burned that belongs to me.' Udānavarga 30.44 has a verse resembling the Uttarajjhayaṇa version: 'Ah, how happily we live, / We who own nothing! / Though Mithilā burns / Nothing burns that belongs to us.' In the Jain text it appears to be spoken by Janaka, a king of Mithilā who is also an enlightened sage. It is also paralleled in the Mahābhārata (Roth op. cit.; see also Brough 1962: 229–30 on the parallel verse, GDhp 168).

STORY: The Buddha goes to a village where he is aware of 500 young women who are ready to benefit by his teaching. Māra turns the villagers against the Buddha, so that he will not receive alms that day. When the young women arrive, Māra taunts the Buddha with the fact that he has not eaten that day, and must be feeling the pangs of hunger. The Buddha points out to Māra that he is content, living on the joy of meditation like the Radiant Gods. The 500 young women attain Stream-Entry.

201. *The victor*: Following K. R. Norman (1997: 30, 111–12), who takes *jayaṃ* as a present participle ('the conquering one') rather than a noun ('victory').
in pain: *dukkhaṃ*.

STORY: The king of Kosala three times goes to war against his nephew Ajātasattu, and each time is defeated. Overcome by grief, he refuses to eat and takes to his bed. The Buddha speaks the verse to console him.

202. *pain*: *dukkha*.
aggregates: *khandha* – see Glossary.

STORY: At a wedding celebration, the bride's parents invite the Buddha and the monks for alms. The bridegroom is so distracted by desire for the bride that he does not pay proper attention to the Buddha. The Buddha, by his psychic power, makes the bride invisible to the groom. He speaks the verse, and both bride and groom attain Stream-Entry. The Buddha now lets him see her once more.

203. Rather a free translation here, since it is impossible to translate literally without writing 'Buddhist Hybrid English'. The words translated as 'worst' and 'greatest' are all forms of *parama*, 'supreme'. Literally, 'Hunger [is] the supreme disease, the *saṅkhāras* the supreme painful (*dukkha*) [things]: knowing this as it is (*yathābhūtaṃ*), [one realizes that] *nibbāna* is the supreme happiness.'
Conditioned things: The *saṅkhāras* or 'conditions', all the components of the conditioned realm.
truly: *yathābhūtaṃ*, 'as it [really] is'.

STORY: A poor farmer comes late to a meeting with the Buddha and the monks, because he has spent the morning searching for his one ox, which has strayed. Realizing that the farmer has had nothing to eat, the Buddha delays his teaching until food has been found for him. There is some criticism of the Buddha for delaying his discourse for just one man. He explains afterwards that if the farmer had tried to listen to the teaching while hungry, he could not have comprehended it. As it is, he has listened intently and gained Stream-Entry.

204. See my comments on v. 203. Literally, 'Gains have absence of disease as their supreme [example]; wealth has happiness as its supreme [example]; a relative has trust as his/her supreme [quality]; *nibbāna* is the supreme happiness.'
Health: Literally, 'Absence of disease' (*ārogya*).
Trust is what makes the truest kin: i.e. it is trustworthiness, not blood relationship, that makes a person into a true relative.

STORY: King Pasenadi has got into the habit of drastically overeating, and finds he has become uncomfortable, short of energy, and inclined to quarrel with members of his family. The Buddha, speaking v. 325, advises him on how to cut down on the amount of rice he is eating. The king learns moderation in eating, and his health and family relationships become better than ever before. The king becomes a devout follower of the Buddha.

205. *Savouring*: Literally, 'Drinking'.
free of fear: *niddaro*. K. R. Norman (1997: 113) takes this as coming from *ni* ('without') + *dara* ('fear' or 'distress', < Sanskrit *dara*), though, as he points out, the reason for the doubling of 'd' is unclear, since it is not required for metrical reasons. It is possible that instead it comes from *ni* + **dvara* = *jvara*, 'burning', 'fever'. This verse is not paralleled in other Dharmapada literature – but see also the notes on *vīta-ddaraṃ* for v. 385.
the taste of joy in the Dhamma: Or 'the taste of drinking the Dhamma'. For the pun on *dhamma-pīti*, see the note on v. 79.

STORY: A similar story to the one for v. 166, but told of the Elder Tissa.

206–8. *If you never see a fool / You'll always be happy*: Literally, 'By the non-seeing of fools one would always be happy.'
So: *tasmā hi*. These words fall outside the metrical verses.
steadfast: Or perhaps 'wise' (*dhīra*).
such a: *tādisaṃ* – cf. the note for v. 76.
As the moon keeps to the zodiac path: Literally, 'As the moon [keeps to] the path of the lunar mansions'. The mansions (*nakkhatta*, Sanskrit *nakṣatra*) are twenty-seven constellations marking the course of the moon round the ecliptic. They form a kind of lunar zodiac, which was known in India before the solar

zodiac of twelve constellations was imported into India from Hellenistic Greek astrology.

STORY: When the Buddha is suffering from dysentery, caused by the illness that will eventually end his life, Sakka himself comes to attend upon him, even emptying his chamber-pot for him. The monks are amazed, because normally the gods find the smell of human beings (even healthy ones) repulsive. But Sakka is grateful to the Buddha because his teaching has enabled him to attain Stream-Entry.

CHAPTER 16
THE DEAR

The dear (*piya*) is that to which one is attached, or what is cherished. K. R. Norman (1997: 32–3) translates it throughout as 'pleasant', but this seems to restrict the meaning to things, rather than people. In many of the following verses, the word could apply equally to either, but the commentarial stories generally take it as applied to people, such as family members. The message is not that one should not feel love for other beings, but rather that one should not be caught up in personal attachment.

209–11. Verse 209 is built round a series of derivatives of the verb *yuj-*, 'to yoke', 'to join', 'to apply oneself' (cf. *yoga*), and is hard to translate into idiomatic English: literally, 'Applying oneself (*yuñjaṃ*) to not-*yoga* (*ayoga*), and non-applying (*ayojanaṃ*) to *yoga*, having abandoned the goal, clinging to what is dear, one would envy the one who applies himself to the goal (*attānuyoginaṃ*) [taking *atta* as equivalent to *attha*: K. R. Norman, 1997: 114].'
In v. 210 Norman, as usual, takes the words as applying to things or states rather than people: 'Do not at any time associate with pleasant (or) unpleasant things. Not seeing pleasant things is painful, and also seeing unpleasant things.'
losing what's dear: Literally, 'the going away of the dear'.

STORY: A young man and his father become monks, and his mother becomes a nun. However, the three do not give up their attachment to one another, and spend their time chatting together. The Buddha speaks the verses to remind them of their proper duties.

212. *If you're freed from the dear / You'll have no grief, let alone fear*: Literally, 'For the one who is freed from the dear, there is no grief, let alone fear.' Similarly in vv. 213–16.

STORY: A layman whose son has died is overcome by grief, so that he gives up eating and working. The Buddha visits him and reminds him that death is common to all beings: the wise do not give themselves up to excessive grief.

213. STORY: Visākhā's granddaughter has died, and she is in mourning. The Buddha asks her if she would like to have as many dear ones as there are people in the city of Sāvatthi. She says that she would. He reminds her that, if this were so, she would be constantly in mourning, as there is always someone dying in Sāvatthi.

214. STORY: The Licchavi princes go off to a festival in their finery, looking like the Thirty-Three Gods. Before nightfall, they are carried home battered and covered in blood, having fought over a beautiful courtesan they met on the way.

215. STORY: A young man called Anitthigandha refuses to marry unless his parents can find a girl as beautiful as a golden statue that he has had made. They send some Brahmins to look for such a girl, and they search, taking the statue with them, until one day a woman mistakes it for her daughter. A date for the wedding is fixed, but on the way to Anitthigandha's home the girl becomes ill and dies.

Hearing of this, Anitthigandha is struck down with grief, and refuses to eat. Aware of his plight, the Buddha calls at his house on his alms-round, and is invited in by the youth's parents. They bring Anitthigandha to meet the Buddha, who teaches him with this verse. Anitthigandha attains Stream-Entry.

216. STORY: A Brahmin farmer promises a share of his crop to the Buddha. The night before it is due to be harvested, it is destroyed by a storm. The farmer is grief-stricken, because he feels that he is breaking his word to the Buddha. The Buddha comforts him by speaking the verse, and he gains Stream-Entry.

217. *firm in the Dhamma*: *dhammaṭṭha* – cf. the introduction to Chapter 19 and the notes to vv. 256–7.

STORY: Five hundred boys take a liking to the Elder Kassapa the Great, and offer him the basket of pancakes they have with them, though they have given none to the Buddha and other monks whom they met previously. Kassapa asks them to offer the pancakes to the Buddha and the monks, and they do so. The other monks are shocked by the boys' favouritism towards Kassapa, but the Buddha does not mind at all. He speaks this verse in praise of Kassapa. Hearing it, the boys all attain Stream-Entry.

218. *who has aroused a wish for the Undeclared*: *chandajāto anakkhāte*, referring to a person who has already attained one of the lower three paths – Stream-Entry, Once-Return or Non-Return – and had a preliminary experience of *nibbāna* ('the Undeclared'). (If he or she had attained Arahatship, the *chanda*, or wish, would no longer be present.)
the Undeclared: *nibbāna*, because it cannot be described.
filled with that consciousness: Literally, 'filled with mind', but referring to the state of mind produced by seeing *nibbāna*. Carter and Palihawadana (1987: 267) translate this as 'clear in mind', but quote the Commentary: 'Who would be filled with the thoughts pertaining to the three prior Paths and Fruits' – i.e. Stream-Entry, Once-Return and Non-Return.
heading upstream: Against the stream of *saṃsāra*. See 'Stream-Enterer' in the Glossary.

STORY: A monk dies without attaining Arahatship, and his followers are distressed. However, the Buddha points out that the monk had attained Non-Return, and had therefore been reborn in the high heavens called the Pure Abodes: he will certainly attain Arahatship in his next birth.

219–20. *good actions*: *puñña*.
the next: Literally, 'the other [world]'.

STORY: A pious layman called Nandiya makes generous offerings to the community of monks. Moggallāna, visiting the Tāvatiṃsa heaven through his psychic powers, sees a wonderful palace there, and enquires for whom it has been built. It turns out that it is for Nandiya.

CHAPTER 17
ANGER

221. *pride*: The Sanskrit and Pali word *māna* is probably derived from *man-*, 'to think': hence, perhaps, 'thinking well of oneself'. In Sanskrit poetry it is often used of the hurt pride of a woman whose

husband favours a rival wife. But the commentator relates *māna* to *mā-*, 'to measure', giving it the meaning of 'measuring oneself against others', 'thinking oneself better/worse/the same as someone else'. (Buddhist thought considers that all these are simply forms of pride or self-conceit.) The commentarial story in fact seems to show both kinds of *māna* in action: that which led Rohiṇī in a former life to disfigure the dancing-girl (see below), and that which leads her in the present life to hide herself from view.

sorrows: *dukkha*.

STORY: Rohiṇī, sister of the Elder Anuruddha, is suffering from a disfiguring skin disease, and hides herself away. Anuruddha encourages her to perform a meritorious act in order to become free of her affliction. She sells her jewellery and with the proceeds has a hall built, to which she invites the Buddha and the monks. After the offerings of food, the Buddha explains the reason for her affliction: in a previous existence as a queen she was jealous of one of the king's dancing-girls, and played an unpleasant trick on her, putting powder from an itching plant in her bed, so that she would develop a disfiguring rash.

The Buddha speaks the verse, on the consequences of anger, and Rohiṇī attains Stream-Entry. At that moment, her disease vanishes and her complexion becomes like gold. Later, when she dies, she is reborn in the heaven of the Thirty-Three Gods, so beautiful that she becomes the darling of Sakka himself.

222. STORY: A monk begins to cut down a tree to build himself a hut. The deity living within the tree tries to stop him, holding up her* baby in front of the monk. The monk does not see the baby, and cuts off its arm. The deity is tempted to kill the monk, but restrains her anger, and instead goes and reports to the Buddha what has happened. The Buddha speaks the verse in praise of the deity's self-restraint, and the deity attains Stream-Entry; however, she still grieves for the loss of her home. The Buddha points out another tree to be the deity's home: because it is the Buddha's gift, no one will be able to damage or remove it. The Buddha makes the Vinaya rule preventing monks from cutting down trees.

*As in the notes on vv. 119–20, the word *devatā* (deity) is used, so it is not explicitly stated that the being is female. However, in the course of this story the deity uses feminine forms in reference to herself.

223. The verse is puzzling, because in all versions it seems to mix abstract nouns with adjectives, and in some cases it is not clear which is intended: see K. R. Norman 1997: 116.

By freedom from anger [literally, 'By non-anger': see the notes on v. 5] *you should conquer anger*: The Commentary takes *akkodhena jine kodhaṃ* as 'By freedom from anger you should conquer the angry person', though *kodha* does not seem elsewhere to be used in this sense.

By good conquer what is not good: Or 'By good conquer the person who is not good'.

miserliness: Or 'the miser'.

the teller of lies: This seems unambiguously to refer to a person, but both the Sanskrit Udānavarga (20.19) and the Gāndhārī Dharmapada (280) have 'one should conquer falsehood by truth'.

STORY: Uttarā, the daughter of a wealthy banker, and a devout Buddhist, is married into a non-Buddhist family. Frustrated at not being able to offer alms to the monks, she pays Sirimā, a beautiful courtesan, to stay with her husband while she organizes an alms-giving. Her husband, presented with a courtesan who is greatly sought after, readily agrees.

Sirimā, it seems, does not realize that she is there merely as a temporary companion, but thinks she is the new mistress of the house. One day the husband sees Uttarā bustling about, preparing for the alms-giving, and laughs. Sirimā, seeing the intimacy between the two of them, becomes jealous and throws hot ghee at Uttarā. Uttarā controls her anger, reflecting on her gratitude at Sirimā for enabling her to give alms. She meditates on loving kindness, and the boiling-hot fat does not harm her. Uttarā's maids begin to beat Sirimā, but Uttarā prevents them. Sirimā, overcome by Uttarā's kindness, begs her forgiveness. Uttarā agrees to forgive her if the Buddha will do so. They go before him, and the Buddha praises Uttarā. Sirimā herself becomes a follower of the Buddha (see also the story for v. 147).

224. *tell the truth*: K. R. Norman (1997: 34, 116), following Brough (1962: 184, on GDhp 22), takes this as 'speak what is pleasant', deriving *saccaṃ* from *sātyaṃ*, not *satyam*. However, the verse specifies *three* practices, and speaking pleasantly seems to be part of the same practice as 'not getting angry'.

even if there's not much: Literally, 'even [if there's] little'.

practices: Literally, 'states'.

STORY: Moggallāna visits a heavenly realm, and sees divine beings enjoying existences of great splendour. When asked what they have done to earn such a reward, they are almost too embarrassed to say. One has simply spoken the truth. One was a servant who did not get angry when her master ill-treated her. Others gave small items of food to monks. The Buddha confirms that even small acts of merit can bring enormous rewards.

225. *Where those who go don't grieve*: Literally, 'Where having gone they would not grieve'.

STORY: An old Brahmin couple, great devotees of the Buddha, continually refer to him as their son, and treat him as such. Both attain Non-Return. When people disapprove of their way of addressing the Buddha, he explains that in 1,500 past lives they have been either his parents, his uncle and aunt, or his grandparents. He stays near them for three months, at the end of which they attain Arahatship and pass away.

226. *go to rest*: *atthaṃ gacchanti* – 'go west', 'set', like the sun and moon.

STORY: A slave woman called Puṇṇā, too tired to sleep, wonders why the Buddha's monks are also wakeful at night. Is one of their number sick? Next day she offers her modest meal of a rice cake to the Buddha. He explains that his monks are wakeful through mindfulness, and Puṇṇā attains Stream-Entry.

227–30. *truth*: Word added for clarity.
When they've observed him day after day: The only way to find out if a person is truly enlightened.
of new gold: *jambonada* – gold that has been worked for the first time.

STORY: Atula, a layman, brings 500 companions to the monastery and requests teaching from various senior followers of the Buddha. Revata is extremely taciturn. Sāriputta expounds the Abhidhamma, at great length. Ānanda gives a very brief and simple talk. Atula goes and complains to the Buddha, who explains that no one in this world escapes criticism: kings, the earth, the sun and moon, even the Buddha himself. Praise or blame from foolish people does not matter, and only praise from the wise and learned is worth paying attention to.

231–4. *anger*: *pakopa*, sometimes translated as 'disturbance', which seems to be how the Commentary is taking it. Presumably the verses are primarily concerned with bad actions, speech and thought that are the result of anger. Carter and Palihawadana (1987: 276–7) have 'intemperance'.
thoroughly restrained: In ll. 1–3 of v. 234 we have *saṃvutā*, 'controlled', 'restrained'. In l. 4 we have *su-pari-saṃvutā*, 'well + all-round + restrained'.

STORY: The Buddha speaks the verses to a group of six monks who are very noisy, clattering about in wooden shoes and disturbing their fellow monks. At the end of his instruction, the six monks attain Stream-Entry.

CHAPTER 18

RUST

Rust: *mala*. The key word in this chapter, the *mala-vagga*, can be used of any kind of impurity or stain, and in the course of the chapter I have varied the translation accordingly. However, in vv. 240–43, it is specifically used of impurities that, like rust in metal, corrode away the sound material that surrounds them.

235–8. *you/You*: A genuine second-person singular: all four verses seem to be addressed to one individual.
at the start of an undertaking: Following K. R. Norman 1997: 36, 119. The Commentary takes *uyyoga-mukhe* as 'on the brink of dissolution', presumably regarding *ud* + *yoga* as the opposite of *yoga*, 'joining'. *Uyyoga* appears not to be found elsewhere in the Pali Canon, but in Sanskrit the normal meaning of *udyoga* is 'effort', 'striving', 'undertaking'. If we take it in that sense here, it would refer to the metaphorical journey to Yama's abode that everyone has one day to take.
provision for your journey: *pātheyya* – literally, 'belonging to the road'. In the metaphorical sense, presumably a store of merit.
So make an island: My 'So' actually represents the Pali *so*, which is a demonstrative adjective or pronoun: 'that [one]'. However, here it emphasizes the 'you' and links it back to the previous verse: 'That very same you must make an island . . .' Carter and Palihawadana (1987: 280) take *dīpa* as 'lamp' (< Sanskrit *dīpa*), but the Commentary takes it as 'island' (< Sanskrit *dvīpa*), thinking of the traveller in the verse as a shipwrecked sailor.

With rust blown away: The metaphor appears to be from the smith's technique for removing impurities from molten metal: cf. v. 239.
to meet Yama: Literally, 'to the presence of Yama'.

STORY: A butcher spends his life killing cows, and never performs any good action. He sells some of the meat, but also insists on eating beef every day himself. One day, when there is no beef for him to eat, he plucks out the tongue of a living cow. His own tongue splits. He begins to crawl around, lowing like a cow, dies, and is reborn in the Avīci hell.

His son, terrified, leaves the town and sets up elsewhere, where he becomes a skilled goldsmith. Although very successful, he too does no meritorious acts. His sons in time become followers of the Buddha, and are worried about their father. On his behalf, they invite the Buddha and the monks for alms. The Buddha gives this teaching to the goldsmith, who attains Stream-Entry.

239. STORY: A Brahmin does a number of kind actions to help the monks and make their lives more comfortable. The Buddha speaks the verse about him, and he gains Stream-Entry.

240. *The one who misuses the requisites*: Following the Commentary, which takes this to refer to the four requisites of the monk: food, clothing, medicine and lodging. K. R. Norman (1997: 36, 120) takes it to mean 'one excessively devoted to ascetic practices'.

STORY: A monk named Tissa becomes possessive about a particularly fine robe that has been offered to him. While dwelling upon this, he dies, and is reborn as a louse in the robe. When the other monks start to divide up the robe, the louse screams in distress, though only the Buddha can hear it. The Buddha knows that, if they divide the robe now, the louse will hold a grudge against them and be reborn in a hell world. Only after seven days, when the former monk has died as a louse and been reborn in the Tusita heaven, will the Buddha allow the monks to divide up the robe. He warns the monks of the danger of excessive attachment to the requisites.

241. *texts*: *manta* (Sanskrit *mantra*), here referring to texts such as Suttas which monks would have needed to learn by heart.
houses: The literal meaning. K. R. Norman (1997: 36, 120) takes it as 'families'. In either case, regular maintenance is needed.

STORY: A monk called Udāyi disparages the teaching of Sāriputta and Moggallāna, and offers to teach and chant in their place; but when he takes the teacher's seat he cannot remember a word. He is driven away, and falls into a cesspit.

242–3. *misconduct*: Presumably sexual misconduct is primarily intended, as in the commentarial story.
ways: *dhamma*, here clearly of a course of conduct rather than a state of mind. I borrow Burlingame's useful rendering (1921: III, 124).

STORY: A husband is so embarrassed by the behaviour of his adulterous wife that he finds it difficult to appear in society. The Buddha tells a Jātaka story concerning the insatiable nature of wicked women, and encourages him to develop wisdom.

244–5. *It's easy to live like a shameless person*: Literally, '[Life is] easily lived by a shameless [one, who is . . .]'; and similarly in the contrasting verse.
A crow-hero: Presumably noisy and loud, but not really brave. The Commentary takes it as referring to a monk who, instead of accepting alms in due measure, wherever they are offered, is constantly looking out for the houses that give the most lavish food. He is compared to a crow which is constantly on the lookout for unguarded food that it can snatch. This does not explain the 'hero' element in the word, unless it means 'a hero among crows'. Carter and Palihawadana (1987: 285–6) translate it as 'crafty as a crow'.

STORY: A monk called Cullasāri accepts food as a payment for giving medical treatment, instead of depending upon alms; he then offers it with boastful words to Sāriputta, who silently refuses it. Cullasāri is unabashed by the fact that he is openly breaking the Vinaya rules, but the Buddha reproaches him with the verses.

246–8. Verses 246–7 summarize the five precepts of lay Buddhist conduct, with a change from the usual order (here 1, 4, 2, 3, 5), no doubt to fit the metre.
Gives himself up to strong drink: *Surā-meraya-pānaṃ . . . anuyuñjati*. Literally, 'Undertakes/Devotes himself to the drinking of *surā* and *meraya*', which are thought to be the names of two different kinds of liquor, perhaps one fermented and one distilled. However, as they occur in the formulation of the fifth precept – *surā-meraya-majja-ppamādaṭṭhānā veramaṇī*

sikkhāpadaṃ samādiyāmi: 'I undertake the precept to avoid states of intoxication and carelessness [caused by] *surā* and *meraya*' – they are clearly intended to symbolize every kind of intoxicant. (In modern English versions of the precepts, they are often translated as 'drink and drugs'.)
my friend: Literally, 'O man' (*bho purisa*). I assume that this is a fairly colloquial greeting, here used in warning. The wide range of ancient Indian greetings, with their different levels of relative status and familiarity, is practically impossible to translate.
Evil states: *pāpadhammā*.
wrongdoing: *adhamma*.
to long suffering: Literally, 'to suffering for a long time (*ciraṃ*)'.

STORY: Some laymen are trying to keep different ones of the five precepts, and argue about which is the most difficult. The Buddha points out that all are difficult and all equally important.

249–50. *clarity of mind*: *pasāda*, with connotations of peace, brightness and lucidity.
this [v. 250, l. 1]: i.e. the discontent.

STORY: A novice called Tissa is always discontented with the alms-food he receives, even the sumptuous offerings of Anāthapiṇḍika and Visākhā. He boasts of the wealth and generosity of his own family. However, when someone visits Tissa's home town and makes enquiries, it turns out that Tissa is a gatekeeper's son who went on the road with a band of wandering carpenters. The Buddha speaks the verses to advise him to eat what is offered and be content.

251. STORY: Despite the Buddha's incomparable skill as a teacher, five laymen cannot concentrate on his words, but spend the time sleeping, fidgeting or daydreaming. The Buddha explains to Ānanda that this comes from habits of lust, hate, delusion or craving built up over many lives.

252. STORY: An elaborate sequence of stories, covering many lives, and full of magic, concerns the banker Meṇḍaka, the grandfather of Visākhā. In a former life, Meṇḍaka and his wife, son, daughter-in-law and slave have all gained psychic powers through their generosity to a Paccekabuddha. Because of their affection for one another, they made a wish to continue to be reborn together in life after life, until the time of the present Buddha, when all five of them attain Stream-Entry.

Some non-Buddhist ascetics try to dissuade Meṇḍaka from going to see the Buddha, finding fault with the Teacher: hence the verse.

253. STORY: A monk keeps finding fault with his fellow monks. As a result, he increases his own defilements instead of conquering them.

254–5 *Outside the Order there is no true wanderer* [*samaṇa*]: 'the Order' and 'true' added for clarity. The idea is that the higher attainments are possible only in the Buddha's dispensation.
proliferation: *papañca* – the tendency of the mind to go after more and more distractions.

STORY: Subhadda, the last follower to achieve liberation in the Buddha's lifetime, asks him the questions that are answered in the verses: Is there a path in the air? Can someone outside the Order be called a monk? Are conditioned things (*saṅkhāras*) eternal?

CHAPTER 19
THE JUST

'The Just' is my translation of *dhammaṭṭha* – one who stands in the Dhamma. However, in vv. 256–7 the word specifically refers to a judge.

256–7. *justice*: *dhammaṭṭha* – see above. Here I have translated it as 'justice' to try to give some sense of the pun.
justly: *dhammena* – 'with *dhamma*'.
What's the case and not the case: *atthaṃ anatthaṃ ca* – 'benefit/right/purpose and not-beneficial/wrong/not to the purpose', with a pun on *attha*, the word used above for the (law) case.

STORY: Some monks, entering a courtroom to keep out of the rain, are shocked to see judges who are taking bribes and trying cases badly.

258. STORY: The words are spoken concerning some boastful monks who talk a lot but know nothing.

259. *Dhamma-bearer*: One who knows and understands the Dhamma, and so can teach it to others.
with his body: Directly, through his own experience.
isn't careless: *na-ppamajjati* – cf. *pamāda*, in the introduction to the notes on Chapter 2.

STORY: A monk known as Ekuddāna ('One Utterance') is an Arahat, though he knows just one verse:

A sage with high thoughts, diligent,
Training in the paths of silence,
Calmed and ever mindful –
Such a one has no sorrows.

When he teaches the Dhamma with this one verse, the forest deities applaud him. Two visiting monks with more to say do not receive the same response.

260–61. *He's just had a long life*: *paripakko vayo tassa* – 'Of him there is fully ripened age.'

STORY: The Buddha explains why he calls Lakuṇṭaka Bhaddiya an Elder, though he's very young. (For Lakuṇṭaka Bhaddiya, see also the stories for vv. 81, 294–5.)

262–3. *fine*: *sādhurūpa* – literally, 'of good appearance': but here the word *rūpa* does not appear to add anything to the meaning of the word (K. R. Norman 1997: 124).
fine words: 'fine' added for clarity.
Verse 263: First half as for v. 250.
free from fault: Or possibly 'free from hatred' – *vanta-doso*. In Pali there are two words *dosa*, one meaning 'hatred', 'ill will' (< Sanskrit *dveṣa*), the other meaning 'fault' (< Sanskrit *doṣa*). Sometimes there is a clear difference between them because of their context, while at others their meanings seem to overlap.

STORY: Some monks hope to gain a reputation through their eloquence, despite their lack of real knowledge.

264–5. Puns on 'wanderer' (*samaṇa*) and 'to cause to become quiet', 'to quell' (*sam-*).

STORY: A monk called Hatthaka uses underhand tactics when taking part in debates. The Buddha reproaches him with these verses.

266–7. Verse 266 is somewhat problematic, and there have been various attempts to explain it. Some read the second half as 'By taking on the whole Dhamma / One becomes a monk, not otherwise.'

This involves taking *vissadhamma* as 'the whole Dhamma', deriving *vissa* from the Vedic Sanskrit *viśva*, 'all', 'whole'. However, it still causes the difficulty of taking *na tāvatā*, 'not thus' (translated here as 'not . . . for all that), as 'not otherwise'. K. R. Norman (1997: 40, 125–6) relates *vissa* to such words as Sanskrit *veśma*, 'dwelling', and regards the verse as an attack on some Brahmins who begged alms while still living the household life.

Rather as in the previous pair of verses, there are wordplays on *bhikkhu*, 'monk', and *bhikkh-*, 'to beg alms'.

living the holy life: *brahmacariyavā* – perhaps meaning specifically 'celibate'.

not . . . for all that: *na tāvatā*, i.e. not even through begging alms.

STORY: A Brahmin ascetic who is not a Buddhist wants the Buddha to address him as 'monk'. With these verses, the Buddha explains why he does not do so.

268–9. Puns on *muni*, 'sage' (literally, 'silent one'), *mona*, 'silence', and *munā-*, 'to understand', 'to measure'.

understands both in the world: i.e. good and evil choices, taking *loke* as locative. The Commentary takes *loke* as plural, giving 'understands both worlds'.

STORY: In the early days, Buddhist monks receive food in silence, leading to unfavourable comparisons with ascetics of other groups, who thank the laypeople politely. The Buddha then institutes the custom of giving a discourse as thanks after a meal. This still leads to criticism. The Buddha explains that people may keep silence for a number of reasons – ignorance, lack of confidence, or even meanness about sharing their knowledge with others. Silence is not what makes a person a real sage.

270. STORY: The verse is spoken to a fisherman called Ariya ('Noble'). The Buddha explains that a person who takes the lives of other beings cannot be truly noble.

271–2. *by much learning*: Literally, 'by much truth'.

Nor has a monk attained confidence: I follow K. R. Norman's interpretation (1997: 40, 127–8), which regards *āpādi* as governed, like *phusāmi*, by the *na* in v. 271.

The Commentary follows a different interpretation of these verses, in which v. 272 would read:

Or by thinking, 'I enjoy the happiness of renunciation
Not known to worldly folk,'
Should a monk rest content
Until he reaches the destruction of the defilements.

STORY: Monks who have achieved the stages of Stream-Entry, Once-Return and Non-Return are feeling satisfied with their progress. The Buddha urges them to press on until they have achieved Arahatship.

CHAPTER 20
THE PATH

273–6. The 'you'/'You' in these verses is a genuine second-person plural: the Buddha is addressing a group of monks.
The Eightfold Path: 'Path' added for clarity.
Four Sayings: The Four Noble Truths – of suffering, the cause of suffering, the cessation of suffering, and the path to the cessation of suffering.
states: *dhammas*, in the sense of 'mental states'.
Seer: *cakkhumā* – literally, 'one who possesses the eye (of insight)', i.e. the Buddha.
are the teachers: i.e they can show you the way, but can't liberate you without your effort.
who enter upon the path: 'the path' added for clarity.

STORY: A group of monks are talking about the state of the paths they have taken to reach the monastery. The Buddha reminds them that these are not the sort of paths with which they should be concerning themselves.

277–9. *you see . . . You grow weary*: Literally, 'one sees . . . One grows weary'. The dictionary definitions of *nibbindati* – 'becomes depressed', 'becomes disgusted' – do not fit its use in Buddhism, since they convey strong negative feeling. The word refers to the moment of realization that suffering has gone on long enough, and one doesn't want to do it any more: cf. in the stories of Paṭācārā (v. 113) and Santati (v. 142) the idea that 'more than the water in the four oceans' is the expanse of tears you have shed over all those past lives in *saṃsāra*. The knowledge acts as a spur to become free of suffering.

The verses are a statement of Buddhist teaching on the three signs of existence:

All conditioned things are impermanent: sabbe saṅkhārā aniccā.

All conditioned things are [subject to] suffering: sabbe saṇkhārā dukkhā.

All dhammas are without self: sabbe dhammā anattā. The phraseology of this last is different, because not just conditioned things (*saṅkhāras*) but also *nibbāna*, the unconditioned *dhamma*, are without self.

STORY: The stories attached to these verses all follow the same pattern: the Buddha considers which meditation object will be most suitable for a group of monks, and sets them, respectively, recollection of impermanence, of suffering, and of no-self.

280. STORY: All but one of a group of monks attain Arahatship: the other misses the opportunity. Seeing how the Buddha greets those who have attained Arahatship, but not himself, the other monk decides to make an effort; however, he has a painful accident which prevents his fellow monks from going on their alms-round when they have to look after him. The Buddha tells the story of a past life when this monk had been a youth who, through his laziness, prevented his fellows from receiving offerings, and he speaks the verse.

281. STORY: As in the stories for vv. 71, 72 and 136, Moggallāna sees a ghost, this time in the form of a giant figure with the head of a pig. It had formerly been a spiritual teacher who tried to break the friendship between two monks and, when rebuked, refused to accept correction.

282. *practice*: *yoga*.

wisdom: *bhūri*, a word that in Sanskrit has many meanings: 'plenty', 'prosperity', 'greatness', even 'the earth' (all ultimately derived from the verb *bhū-*, 'to be'). The meaning 'wisdom' is given by the Commentary, which explains that wisdom is as extensive as the earth.

Leading to gain and loss: *bhavāya vibhavāya ca* – '[Leading] to existence and non-existence [of wisdom]'.

STORY. A monk called Poṭhila has studied the teaching throughout the ages of seven Buddhas, but has still not made the effort to gain freedom. The Buddha spurs him to act by repeatedly calling him 'Tucchapoṭhila' – 'Empty Poṭhila'. Poṭhila tries to find a learned teacher, but, because of his pride, he is sent to learn from a seven-year-old novice. Receiving the boy's basic teaching, and urged on by the Buddha with this verse, he attains Arahatship.

283–4. These two verses depend on a complex series of puns on the word *vana* = (1) 'wood' (i.e. small forest, not timber), (2) 'desire', 'yearning'; *vanatha*, 'brushwood'; and *nibbana*, 'without wood' or 'without desire', but perhaps with a reminiscence of *nibbāna*, which could punningly be taken as 'state of being without wood/desire'.
towards women: *nārisu*. The Patna Dharmapada (362) has *ñātisu*, the Udānavarga (18.4) *bandhuṣu*, both of which mean 'towards relatives'.

STORY: A group of men become monks late in life. The former wife of one of them continues to be their loyal supporter. When she dies, all are very distressed. The Buddha tells them that in a previous life, when they were crows, she was drowned in the sea, and they could not save her. They are suffering because they have not eradicated the forest of greed, hatred and delusion.

285. *affection towards yourself*: Or perhaps just 'your own affection': *sineham attano*, 'affection of [one]self'. *Sineha* is personal attachment – not loving kindness, which is free of clinging. (This 'you' is a genuine second-person singular: the verse is addressed to one individual.)
you'd pluck: Added for clarity.
lily: *kumuda* – a water lily, not a lotus, as sometimes translated. (They are distinct species of water plants.)
the Well-Gone: *sugata* – the Buddha.

STORY: A young monk who was a goldsmith in lay life cannot make any progress with meditation on foulness, a subject given to him by Sāriputta (cf. the notes on vv. 7–8). The Buddha realizes that this is because in his present life and many previous ones the youth has spent his time working with beautiful things. He creates the form of a large and beautiful red lotus, and tells the monk to use that as his subject. Contemplating it, the monk attains all the stages of *jhāna*. The Buddha then causes the lotus to wither. The monk realizes the three signs of existence: impermanence, suffering and no-self. As the young monk meditates, the Buddha sends a luminous image of himself to appear before him and speak the verse, and the monk attains Arahatship.

286. STORY: A wealthy merchant makes plans for the future of his business. The Buddha remarks to Ānanda that in fact the merchant will die in seven days. When Ānanda passes this on to the merchant, he determines to spend the rest of his time giving alms, and he attains the state of Stream-Entry. At the end of the seven days, he feels ill, goes to bed, and dies.

287. Apart from first half-line, this verse is identical with v. 47.
sons: This of course may refer to offspring in general.

STORY: That of Kisā Gotamī – see the story for v. 114.

288–9. *Sons*: As in v. 287.
good conduct: *sīla*, which protects one in a way that relatives cannot.
The path that leads to nibbāna: *nibbāna-gamanaṃ maggaṃ*. The Patna Dharmapada (368–9) has *saggagamanaṃ maggaṃ*, 'the path that leads to heaven', but the Udānavarga (6.15) has the equivalent to the Pali version: *nirvāṇagamanaṃ mārgaṃ*.

STORY: That of Paṭācārā – see the story for v. 113.

CHAPTER 21
MISCELLANEOUS

290. *happiness from material things*: Following K. R. Norman 1997: 43, 132. Others take *mattāsukha* as 'limited happiness'.

STORY: The city of Vesāli is afflicted by drought, followed by famine, plague and an influx of evil spirits. The Buddha is invited to the city to chant a blessing. He teaches the Ratana (Jewel) Sutta – still a very popular blessing – to Ānanda, and tells him to recite it. As soon as Ānanda begins to recite, rain falls and the troubles of the city are over. People marvel at the power of the Buddha, but he explains that it is the result of relatively small acts of service in a previous life.

291. *happiness*: *sukha*.
pain: *dukkha*.

STORY: A girl likes eating eggs. Her hen conceives a grudge against her, and determines that in a future life she will eat the girl's young. The rest of the story follows a similar pattern to the one in the Commentary for v. 5.

292–3. *go to rest*: cf. the note on v. 226.

STORY: A group of monks are in the habit of wearing sandals of fancy pattern. The Buddha speaks the verses to recall them to their proper duties, after which they attain Arahatship.

294–5. These notorious verses must surely always have been accompanied by a commentary, though the actual explanation of the symbolism may have varied from one tradition to another. There is no evidence that they were ever taken literally, in an antinomian sense.
mother = craving (*taṇhā*, fem.).
father = conceit (*anumāna*, masc.).
two royal [*khattiya* = *kṣatriya*] *kings/two Brahmin kings* = the extreme views of eternalism and annihilationism.
a kingdom = sense-avenues and sense-desires.
tax-gatherers = clinging to life. It is not possible to tell from the verse whether the tax-gatherer is singular or plural, but clearly he (or they) represents something quite difficult to get away from.
tiger-man, or perhaps 'tiger-forest' = the hindrances (see Glossary). Following K. R. Norman (1997: 134), I have taken *veyaggha-pañcamaṃ* as 'tiger-like [man] as fifth' rather than the grammatically unlikely 'five-fold tiger-forest' – the usual translation. The Sanskrit Udānavarga (33.62) has *vyāghraṃ ca pañcamaṃ hatvā*: 'and killing a tiger as fifth'.

STORY: The Buddha is said to have spoken these two verses on different occasions about the monk Lakuṇṭaka Bhaddiya, apparently a tiny man who was subject to teasing, though he was a great Arahat.

296–301. *Are always wide awake*: Literally, 'Wake always well-awakened'. Clearly it is intended figuratively, though there may be the implication that there is a level of awareness present even in sleep.
Both day and night they are ever / Mindful of the Buddha [/Dhamma/Saṅgha]: Literally, 'Of whom, both day and night, there is mindfulness constantly gone to the Buddha[/Dhamma/Saṅgha]'.
meditation: *bhāvanā* – literally, 'causing-to-be', 'development [of the mind]'. The word is used of meditative practice in a broad sense, not just of formal sessions of meditation.

STORY: A boy who is devoted to the Buddha is left alone at night outside a city and near a cremation ground. He is protected by two spirits (*amanussā*, non-human beings), who appear to him in the form of his parents. When the king learns of this, he asks whether it is only contemplation of the Buddha that gives protection in this way. The Buddha explains that any of the six forms of meditation listed in the verses will have the same effect.

302. This verse is problematic, but seems to point out difficulties in both the householder's and the renouncer's lives.
So you shouldn't be a wayfarer: Burlingame (1921: III, 183) takes this as '. . . such a wayfarer', to resolve the apparent contradiction in the last line.

STORY: A monk, formerly a prince, becomes discontented when he hears the sounds of a festival taking place nearby. He feels that monks have a very hard life. A spirit appears and reminds him that there are other beings who would envy his state. The Buddha speaks the verse in confirmation of this.

303. STORY: See the story for vv. 73–4.

304. *Himavat*: 'Snowy', another name for *Himālaya*, 'Abode of Snow'.
even: Added for clarity.

STORY: Anāthapiṇḍika's second daughter, Cullasubhaddā (see the story for v. 18), is married to the son of another banker, and sent to live a long way from her parents. Her in-laws are followers of a group of naked ascetics. She refuses to visit those ascetics, despite the anger of her parents-in-law, and speaks in praise of the Buddha, until they too become interested and wish to see him. She visualizes the Buddha and offers him an invitation, which he accepts. The Buddha explains in the verse how he was aware of Cullasubhaddā's invitation, even at a distance. Her in-laws are very impressed by the Buddha and his monks, and become devout followers.

305. STORY: The Buddha speaks the verse in praise of a monk who lives a solitary, hermit-like existence.

CHAPTER 22
HELLS

Niraya, literally, 'down-going', is used in Pali as an equivalent of Sanskrit *naraka*, 'hell'. The difference between the hells of Buddhist and Western traditions is that those of the Buddhist (and other South

Asian) traditions are subject to impermanence, as are the heavens, and, after undergoing the results of their actions, beings are reborn elsewhere. The hell most frequently mentioned in the Dhammapada Commentary is the Avīci (see Glossary). In this section I have generally translated *niraya* as 'hell world', to try to suggest the distinction between this and the Christian view. Strictly speaking, the Buddhist 'hells' are more like purgatories.

306. STORY: Some ascetics, jealous of the alms and reputation of the Buddha, plot against him, with the aid of the ascetic woman Sundarī ('Beautiful'), who pretends to be having an affair with him (cf. Ciñcā in the story for v. 176). Once the rumour has started to get about, the ascetics pay some criminals to murder Sundarī and throw her body on a rubbish pile near to the place where the Buddha is staying. They then go to the king and accuse the Buddhist monks of killing her to cover up their teacher's misconduct. When the Buddha is told about this, he calmly utters the verse.

The king, doubting the word of the ascetics, sends officers to find out what has really happened. They find the hired killers drinking the proceeds of their crime, and boasting about what they have done. The lying ascetics are punished, and the Buddha's reputation increases.

307. *their backs*: Literally, 'their necks', but I have used the equivalent colloquial usage in English. Here the monk's robe is being worn only externally, and does not correspond to a proper attitude within.
of evil character: *pāpadhammā*.

STORY: Moggallāna and Lakkhaṇa see some skeletal ghosts with the attributes of monks. Moggallāna explains that these were monks who were ordained in the time of the Buddha Kassapa, but did not live up to their vows. (Cf. the stories for vv. 71, 72, 136, 281.)

308. *Hot as flames of fire*: Literally, 'Like a flame of fire'. The image of swallowing a red-hot ball of iron is commonly used of the dangers of eating alms-food to which one is not entitled.
eat the alms of the kingdom: i.e. accept the support of laypeople while not living as a monk should.

STORY: The Buddha speaks the verse as a warning to some

monks who have been claiming spiritual attainments they do not possess in order to get alms.

309–10. *reckless*: *pamatto* – literally, 'unaware'. (See the introduction to the notes on Chapter 2.)
Ill fortune earned: *apuññalābha* – literally, 'acquisition of demerit', the kammic consequences of wrong action.

STORY: Khema, a banker's son, is constantly getting into trouble with married women. He is caught three times, and each time the king lets him go out of sympathy for his father; but Khema will not learn his lesson. His father takes him to the Buddha, who speaks these verses, bringing the young man to his senses.

311–13. *wanderer's life*: *sāmañña*, the condition of a *samaṇa* – see Glossary.
kusa grass: See the notes on v. 70.
spiritual practice: Or celibacy (*brahmacariya*).
doubtful: Following the Commentary, which takes *saṅkassara* as being from *saṅkā*, 'doubt'. K. R. Norman (1997: 45) takes it in the alternative sense as 'vile' (perhaps from Vedic Sanskrit *saṅkasuka*, though he does not comment on this).
Just scatters more dust on himself: 'on himself' added for clarity.

STORY: Contrary to the monastic rule, a monk pulls up a blade of grass. He is remorseful, but another monk says that it does not matter, pulling up a whole clump of grass to make his point. The Buddha speaks the verses in rebuke. (As usual, the fault of denying the difference between right and wrong is regarded as more serious than making a mistake and honestly acknowledging the fact.)

314. STORY: A woman finds that her husband has been having sexual relations with their slave woman. In her jealousy, she punishes the woman cruelly, mutilating her face and locking her in the house. Then she goes off with her husband (who is apparently unaware of what she has done) to hear the Buddha's teachings.

In their absence, some relatives visit the house, discover what has happened, and release the slave woman. In front of the assembled people, she reports the matter to the Buddha. He speaks the verse; the couple attain Stream-Entry, and immediately set free the slave woman, who herself becomes a follower of the Buddha.

315. STORY: Some monks have an uncomfortable time because the city where they are staying is expecting an attack, and the citizens are mainly concerned with fortifying it. The Buddha counsels them to endure the situation, but reminds them that they too should fortify themselves.

316–17. *where there is no danger*: Literally, 'in non-danger'.
where danger exists: Literally, 'in danger'.

STORY: Arguments break out between ascetics who go completely naked and ascetics who wear a small loincloth. The verses are said to be the Buddha's comment on this.

318–19. *where there is no fault*: Literally, 'in the non-blamable'.
where fault exists: Literally, 'in the blamable'.

STORY: Some parents who are followers of other teachers are unhappy when their young children become devotees of the Buddha; but wise neighbours calm their fears.The parents go to pay homage to the Buddha, who teaches them with these verses.

CHAPTER 23
THE ELEPHANT

Nāga has many meanings, including 'serpent-deity' and 'hero', but in this chapter it clearly means 'elephant', and the majority of the verses mention this animal.

320–22. *arrows*: Taking *saraṃ* as plural (as it is in Uv 19.21).
abusive speech: *ativākyaṃ* – speech beyond the normal bounds.
Sindh: Pali/Sanskrit *Sindhu* – the area of the Indus river, proverbial home of the finest horses in ancient India.

STORY: Instigated by Māgandiyā (see the stories for vv. 21–3, 179–80), people shout abuse at the Buddha wherever he goes. Ānanda wants him to leave, but the Buddha asks him what they will do if they meet similar abuse elsewhere. Will they keep moving on? He compares himself to a well-trained elephant, who endures arrows with patience. The mob are won over by the Buddha's patience, and many of them attain higher states.

323. *to the place where none has gone*: *agataṃ disaṃ*, taking *agata* as 'not gone to'. K. R. Norman (1997: 47, 139) translates this as 'to

the region where there is no rebirth', taking *agata* as 'without *gati* [place of rebirth – see Glossary]'. In either case, it means the unconditioned, *nibbāna*.

STORY: A monk who was an elephant-trainer in lay life sees a man trying to teach a trick to an elephant, and gives him advice. The Buddha reproaches him for troubling himself with mounts which cannot help him get to his goal as a monk.

324. *must*: A fluid (sometimes spelled 'musth') secreted from the forehead by some bull elephants during rut.
in captivity: Literally, 'bound'.

STORY: An elderly Brahmin gives up his property to his sons and daughters-in-law, on the understanding that they will take care of him. Soon, however, they begin to ill-treat him. The Buddha shames them by telling the story of the captive elephant Dhanapālaka, who weeps for his parents left behind in the jungle.

325. STORY: A shortened version of that for v. 204.

326. *mahout*: Literally, '*aṅkusa*-holder', the *aṅkusa* (Sanskrit *aṅkuśa*) being the hooked stick used by an elephant-driver.

STORY: A novice monk called Sānu practises eagerly, constantly offering the merit of his actions to his parents. His present, human, parents are not aware of it, but a *yakkhinī*, his mother in a previous birth, greatly appreciates it. When he becomes discontented and wishes to return to the household life, both his mothers do their best to dissuade him: his human mother by pointing out the disadvantages of the household life, and his *yakkhinī* mother by possessing him and causing him to have a fit. Both in their own ways warn him of the dangers of leaving the Buddha's path.

Sānu recovers, and returns to the Order. He is ordained as a monk, and becomes an Arahat and a famous teacher.

327. *Awareness*: *appamāda* – see the introduction to the notes on Chapter 2.

STORY: An old war-elephant, formerly very strong, but now grown weak with age, gets stuck in the mud of a lake. The trainer has drums beaten, as though for battle, rousing the elephant's pride so that it manages to extricate itself. The Buddha points it out as an example to the monks.

328–30. *skilful*: K. R. Norman (1997: 47, 141) takes *nipaka* in its alternative sense as 'zealous'.
conquered territory: *vjita* – cf. *jita* in v. 40 and its notes. Here, however, there still seems to be a memory of the original meaning.
like an elephant in an elephant-forest: Norman splits the words *mātaṅg'araññe va nāgo* differently, reading them as 'like a mātaṅga nāga elephant [which he takes as a particular kind or breed of elephants] in the forest'.
It's better to walk alone: Literally, 'Better is walking of one alone'.
with fools: Taking *bāle* as instrumental plural rather than locative singular – otherwise, 'in a fool'.

STORY: The Buddha has gone to the forest to get away from the quarrelling monks, and an old elephant has gone there to get away from the constant noise and jostling of the herd. The Buddha praises the elephant, which provides him with water and protects him in the forest (see the story for v. 6).

331–3. *pleasant*: *sukha*, here implying 'bringing happiness'.
caring for your mother . . . caring for Brahmins: All traditional sources agree that the abstract nouns *matteyyatā*, *petteyyatā*, *sāmaññatā*, *brahmaññatā* here mean 'care for mother', 'care for father', 'care for wanderers (*samaṇa*)', 'care for Brahmins', rather than 'motherhood', 'fatherhood', 'wanderer's state', 'Brahminhood'. As K. R. Norman (1997: 142–3) points out, *sāmaññatā* and *brahmaññatā* are double abstract nouns, since *sāmañña* and *brahmañña* are already abstracts ('*samaṇa*-hood', 'Brahminhood'), and *-tā* is a further abstract suffix; the same is perhaps true of *matteyyatā* and *petteyyatā*, suggesting that none of these words is to be taken in an obvious sense.

STORY: The Buddha is thinking about unjust kings who oppress their subjects. Māra mistakenly supposes that he still has a craving for kingship, and tries to tempt him back to the household life. The Buddha tells him that no amount of power or wealth is enough to satisfy a person who is not free from craving.

CHAPTER 24
CRAVING

Craving – literally, 'thirst' (*taṇhā*) – is what, in Buddhist teaching, keeps us trapped in the realm of birth and death.

334–7. *māluvā creeper*: See the notes on v. 162.
If someone is overpowered: Literally, 'The one whom this fierce (*jammī*) craving overpowers'.
bīraṇa grass after rain: Literally, '*bīraṇa* grass [that has been] rained on'. *Bīraṇa* grass (Sanskrit *vīriṇa*) = *Andropogon muricatum*.
venerable sirs: As K. R. Norman points out, the expression *bhaddaṃ vo*, which looks as though it means 'good luck to you [pl.]', is in fact functioning like a vocative – 'good sirs'. See K. R. Norman 1997: 144, and Brough 1962: 264.
usira root: Sanskrit *uśīra* – the fragrant root of the *bīraṇa* grass (see above), believed to have medicinal properties.

STORY: A monk in the Buddha Kassapa's time falls away and begins to give false teaching. After a stay in the Avīci hell, he is reborn in the present Buddha's time as a talking fish with beautiful golden scales (because of his previous practice as a follower of a Buddha) but a foul breath (because of his false teaching). After telling his story, the fish dies, overcome by remorse, and is reborn in a hell world again.

338–43. *Just as a tree ... grows again*: Strongly reminiscent of Bṛhadāraṇyaka Upaniṣad III.9.28 (tr. Roebuck 2000: 69; 2003: 59).
tendency to craving: *taṇhānusaya*. The *anusayas* are latent tendencies to which the mind is liable to return, and in later Buddhism are often listed as seven: tendencies towards sense-desire, desire for existence, anger, pride (*māna* – see the notes on v. 221), views, doubt and ignorance. The Commentary takes the tendency to craving as comprising the first two on the list, but it is not clear whether the theory was fully developed when the Dhammapada was composed (Carter and Palihawadana 1987: 497).
thirty-six streams: According to Carter and Palihawadana (1987: 359; 497, n. 9), the various possible activations of craving: 'eighteen activations dependent on the internal [*āyatanas*] and eighteen on the external'. There are a number of possible interpretations of the thirty-six, but clearly they are related to the operation of the six senses. (In Buddhist thought, the mind is considered a sense along with sight, hearing etc., with *dhammas* as its objects.) Each sense may be associated with craving for inner or outer objects in the past, present or future, and in three modes – craving for sense-pleasures, craving for existence and craving for the cessation of existence – giving various ways of arriving at thirty-six.

Floods: Reading *vāhā*, rather than *mahā*, 'great', which does not fit the syntax here.
stands tall: 'tall' added for clarity.
Crawl around like a trapped hare: Following Carter and Palihawadana (1987: 359–60). K. R. Norman (1997: 50) has 'run around like a hunted hare', but the verb *parisappati* comes from the root *sṛp-*, 'to creep', and the imagery of a hare caught in a snare seems more appropriate here.

STORY: The Buddha, seeing a young sow, is observed to smile. He explains that in the time of the Buddha Kakusandha she was a hen who used to enjoy the sound of a monk teaching. When she died, because of this wholesome activity, she was reborn as a princess. After seeing some maggots (leading to an understanding of foulness, or impermanence?) she achieved the first meditation (*jhāna*) and was then reborn in a Brahmā world. From there she fell to her current state. Understanding this, the Buddha smiled. He speaks the verses.

The commentator then takes the sow's story on through a series of births to Sri Lanka in his own time, where she is again a woman of high station. She becomes a nun, and attains Arahatship. She recollects her previous births and recounts them before passing into *nibbāna*.

344. Puns on *vana*, 'wood'/'desire', as in vv. 283–4: 'without brushwood', *nibbanatha*; 'committed to the wood', *vanādhimutto*. K.R. Norman (1997: 145–7), pointing out that the commentarial story does not take account of the puns, regards the verse as an attack on Brahmins who, though living in the forest, maintain their family commitments.

STORY: A monk, a follower of the Arahat Kassapa, returns to the lay life. Falling into bad company, he becomes a bandit. When he is captured and is awaiting execution, Kassapa sees his plight and tells him to take up his former meditation subject again. The bandit does so, and his fearlessness impresses his captors. Kassapa reports the matter to the Buddha, who sends his likeness to appear before the condemned man and teach him with this verse. At the moment of execution, the former monk attains Arahatship.

345–6. *rope*: *babbaja*, made of plaited reeds or grass (K. R. Norman 1997: 146).
hard to escape for the slack: Following K. R. Norman (1997: 50,

146–7), who takes *sithilaṃ duppamuñcaṃ* as a compound, with *ṃ* inserted for metrical reasons. The Commentary tries to explain *sithilaṃ*, 'slack', 'lax', as an epithet for the chain, perhaps referring to a bond that is supple like leather. It is followed by Carter and Palihawadana (1987: 362–3), who have 'lax [and yet] hard to loosen'.

STORY: The monks see some convicts in chains, and ask the Buddha whether there are any stronger chains than these. He replies that the bonds of passion and attachment are far stronger than physical chains.

347. STORY: Queen Khemā avoids hearing the Buddha's teaching, fearing that he will disparage her beauty. When she is eventually persuaded to hear him, he causes the figure of an extremely beautiful woman to appear before her, to grow old and to die (cf. the story of Nandā for v. 150). Seeing this, she attains Stream-Entry. Then the Buddha speaks this verse, and she attains Arahatship. The Buddha tells the king, her husband, that she will either have to ordain as a nun or pass away in *parinibbāna*. With his permission, Khemā joins the Order and becomes chief among the nuns, supreme in insight.

348. STORY: Uggasena, a banker's son, falls in love with a woman acrobat and runs away to join her troupe. They marry. First of all Uggasena just looks after their carts and oxen, and carries their equipment – surely one of the earliest descriptions of a roadie in literature. But when one day he hears his wife playfully calling their child 'son of a cart-driver' he determines to prove his worth, and sets about learning one of the acrobats' most difficult tricks, a routine of seven somersaults on top of a very tall bamboo pole. It takes him a year to learn, but when he has perfected it he announces a public performance.

The Buddha realizes that Uggasena has the ability to attain Arahatship, and goes to see him. Uggasena performs his seven somersaults, only to find that the audience has been looking at the Buddha, who has just arrived, and not at him. He is greatly disappointed. Understanding his thought, the Buddha sends Moggallāna to request him to perform again. Delighted, Uggasena now performs fourteen somersaults and lands back on top of his pole. At this moment, the Buddha speaks the verse, and Uggasena attains Arahatship; he comes down from the pole to pay homage to the Buddha, and is ordained as a monk.

When Uggasena is asked whether he felt any fear when he came down from the pole, he declares that he did not – tantamount to a claim of Arahatship. When others express doubts about this, the Buddha confirms his attainment with v. 397.

Later, the Buddha recounts the actions, good and bad, in a past life that led Uggasena and his wife to their present situation. Uggasena's wife decides that she too will attain whatever her husband has attained, is ordained as a nun, and attains Arahatship.

349–50. *the fair . . . the foul*: cf. the notes on vv. 7–8.

STORY: The monk Dhanuggaha is distracted by a beautiful laywoman, and becomes discontented. The Buddha reveals that in a previous life she had been Dhanuggaha's wife, but had betrayed him to his death for love of a bandit.

351–2. *This accumulation*: i.e. the body, as in the following verse.
Skilled in etymology and words, / Who knows the order of letters: The words used here are normally technical terms of grammar, but in this context must refer to the skills necessary to understand and teach the Dhamma (Carter and Palihawadana 1987: 500, n. 29). 'letters' is literally 'syllables'. Indian scripts, including Brāhmī and Kharoṣṭhī, are written in syllables, which in turn are built up of symbols for the individual phonemes. So it is not absolutely certain that written language is meant here.
a great person – / So he is called: Overruns the metre. Probably 'a great person' has been added from an early commentary.

STORY: Māra takes the form of a gigantic elephant and tries to frighten Rāhula, the Buddha's son, now ordained. But, though Rāhula is only eight years old, he is an Arahat, and Māra cannot frighten him.

353. *through the destruction of craving*: Literally, 'in the destruction of craving'.
as teacher: Added for clarity.

STORY: After the Buddha's enlightenment, and his stay of seven weeks at Bodh Gaya, he goes to meet the five ascetics with whom he previously practised asceticism. On the way he meets Upaka, an Ājīvika ascetic, who sees the Buddha's radiant appearance and asks the name of his teacher. The Buddha replies with this verse. Upaka neither accepts nor rejects the statement, but goes on his way.

354. *conquers*: *jināti*, used in two different senses in the verse. In ll. 1–3 it means 'surpasses', while in l. 4 it means 'destroys'.

STORY: The gods are debating about which gift is best, which flavour is best, which pleasure is best, and why the destruction of craving is supreme. Eventually they go to the Buddha, who answers with the verse.

355. STORY: A banker has died without leaving an heir, and his immense wealth has gone to the king. It turns out that, far from enjoying his good fortune, he was a miser with an evil temper. The Buddha tells the stories of the past lives that brought him to that state.

356–9. STORY: Aṅkura has given alms in various existences for 10,000 years, while Indaka gave a spoonful of his own food to the Arahat Anuruddha. The Buddha points out that giving to such a one brings far more merit than giving indiscriminately.

CHAPTER 25
THE MONK

360–61. STORY: Five monks try each to guard one of the sense-doors, and argue among themselves who has the most difficult task.

362. STORY: A young monk, showing his prowess at throwing stones, hits a goose and kills it, so violating one of the gravest Vinaya rules. The Buddha recounts the Kurudhamma Jātaka, which illustrates the care with which people in former times kept the precepts.

363. *A gentle speaker*: Taking *manta-bhāṇī* from Sanskrit *mandra-bhāṇin*, not *mantra-bhāṇin*, which would mean 'a speaker of mantras/sacred texts' (K. R. Norman 1997: 149).

STORY: A monk called Kokālika repeatedly disparages Sāriputta and Moggallāna, and in consequence of his wicked behaviour is swallowed by the earth (cf. the story for v. 17).

The Buddha explains that this is not the first time that Kokālika has got into trouble through failure to hold his tongue, and recounts the well-known fable of a tortoise carried through the air by holding on with his teeth to a pole carried between two geese. When someone makes a remark about this strange sight, the tortoise is unable to resist opening his mouth to reply, and tumbles to his death. The tortoise was Kokālika in a previous birth.

364. *Dwelling in Dhamma*: Literally, 'Having Dhamma as his pleasure-garden' (*dhammārāma*).

STORY: This concerns a monk called Dhammārāma, who, during the last four months of the Buddha's life, behaves in the same way as Attadattha (story for v. 166) and Tissa (story for v. 205).

365–6. STORY: A monk is close friends with a follower of Devadatta, and stays with Devadatta's monks, partly because of the rich gifts they receive. When the Buddha reproaches him, he explains that he does not share their views, but stays with them because of this friendship.

The Buddha points out the dangers of living with bad people, telling the story of a previous existence in which the monk had been an elephant. Normally well controlled, the elephant overheard the conversation of some bandits and, under their influence, went wild and killed his keepers. When it was arranged that he should hear the conversation of sages, he recovered his former good qualities. The Buddha advises the monk to avoid bad company, and to be content with what he receives.

367. STORY: The Buddha accepts food from a Brahmin, and teaches him about 'name and form' (*nāma-rūpa*), the mental and physical aspects of existence.

368–76. *conditioned things*: The *saṅkhāras*.

Cut off five, give up five: The five lower and higher fetters (see Glossary under *saṃyojana*).

Develop five to the highest: The five *indriyas* (faculties): (1) *saddhā*, 'faith'/'confidence'; (2) *viriya*, 'energy'/'courage'; (3) *sati*, 'mindfulness'; (4) *samādhi*, 'concentration'; (5) *paññā*, 'wisdom'.

five bonds: Greed, hate, delusion, pride and views.

Don't let your mind wander: Literally, 'Don't cause your mind to wander'.

Don't . . . swallow an iron ball: See the notes on v. 308.

recklessly: *pammatto*, '[being] unaware'.

There's no meditation . . . close to nibbāna: This verse is found in the surviving literature of many of the early Buddhist schools: see Skilling 2006: 111, n. 47.
an empty house: Perhaps literally a secluded place, suitable for meditation (Carter and Palihawadana 1987: 382; K. R. Norman 1997: 53), or perhaps a symbol for the unattached mind itself.
Who has right insight into dhammas: Literally, 'Seeing rightly into *dhammas*', with connotations of *vipassanā*, the insight aspect of meditation.
dhammas: Or 'the Dhamma', but here *dhammaṃ* is probably being used as an accusative plural (as in Uv 32.9, which has *dharmān*).
beyond the human: Literally, 'not-human' (*amānusī*), a word generally used of divine beings.
contemplates: *sammasati*, implying repeated and intense meditative activity.
aggregates: *khandhas* – see Glossary.
So this is how the wise monk / Can make a beginning here: Literally, 'In that respect, this is the beginning here / For the wise monk.'
monastic rule: *pātimokkha*, the basic code of the monastic life, with 227 rules for monks and 311 for nuns.
Find friends . . . livelihood: Some editions place this at the start of the following stanza.
friends . . . good for you: *mitte kalyāṇe*. K. R. Norman (1997: 152–3) takes 'Of pure livelihood' (*suddhājīve*) and 'unwearied' (*atandite*) in the next line as Eastern forms of the nominative singular, referring to the subject of *bhajassu* (imperative, 'resort to' friends etc.). He demonstrates that in the earlier versions (and preserved in Uv 32.27 c–d) the reference was to knowing measure, i.e. moderation (*mitta* < *mātra*), in food (cf. vv. 7–8, where the word occurs as *matta*), rather than to friends (*mitta* < *mitra*). However, the use of the word *kalyāṇa*, normally paired with *mitta*, 'friend', rather than *pratirūpa* (or its derivatives), 'suitable', shows that this possible meaning of *mitta* has been lost in the Pali Dhammapada. I therefore translate it as it has been traditionally understood. Norman takes the Pali line as it now stands as 'Being of good livelihood and unwearied, associate with friends who are noble.'

STORY: Some burglars break into the house of a wealthy laywoman, who is away listening to her son, an Arahat, teaching the Dhamma. If she comes back, the chief burglar is determined to kill her. However, though three times a servant comes to tell her that there are burglars in the house – first in the strongroom for copper coins, then in the one for silver, and then in the one for gold – the laywoman sends the servant away, telling her not to bother her while she is listening to the Dhamma.

Hearing of this, the burglars think that if they were to rob a woman like this they would be struck by thunderbolts; so the chief orders the other burglars to put back what they have already stolen. Then they go to the woman and confess their fault. She forgives them, and asks her son to ordain them as monks. Becoming aware of what has happened, the Buddha sends a likeness of himself to appear before the new monks and teach them with these verses.

377. STORY: A group of 500 monks see that jasmine flowers which have bloomed in the morning are dropping in the evening. They resolve that, before the flowers have fallen, they will have let go of greed, hatred and delusion. The Buddha appears and encourages them with the verse, and all attain Arahatship.

378. *Peaceful in mind, concentrated*: Following K. R. Norman, one of the manuscripts, and apparently the Commentary, and reading *santamano samāhito*. Most versions have *santavā susamāhito*, 'peaceful(?), well-concentrated'. But *santavā* is problematic. The final element *-vā* has been taken to represent either a possessive form or a past participle (hence, 'having peace' or 'having become peaceful'), but it probably originally represented < *vāk*, 'speech'. Presumably once this had been forgotten this word was taken to refer to the mind, and the first *pāda* was emended to refer to speech to complete the usual triad (K. R. Norman 1997: 153).

at peace: *upasanta*, 'thoroughly peaceful'. Cf. *upasama* in the note to vv. 3–4.

STORY: A monk called Santakāya ('Of Peaceful Body') was miraculously born of a lioness. Like his mother, he is peaceful and composed in all his actions, making him an exemplary monk.

379–80. STORY: A poor ploughman gives up his hard life to become a monk. When he puts on the robes, he leaves his tattered old loincloth hanging on a tree. Whenever he becomes discontented with the monastic life, he visits the old loincloth, which he calls his 'teacher', and reproaches himself. He soon attains Arahatship, and no longer needs to visit this 'teacher'. The Buddha confirms his attainment with the verses.

381. STORY: Vakkali loves the physical beauty of the Buddha, and becomes ordained in order to be able to gaze on him at all times. When the Buddha perceives that Vakkali is ready to understand, he reproves him, asking why he wants to gaze on the mass of corruption which is the body: 'Whoever sees the Dhamma, sees me.' But Vakkali continues to follow the Buddha wherever he goes. When the Buddha orders Vakkali back to his monastery at the start of the Rains Retreat (which means that he will not see him for three months), Vakkali determines to commit suicide. He climbs Vulture Peak, intending to throw himself off. However, the Buddha sends his likeness to appear before him and speak the verse.

After further encouragement, Vakkali becomes an Arahat with great psychic powers. The Buddha names him the foremost of the monks possessing faith.

382. STORY: The Arahat Anuruddha, the foremost of the monks for the divine eye – the power to see what is happening at a distance – has a novice called Sumana. At seven years old, Sumana has such remarkable psychic powers that, when Anuruddha is ill, he is able to fly to Lake Anotatta, in the Himalayas, to fetch him healing water to drink. The *nāga* king who lives there is reluctant to let him have it, but Sumana has the power to compel him.

Later, the Buddha sees adult monks patting the novice on the head and tweaking his ears, so decides to teach them a lesson. He asks Ānanda to tell the novices to bring water from Lake Anotatta so that he can bathe his feet. Of course, none of the other novices can do it, but Sumana, the youngest of them, manages without difficulty. Sumana receives his full ordination, and the Buddha speaks this verse.

CHAPTER 26
THE BRAHMIN

383. *Strive, and cut across the stream*: Literally, 'Having striven/Striving, cut across the stream', taking *parakkamma* as an indeclinable participle ('absolutive'), 'having striven/striving'. Alternatively, taking it as an imperative (equivalent to *parakkama*), 'Cut across

the stream, strive'. See Carter and Palihawadana 1987: 391, 505, and K. R. Norman 1997: 154.
conditioned things: The *saṅkhāras*.
You'll know the unmade: 'You'll be *akataññū*,' a knower of the unmade – cf. the notes on v. 97.

STORY: A generous Brahmin gives alms to monks and addresses them all as Arahats. Those who are not yet Arahats feel uncomfortable about this, and stop going to his house. The Buddha explains that the Brahmin is simply expressing his joy at giving alms, and urges them all to attain Arahatship.

384. *twofold states* [*dhammas*]: e.g. pleasure and pain, praise and blame. The equivalent verse in the Udānavarga (33.68) has *sveṣu dharmeṣu* ('among [his] own *dharmas*') instead of the expected *dvayeṣu dharmeṣu*: see K. R. Norman 1997: 154–5. The Commentary here seems to take *dvaya*, 'twofold', as simply equivalent to 'two', and takes it to refer to the two means to liberation rather than the twofold states characteristic of *saṃsāra* (Carter and Palihawadana 1987: 392).
go to rest: *atthaṃ gacchanti* – see the note on v. 226.

STORY: At Sāriputta's request, the Buddha gives a discourse about the two states (*dhammas*) – calm (*samatha*) and insight (*vipassanā*) – through which a meditator can attain liberation.

385–6, 395–423. *Him I call a Brahmin*: *tam ahaṃ brūmi brāhmaṇaṃ*. Although this refrain (which could also be translated as 'That one I call a Brahmin') is in the masculine gender, the words are of course intended to be taken in an inclusive sense, and several of the commentarial stories attached to these verses are about women (vv. 391, 395, 401, 403, 421).

385. *The far shore . . . near shore*: K. R. Norman (1997: 155, referring to Brough 1962: 202) considers that here *pāra* ('other shore', 'further shore') and *apāra* ('this shore', 'nearer shore') refer to the next life and the present life. The Commentary takes them as referring to the internal and external sense-bases (*āyatana*): see Carter and Palihawadana 1987: 392–3. However, the story suggests the symbolism of *nibbāna* and *saṃsāra*.
Free of fear: *vīta-ddaraṃ* – see the notes on v. 205. The parallel versions to the present verse have *vīta-jjaraṃ* (PDhp 40) and *vikada-dvara* (GDhp 35; Brough 1962: 186), 'free of fever'.

STORY: Māra, in disguise, questions the Buddha about 'the other shore'. The Buddha, recognizing him, says that it has nothing to do with Māra, since it can be attained only by one who is freed from desires.

386. STORY: A Brahmin wonders why the Buddha calls his own followers 'Brahmins', regardless of their birth, yet does not call *him* a Brahmin. The Buddha explains that he uses the word only for those who have attained Arahatship.

387. STORY: During a great festival, four glorious sights can be seen all at once: King Pasenadi, in his royal splendour; the golden-skinned Arahat Elder Kāḷudāyi, seated in meditation; the setting sun; and the rising moon. But the Buddha outshines them all. When Ānanda afterwards mentions this to him, the Buddha confirms it with the verse. (Kāḷudāyi – 'Dark Udāyi' – formerly a minister to King Suddhodana, is not the same as the monk(s) named Udāyi mentioned in the notes to vv. 64, 152, 241.)

388. A series of wordplays: on 'Brahmin' (*brāhmaṇa*) and 'get rid of' (*bāh-*); on 'wanderer' (*samaṇa*) and 'even/peaceful conduct' (*samacariyā*); and on 'giving up' (*pabbājā*) and 'renouncer' (*pabbajita*).

STORY: As for v. 386, but here a follower of another tradition wonders why the Buddha does not address him as *pabbajita*.

389–90. There are problems with both these verses in the form in which we have them.
anger: Word added twice for clarity.
him who strikes a Brahmin: Or 'a Brahmin-slayer', but in context it appears that a lesser assault is intended.
More shame on him who unleashes his anger: Presumably, in response. It would hardly make sense for the verse to say that it is more serious for the first Brahmin to use harsh words to the second Brahmin than to beat him. Rather, the verse is warning the second Brahmin not to retaliate. (For a detailed discussion of this verse and its variants, see Carter and Palihawadana 1987: 507–8.)
Verse 390 is obscure and probably corrupt. K. R. Norman (1997: 55) translates the first two lines as 'This is no advantage for a brahman, when there is restraint of mind from pleasant things,' taking 'This' presumably as referring back to the actions mentioned in the previous verse.

To have restraint of mind: Literally, 'When he has restraint of mind'.
The more the will to harm ceases, / The more is sorrow calmed: Here I translate the Pali version as we have it, where it is part of a discussion of anger and retaliation. K. R. Norman (1997: 156–7) reads *hiṃsa-mano* as derived from *hi ssa mano*, 'indeed . . . the mind', rather than following the Commentary and taking it as equivalent to *hiṃsā-mano*, 'the will to harm', for which, as he points out, there is no warrant in the parallel verses in the Sanskrit Udānavarga and the Gāndhārī Dharmapada. Originally, it seems, v. 390 was concerned with attachment, rather than ill will, but the Commentary (or even, perhaps, the compiler of the Pali Dhammapada) has taken it as following on from v. 389. (For the Gāndhārī version, see Appendix 1, v. 15 and note.)
things that are dear: Or 'people that are dear'. The text just has *piya* in the plural – see the introduction to the notes on Chapter 16.
sorrow: *dukkha*.

STORY: A Brahmin tests Sāriputta's self-control by coming up behind him and hitting him with a stick. The Elder is completely untroubled. The Brahmin, filled with remorse, begs his pardon and invites him for a meal. Sāriputta's followers want to punish the man, but Sāriputta stops them, asking them who has been hit.

391. *ways*: Literally, 'places' – i.e. body, speech and mind.

STORY: The verse is spoken in praise of the Arahat Mahāpajāpati, the first *bhikkhunī*. (She had been the sister and co-wife of the Buddha's mother, and had brought him up as her own after his mother died.) Some of the other nuns question whether her ordination was properly carried out; the Buddha confirms that he himself ordained her, and speaks the verse in praise of her.

392. STORY: Every night, before going to sleep, Sāriputta bows towards the direction in which the Elder Assaji is living. Some monks complain that Sāriputta is paying respect to the cardinal points, but the Buddha explains that he is in fact paying respect to the person who first passed on to him the Buddha's teaching.

393. *matted locks*: *jaṭā* – the piled-up matted hair that is the symbol of the ascetic, especially in many Hindu traditions.
lineage: *gotta* (Sanskrit *gotra*) – the exogamous family unit to which Brahmins belong, each one thought to be descended from one of the ancient sages.

caste: Or perhaps simply 'birth' (*jāti*).

STORY: Similar to that for v. 386.

394. *antelope-skin garment*: Another symbol of the ascetic.
mess: The dictionary meaning of *gahana* is 'a thicket, tangle, or obstruction'. Carter and Palihawadana (1987: 398–9) have, 'Within you is the jungle' K. R. Norman (1997: 56) has, 'There is a thicket inside you.' But the reference here is to something that needs thorough cleaning or polishing (*pari-majj-* in the following line), rather than cutting through. The Commentary repeats the word *gahana* without giving an alternative, glossing the sentence as 'Within you is a *gahana* of defilements, passion etc.: you clean it [so that it is] polished like elephant-dung or horse-dung', which, as Carter and Palihawadana point out, 'does not appear ugly to the onlooker'. So I have assumed that *gahana* must mean primarily something dirty, rather than something tangled.

STORY: A Brahmin, a false ascetic, tricks people out of money and valuables.

395. STORY: Spoken in praise of Kisā Gotamī – cf. the stories for vv. 114, 287. The ascetic described in the verse is *kisa*, 'lean', like her.

396. *Brahmin womb or mother*: 'Brahmin' added for clarity.
a man who says 'good sir': *bhovādin*, 'bho' being a greeting used by Brahmins. Some have taken this as a disrespectful or patronizing address to non-Brahmins, but there seems no evidence for this. In the Laws of Manu (2.122) the word *bho* is actually prescribed as a greeting between Brahmins.

STORY: Similar to that for v. 386.

397. STORY: Spoken in praise of Uggasena, the former acrobat – see the story for v. 348.

398. *cut the strap and the girth, / The thong with its attachments*: The Commentary equates the strap with hate, the girth with craving, the thong with wrong views, and the attachments with the latent tendencies (see the notes on v. 338): see Carter and Palihawadana 1987: 401.
the door-bar: Symbolizing ignorance (ibid.).
awakened: *buddha*.

STORY: Two Brahmins compete to see which of their oxen is stronger, by organizing a tug of war between them. The oxen are harnessed to opposite ends of the same cart, which is loaded with sand. The Brahmins whip the oxen, but the cart does not move, and the harnesses break.

When the Buddha hears his monks discussing this, he points out that these are merely external straps and thongs: it is more important to break the internal ones, which represent anger and craving.

399. There are problems with the text of this verse.
Abuse, beating and imprisonment: *akkosaṃ vadhabandhañ ca* – possibly intended as accusative plurals, as they are in the equivalent Udānavarga verse (33.18).
Whose strength is patience, whose army is his strength: Or perhaps, taking *khantībalaṃ balānīkaṃ* as a compound, 'Whose power of patience is his strong army'. K. R. Norman (1997: 159) considers that the second occurrence of *bala* in the Pali probably represents *vrata*, 'vow', 'observance', via a form such as *vada* or *vala*. The Udānavarga (33.18) has *kṣāntivratabalopetaṃ*, 'endowed with the strength of his vow of patience'.

STORY: A Brahmin is angry because his wife constantly praises the Buddha. He determines to beat the Buddha in argument, and asks him a question: What must one do to live happily? The Buddha replies that one must destroy anger. The Brahmin is ordained as a monk and attains Arahatship, and the same afterwards happens to his brothers.

400. *bearing his last body*: Because he won't be reborn after death.

STORY: Sāriputta's mother, Rūpasārī ('Sārī the Beautiful'), a Brahmin woman, gives alms to him and his monks, but keeps abusing them while she does so, because she resents his having left the household life to become a monk. He bears it all without ill feeling.

401. *needle's point*: *āragga*. Most translators (e.g. K. R. Norman 1997: 56) have 'the point of an awl', perhaps because of the etymological relationship between *ārā* and the English word 'awl', normally used of the large needle used by a leather-worker. But the simile seems to envisage a small needle.

STORY: Spoken in praise of the leading nun Uppalavaṇṇā: see the story for v. 69.

402. STORY: A runaway slave is ordained as a monk and becomes an Arahat. When his former master tries to seize him, the Buddha explains that the man's burden has fallen away from him. The master realizes that the man can no longer be his slave.

403. STORY: Spoken in praise of the leading nun Khemā: see the story for v. 347.

404. STORY: A monk goes to a deserted place to meditate, and the local deity (not necessarily a goddess, as Burlingame has it: see the notes on vv. 119–120), feeling inconvenienced by his presence, tries to get rid of him by tricking him into breaking the monastic code. He/she is unsuccessful, and the monk orders him/her to leave. However, he does not at any time become angry with the deity.

405. STORY: A monk, meditating in the forest, attains Arahatship, and sets off to report the matter to the Buddha. Meanwhile, a wife has run away after quarrelling with her husband, determined to go back to her parents' home. Afraid to enter the forest alone, she walks closely behind the monk, who does not so much as look at her. The husband, finding them, thinks that the monk has gone off with his wife, and beats him badly. The monk does not at any point become angry.

406. STORY: A Brahmin woman wishes to offer food to four old monks, and is furious when four little boy novices, Saṃkicca (story for v. 110), Paṇḍita (story for v. 80), Sopāka and Revata (story for v. 98), are sent instead. She leaves them unfed, and tries to find an older monk to feed in their place; but Sāriputta and Moggallāna in turn refuse to eat there and depart.

Realizing that the boys are now extremely hungry, the god Sakka takes the form of an old Brahmin and goes to the house. When he pays respect to the novices, the woman and her husband are outraged: they beat him and try to throw him out. Sakka reveals his identity, and the couple feed him and the novices.

When asked afterwards whether they had got angry about any of this, the novices reveal that they had not – so confirming that they are Arahats, and thus supremely venerable.

407. *needle's point*: See the note on v. 401.

STORY: A reflection on the tale of Mahāpanthaka and Cūḷapanthaka (see the story for v. 25). When Mahāpanthaka turned Cūḷapanthaka out of the monastery, was he motivated by anger? No, an Arahat does not have such defilements: he was acting from concern for the Dhamma.

408. *truthful*: Or perhaps 'pleasant' (*saccaṃ* – see the notes on v. 224).

STORY: The monk Vaccha addresses everyone as *vasali*, 'little man', 'low person', a term of contempt. The other monks are offended, but the Buddha, reflecting on Vaccha's previous births, realizes that for 500 lives he has been born in Brahmin families, where it has been the custom to use this term for others. He explains that Vaccha is free of ill will, and is simply using this expression out of long habit.

409. *Takes nothing that is not given*: *adinnaṃ nādiyate* – a reference to the traditional second of the five precepts. See vv. 246–7 and notes.

STORY: An Arahat monk takes a cloth that has been laid outside by a Brahmin, thinking that it has been thrown away. Proclaiming him guiltless of theft, the Buddha speaks the verse.

410. STORY: At the Rains Retreat ceremony, when laypeople bring robes and other requisites in alms for the monks, Sāriputta gives instructions that he should be informed when the requisites arrive. He is planning to distribute them among the young monks and novices, but some hearers think he must still suffer from craving for such things. The Buddha explains the true situation, and speaks the verse.

411. *Plunged into the deathless, not arising again*: *amatogadham anuppattaṃ*. K. R. Norman (1997: 57, 161) translates this as 'arrived at the firm foundation of the death-free', taking *ogadha* as equivalent to *ogādha*, 'firm foundation'.

STORY: As for v. 410, but told of Moggallāna.

412. *here*: i.e. in this world, taking *'dha* as *idha*. K. R. Norman (1997: 58, 162) takes it as *adha*, 'but'.

. *Both kinds of clinging*: Literally, 'Both clingings' – following K. R. Norman (1997: 58, 161), who takes *saṅgaṃ* as masculine plural. This has the backing of the Udānavarga (33.29), which has the dual form (*ubhau saṅgāv* < *saṇgau*), not available in Pali.

STORY: Spoken of Revata, in the story told for v. 98.

413. *With indulgence and existence exhausted*: *nandī-bhava-parikkhīṇa* – *nandī*, often translated as 'relishing', is not joy itself, but the tendency to hold on to such feelings; *bhava*, 'being' or 'becoming', is the tendency to be bound to future existence.

STORY: As a result of generosity to a previous Buddha, the Brahmin Candābha ('Moonlight') emits a radiance like moonlight from his navel. Some ascetics take him around with them as a means of impressing people and getting alms. But Candābha finds that when he goes into the presence of the Buddha the radiance disappears, and when he leaves it reappears. He studies with the Buddha to learn the spell that makes this happen, but within a few days achieves Arahatship and sends his former companions away. He is no longer interested in the power to emit moonlight.

414. STORY: That of Sīvali, who spent seven years in the womb. His mother, Suppavāsā, a Buddhist laywoman, is finally released from the pain of the extended pregnancy when offering alms to the Buddha. Later, Sīvali becomes a monk and attains Arahatship. The other monks remark on the suffering that Sīvali must have endured during his prolonged stay in the womb. The Buddha says that this is indeed so, but Sīvali has now become free of suffering.

415. *here*: As in v. 412.

STORY: A handsome young man called Sundarasamudda ('Ocean of Beauty') becomes a monk. His parents later regret having allowed him to be ordained, and his mother enlists a courtesan to try to make him come back to the household life. This woman tries all her wiles to seduce Sundarasamudda, but as he begins to waver the Buddha sends his likeness before him to speak this verse. Sundarasamudda attains Arahatship.

416. *here*: As in v. 412.

STORY: A complicated sequence of stories of the lives (including the past lives) of two bankers, Jotika and Jaṭila, who enjoy existences of extraordinary and magical luxury before renouncing everything to become monks. Both become Arahats. Each in turn is asked whether he still feels attachment to his family and his former wealth; each says that he does not, and the Buddha confirms it with the verse.

417. STORY: A wandering actor gives up his profession to become a monk, and attains Arahatship. When the monks see another actor putting on the same kind of performance that he used to do, they ask him whether he still longs for the actor's life. He declares that he does not, and the Buddha confirms it with the verse.

418. *with no remnant of craving*: *nirūpadhi*, 'without *upadhi* [the trace of attachment that can lead to future rebirth]'.

STORY: Similar to that for v. 417.

419–20. *awakened*: *buddha*, which can be applied to Arahats as well as to Buddhas.
destination: *gati* – see Glossary.
spirits: *gandhabbas* – see Glossary.

STORY: Vaṅgīsa, a Brahmin psychic, claims to be able to tell where people have been reborn after death by tapping on their skulls. The Buddha tests him by getting hold of five skulls: four from men who have been reborn, respectively, in a hell world, as an animal, as a human being and as a deity, and one from a man who has attained Arahatship. Vaṅgīsa correctly identifies the first four, but does not know what has happened to the last. The Buddha offers to teach him about this if he becomes ordained as a monk. Vaṅgīsa does so, and himself attains Arahatship.

421. STORY: A man called Visākha hears the Buddha's teaching and attains the state of Non-Return. When he returns home, his wife, Dhammadinnā, thinks at first that he must be angry with her, since he no longer shows desire towards her. He offers all his possessions to her, saying that he no longer wishes to engage in worldly matters. Dhammadinnā refuses his wealth and becomes a nun. She soon attains Arahatship. Visākha remains a devout layman.

One day Visākha sees Dhammadinnā at the nuns' residence and asks her a series of questions about the four Higher Stages. She answers every one, including one about Arahatship, with ease and clarity. She adds, however, that if he wishes to know about Arahatship he should go to the Buddha. But when Visākha reports the conversation, the Buddha tells him that what 'my daughter Dhammadinnā' has said was right, and that, if asked, he himself would answer in the same way. He praises Dhammadinnā with this verse.

Though the content of the discourse is not given here, it is recounted in full in the Cūḷavedalla Sutta (Majjhima Nikāya 1.299ff.: Sutta 44).

422. *bull*: Laudatory epithet for a leader or hero.
bathed: *nhātaka* (Sanskrit *snātaka*) – normally used of one who has completed his studies and ritually bathed to mark the end of his period of studentship. So there are connotations of his having completed his learning, as well as of his being washed clean.
awakened: As in v. 419.

STORY: After the incident recounted in the story for v. 177, Aṅgulimāla is asked whether he felt any fear when faced by the rogue elephant; when he declares that he did not, he is accused by some of speaking a falsehood. The Buddha confirms the truth of what he says with this verse.

423. *perfect in knowledge*: *abhiññā-vosito* – possessing the special knowledges characteristic of a Buddha.

STORY: When the Buddha is ill, the Brahmin Devahita gives him the medicine he needs, and hot water to bathe in. The Buddha is cured. Devahita asks who is the best person to give alms to, and receives his answer in the form of the verse.

SUMMARY VERSES

These verses are not found in all manuscripts of the Dhammapada, and are presumably later than the main body of the text. However, they are highly characteristic of South Asian literature, representing an aide-memoire for those learning the texts by heart.

3. *the Kinsman of the Sun*: *ādiccabandhu*. The Buddha is said to have been born in the royal dynasty that claimed descent from the Sun God.

Index of Names in Stories

Numbers refer to verse numbers in the Notes section.

General Index

Principal glossary entries are shown in **bold**. For individuals mentioned in commentarial stories see also the Index of Names in Stories.